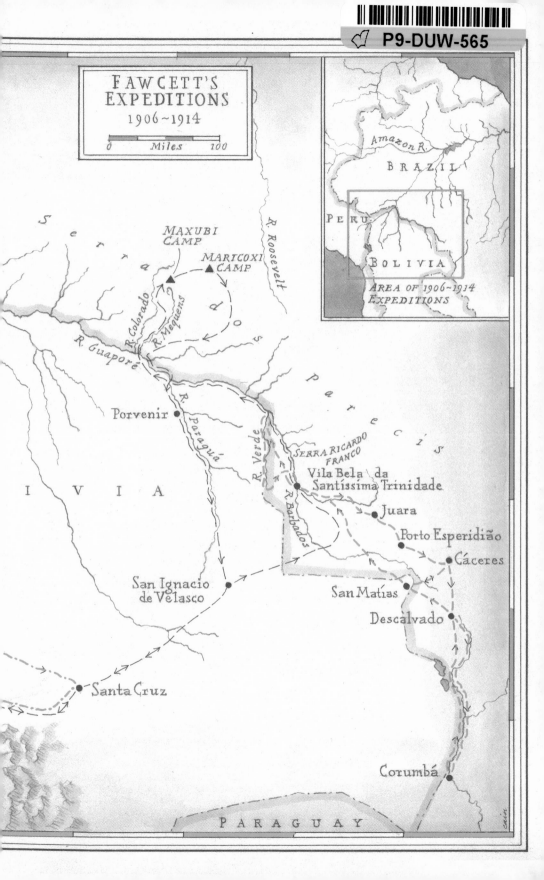

FAWCETT'S EXPEDITIONS
1906~1914

0 — Miles — 100

R. Roosevelt

MAXUBI CAMP

MARICOXI CAMP

S e r r a

d o s

P a r e c i s

R. Colorado

R. Mequens

R. Guaporé

R. Paraguá

R. Verde

R. Barbados

SERRA RICARDO FRANCO

Porvenir

Vila Bela da Santíssima Trinidade

Juara

Porto Esperidião

Cáceres

I V I A

San Ignacio de Velasco

San Matías

Descalvado

Santa Cruz

Corumbá

P A R A G U A Y

Amazon R.

B R A Z I L

P E R U

B O L I V I A

AREA OF 1906~1914 EXPEDITIONS

THE LOST CITY
OF Z

DAVID GRANN

DOUBLEDAY

New York London Toronto Sydney Auckland

The Lost City of Z

Z

A TALE OF DEADLY OBSESSION
IN THE AMAZON

Copyright © 2005, 2009 by David Grann

Published in the United States by Doubleday, an imprint of The Doubleday
Publishing Group, a division of Random House, Inc., New York.
www.doubleday.com

DOUBLEDAY and the DD colophon are registered trademarks
of Random House, Inc.

Grateful acknowledgment is made to Rolette de Montet-Guerin for
permission to repoduce text, photographs, and drawings controlled by the
Fawcett estate. Copyright © R. de Montet-Guerin

Book design by Maria Carella

Endpaper maps designed by David Cain
Title page photograph © Beth Wald/Aurora Photos
Background photograph on photo insert pages by Nigel Hicks/Alamy

Library of Congress Cataloging-in-Publication Data
Grann, David.
    The lost city of Z : a tale of deadly obsession in the Amazon / by David
Grann. — 1st ed.
        p. cm.
    Includes bibliographical references.
    1. Amazon River Region—Description and travel. 2. El Dorado.
3. Fawcett, Percy Harrison, 1867–1925?—Travel—Amazon River Region.
4. Fawcett, Percy Harrison, 1867–1925?—Death and burial. 5. Grann,
David—Travel—Amazon River Region. 6. Explorers—Amazon River
Region. I. Title.
    F2546.G747 2008
    918.1'1046—dc22   2008017432

ISBN 978-0-385-51353-1

For my intrepid Kyra

At times all I need is a brief glimpse, an opening in the midst of an incongruous landscape, a glint of lights in the fog, the dialogue of two passersby meeting in the crowd, and I think that, setting out from there, I will put together, piece by piece, the perfect city . . . If I tell you that the city toward which my journey tends is discontinuous in space and time, now scattered, now more condensed,

you must not believe the search for it can stop.

———•·•———

Italo Calvino, *Invisible Cities*

CONTENTS

Contents

Contents

THE LOST CITY
OF Z

PREFACE

I pulled the map from my back pocket. It was wet and crumpled, the lines I had traced to highlight my route now faded. I stared at my markings, hoping that they might lead me out of the Amazon, rather than deeper into it.

The letter *Z* was still visible in the center of the map. Yet it seemed less like a signpost than like a taunt, another testament to my folly.

I had always considered myself a disinterested reporter who did not get involved personally in his stories. While others often seemed to succumb to their mad dreams and obsessions, I tried to be the invisible witness. And I had convinced myself that that was why I had traveled more than ten thousand miles, from New York to London to the Xingu River, one of the longest tributaries of the Amazon, why I had spent months poring over hundreds of pages of Victorian diaries and letters, and why I had left behind my wife and one-year-old son and taken out an extra insurance policy on my life.

I told myself that I had come simply to record how generations of scientists and adventurers became fatally obsessed with solving what has often been described as "the greatest exploration mystery of the twentieth century"—the whereabouts of the lost City of Z. The ancient city, with its network of roads and bridges and temples, was believed to be hidden in the Amazon, the largest jungle in the world. In an age of airplanes and satellites, the area remains one of the last blank spaces on the map. For hundreds of years, it has haunted geographers, archaeologists, empire builders, treasure hunters, and philosophers. When Europeans first arrived in South America, around the turn of the sixteenth century, they were convinced that the jungle contained the glittering kingdom of El Dorado. Thousands died looking for it. In more recent times, many scientists have concluded that no complex civilization could have emerged in so hostile an environment, where the soil is agriculturally poor, mosquitoes carry lethal diseases, and predators lurk in the forest canopy.

The region has generally been regarded as a primeval wilderness, a place in which there are, as Thomas Hobbes described the state of nature, "no Arts; no Letters; no Society; and which is worst of all, continuall feare, and danger of violent death." The Amazon's merciless conditions have fueled one of the most enduring theories of human development: environmental determinism. According to this theory, even if some early humans eked out an existence in the harshest conditions on the planet, they rarely advanced beyond a few primitive tribes. Society, in other words, is a captive of geography. And so if Z was found in such a seemingly uninhabitable environment it would be more than a repository of golden treasure, more than an intellectual curiosity; it would, as one newspaper declared in 1925, "write a new chapter of human history."

For nearly a century, explorers have sacrificed everything, even their lives, to find the City of Z. The search for the civilization, and for the countless men who vanished while looking for it, has eclipsed the Victorian quest novels of Arthur Conan Doyle and H. Rider Haggard—both of whom, as it happens, were drawn into the real-life hunt for Z. At times, I had to remind myself that everything in this story is true: a movie star really was abducted by Indians; there were cannibals, ruins, secret maps, and spies; explorers died from starvation, disease, attacks by wild animals, and poisonous arrows; and at stake amid the adventure and death was the very understanding of the Americas before Christopher Columbus came ashore in the New World.

Now, as I examined my creased map, none of that mattered. I looked up at the tangle of trees and creepers around me, and at the biting flies and mosquitoes that left streaks of blood on my skin. I had lost my guide. I was out of food and water. Putting the map back in my pocket, I pressed forward, trying to find my way out, as branches snapped in my face. Then I saw something moving in the trees. "Who's there?" I called. There was no reply. A figure flitted among the branches, and then another. They were coming closer, and for the first time I asked myself, *What the hell am I doing here?*

We Shall

Return

On a cold January day in 1925, a tall, distinguished gentleman hurried across the docks in Hoboken, New Jersey, toward the SS *Vauban*, a five-hundred-and-eleven-foot ocean liner bound for Rio de Janeiro. He was fifty-seven years old and stood over six feet, his long arms corded with muscles. Although his hair was thinning and his mustache was flecked with white, he was so fit that he could walk for days with little, if any, rest or nourishment. His nose was crooked like a boxer's, and there was something ferocious about his appearance, especially his eyes. They were set close together and peered out from under thick tufts of hair. No one, not even his family, seemed to agree on their color— some thought they were blue, others gray. Yet virtually everyone who encountered him was struck by their intensity: some called them "the eyes of a visionary." He had frequently been photographed in riding boots and wearing a Stetson, with a rifle slung over his shoulder, but even in a suit and a tie, and without his customary wild beard, he could be recognized by the crowds on the pier. He was Colonel Percy Harrison Fawcett, and his name was known throughout the world.

He was the last of the great Victorian explorers who ventured into uncharted realms with little more than a machete, a compass, and an almost divine sense of purpose. For nearly two decades, stories of his adventures had captivated the public's imagination: how he had survived in the South American wilderness without contact with the outside world; how he was ambushed by hostile tribesmen, many of whom had never before seen a white man; how he battled piranhas, electric eels, jaguars, crocodiles, vampire bats, and anacondas, including one that almost crushed him; and how he emerged with maps of regions from which no previous expedition had returned. He was renowned as the "David Livingstone of the Amazon," and was believed to have such unrivaled powers of endurance that a few colleagues even claimed he was immune to death. An American explorer described him as "a man of indomitable will, infinite resource, fearless"; another said that he could "outwalk and outhike and outexplore anybody else." The London *Geographical Journal*, the preeminent publication in its field, observed in 1953 that "Fawcett marked the end of an age. One might almost call him the last of the individualist explorers. The day of the aeroplane, the radio, the organized and heavily financed modern expedition had not arrived. With him, it was the heroic story of a man against the forest."

In 1916, the Royal Geographical Society had awarded him, with the blessing of King George V, a gold medal "for his contributions to the mapping of South America." And every few years, when he emerged from the jungle, spidery thin and bedraggled, dozens of scientists and luminaries would pack into the Society's hall to hear him speak. Among them was Sir Arthur Conan Doyle, who was said to have drawn on Fawcett's experiences for his 1912 book *The Lost World*, in which explorers "disappear into the unknown" of South America and find, on a remote plateau, a land where dinosaurs have escaped extinction.

As Fawcett made his way to the gangplank that day in January, he eerily resembled one of the book's protagonists, Lord John Roxton:

Something there was of Napoleon III, something of Don Quixote, and yet again something which was the essence of the English country gentleman . . . He has a gentle voice and a quiet manner, but behind his twinkling blue eyes there lurks a capacity for furious wrath and implacable resolution, the more dangerous because they are held in leash.

None of Fawcett's previous expeditions compared with what he was about to do, and he could barely conceal his impatience as he fell into line with the other passengers boarding the SS *Vauban*. The ship, advertised as "the finest in the world," was part of the Lamport & Holt elite "V" class. The Germans had sunk several of the company's ocean liners during World War I, but this one had survived, with its black, salt-streaked hull and elegant white decks and striped funnel billowing smoke into the sky. Model T Fords shepherded passengers to the dock, where longshoremen helped cart luggage into the ship's hold. Many of the male passengers wore silk ties and bowler hats; women had on fur coats and feathered caps, as if they were attending a society event, which, in some ways, they were—the passenger lists of luxury ocean liners were chronicled in gossip columns and scoured by young girls searching for eligible bachelors.

Fawcett pushed forward with his gear. His trunks were loaded with guns, canned food, powdered milk, flares, and handcrafted machetes. He also carried a kit of surveying instruments: a sextant and a chronometer for determining latitude and longitude, an aneroid for measuring atmospheric pressure, and a glycerin compass that could fit in his pocket. Fawcett had chosen each item based on years of experience; even the clothes he had packed were made of lightweight, tear-proof gabardine. He had seen men die from the most innocuous-seeming oversight—a torn net, a boot that was too tight.

Fawcett was setting out into the Amazon, a wilderness nearly the size of the continental United States, to make what he called "the great discovery of the century"—a lost civilization. By then, most of the world had been explored, its veil of enchantment lifted, but the Amazon remained as mysterious as the dark side of the moon. As Sir John Scott Keltie, the former secretary of the Royal Geographical Society and one of the world's most acclaimed geographers at the time, noted, "What is there no one knows."

Ever since Francisco de Orellana and his army of Spanish conquistadores descended the Amazon River, in 1542, perhaps no place on the planet had so ignited the imagination—or lured men to their deaths. Gaspar de Carvajal, a Dominican friar who accompanied Orellana, described woman warriors in the jungle who resembled the mythical Greek Amazons. Half a century later, Sir Walter Raleigh spoke of Indians with "their eyes in their shoulders, and their mouths in the middle of their breasts"—a legend that Shakespeare wove into *Othello*:

> And of the Cannibals that each other eat,
> The Anthropophagi, and men whose heads
> Do grow beneath their shoulders.

What was true about the region—serpents as long as trees, rodents the size of pigs—was sufficiently beyond belief that no embellishment seemed too fanciful. And the most entrancing vision of all was of El Dorado. Raleigh claimed that the kingdom, which the conquistadores had heard about from Indians, was so plentiful in gold that its inhabitants ground the metal into powder and blew it "thorow hollow canes upon their naked bodies untill they be al shining from the foote to the head."

Yet each expedition that had tried to find El Dorado ended in disaster. Carvajal, whose party had been searching for the kingdom, wrote in his diary, "We reached a [state of] privation so great that we were eating nothing but leather, belts and soles of shoes, cooked with certain herbs, with the result that so great was our weakness that we could not remain standing." Some four thousand men died during that expedition alone, of starvation and disease and at the hands of Indians defending their territory with arrows dipped in poison. Other El Dorado parties resorted to cannibalism. Many explorers went mad. In 1561, Lope de Aguirre led his men on a murderous rampage, screaming, "Does God think that, because it is raining, I am not going to . . . destroy the world?" Aguirre even stabbed his own child, whispering, "Commend thyself to God, my daughter, for I am about to kill thee." Before the Spanish crown sent forces to stop him, Aguirre warned in a letter, "I swear to you, King, on my word as a Christian, that if a hundred thousand men came, none would escape. For the reports are false: there is nothing on that river but despair." Aguirre's companions finally rose up and killed him; his body was quartered, and Spanish authorities displayed the head of the "Wrath of God" in a metal cage. Still, for three centuries, expeditions continued to search, until, after a toll of death and suffering worthy of Joseph Conrad, most archaeologists had concluded that El Dorado was no more than an illusion.

Fawcett, however, was certain that the Amazon contained a fabulous kingdom, and he was not another soldier of fortune or a crackpot. A man of science, he had spent years gathering evidence to prove his case— digging up artifacts, studying petroglyphs, and interviewing tribes. And after fierce battles with skeptics Fawcett had received funding from the most respected scientific institutions, including the Royal Geographical Society, the American Geographical Society, and the Museum of the American Indian. Newspapers were proclaiming that he would soon startle the world. The *Atlanta Constitution* declared, "It is perhaps the most hazardous and certainly the most spectacular adventure of the kind ever undertaken by a reputable scientist with the backing of conservative scientific bodies."

Fawcett had determined that an ancient, highly cultured people still existed in the Brazilian Amazon and that their civilization was so old and sophisticated it would forever alter the Western view of the Americas. He had christened this lost world the City of Z. "The central place I call 'Z'— our main objective—is in a valley . . . about ten miles wide, and the city is on an eminence in the middle of it, approached by a barreled roadway of stone," Fawcett had stated earlier. "The houses are low and windowless, and there is a pyramidal temple."

Reporters on the dock in Hoboken, across the Hudson River from Manhattan, shouted questions, hoping to learn the location of Z. In the wake of the technological horrors of World War I, and amid the spread of urbanization and industrialization, few events so captivated the public. One newspaper exulted, "Not since the days when Ponce de León crossed unknown Florida in search of the Waters of Perpetual Youth . . . has a more alluring adventure been planned."

Fawcett welcomed "the fuss," as he described it in a letter to a friend, but he was careful about how he responded. He knew that his main rival, Alexander Hamilton Rice, a multimillionaire American doctor who commanded vast resources, was already entering the jungle with an unprecedented array of equipment. The prospect of Dr. Rice finding Z terrified Fawcett. Several years earlier, Fawcett had watched as a colleague from the Royal Geographical Society, Robert Falcon Scott, had set out to become the first explorer to reach the South Pole, only to discover when he got there, and shortly before he froze to death, that his Norwegian rival, Roald Amundsen, had beaten him by thirty-three days. In a recent letter to the Royal Geographical Society, Fawcett wrote, "I cannot say all I know, or even be precise as to locality, for these things leak out, and there can be nothing so bitter to the pioneer as to find the crown of his work anticipated."

He was also afraid that if he released details of his route, and others attempted to find Z or rescue him, it would result in countless deaths. An expedition of fourteen hundred armed men had previously vanished in the same region. A news bulletin telegraphed around the globe declared, "Fawcett Expedition . . . to Penetrate Land Whence None Returned." And Fawcett, who was determined to reach the most inaccessible areas, did not intend, like other explorers, to go by boat; rather, he planned to hack straight through the jungle on foot. The Royal Geographical Society had warned that Fawcett "is about the only living geographer who could successfully attempt" such an expedition and that "it would be hopeless for any people to follow in his footsteps." Before he left England, Fawcett confided to his younger son, Brian, "If with all my experience we can't make it, there's not much hope for others."

As reporters clamored around him, Fawcett explained that only a small expedition would have any chance of survival. It would be able to live off the land, and not pose a threat to hostile Indians. The expedition, he had stated, "will be no pampered exploration party, with an army of bearers, guides and cargo animals. Such top-heavy expeditions get nowhere; they linger on the fringe of civilization and bask in publicity. Where the real wilds start, bearers are not to be had anyway, for fear of the savages. Animals cannot be taken because of lack of pasture and the attack of insects and bats. There are no guides, for no one knows the country. It is a matter of cutting equipment to the absolute minimum, carrying it all oneself, and trusting that one will be able to exist by making friends with the various tribes one meets." He now added, "We will have to suffer every form of exposure . . . We will have to achieve a nervous and mental resistance, as well as physical, as men under these conditions are often broken by their minds succumbing before their bodies."

Fawcett had chosen only two people to go with him: his twenty-one-year-old son, Jack, and Jack's best friend, Raleigh Rimell. Although they had never been on an expedition, Fawcett believed that they were ideal for the mission: tough, loyal, and, because they were so close, unlikely, after months of isolation and suffering, "to harass and persecute each other"—or, as was common on such expeditions, to mutiny. Jack was, as his brother, Brian, put it, "the reflection of his father": tall, frighteningly fit, and ascetic. Neither he nor his father smoked cigarettes or drank. Brian noted that Jack's "six feet three inches were sheer bone and muscle, and the three chief agents of bodily degeneration—alcohol, tobacco and loose living—were revolting to him." Colonel Fawcett, who followed a strict Victorian code, put it slightly differently: "He is . . . absolutely virgin in mind and body."

Jack, who had wanted to accompany his father on an expedition since he was a boy, had spent years preparing—lifting weights, maintaining a rigid diet, studying Portuguese, and learning how to navigate by the stars. Still, he had suffered little real deprivation, and his face, with its luminescent skin, crisp mustache, and slick brown hair, betrayed none of the hardness of his father's. With his stylish clothes, he looked more like a movie star, which is what he hoped to become upon his triumphant return.

Raleigh, though smaller than Jack, was still nearly six feet tall and muscular. (A "fine physique," Fawcett told the RGS.) His father had been a surgeon in the Royal Navy and had died of cancer in 1917, when Raleigh was fifteen. Dark haired, with a pronounced widow's peak and a riverboat gambler's mustache, Raleigh had a jocular, mischievous nature. "He was a born clown," said Brian Fawcett, the "perfect counterpart of the serious Jack." The two boys had been virtually inseparable since they roamed the countryside around Seaton, Devonshire, where they grew up, riding bicycles and shooting rifles in the air. In a letter to one of Fawcett's confidants, Jack wrote, "Now we have Raleigh Rimell on board who is every bit as keen as I am . . . He is the only intimate friend I have ever had. I knew him before I was seven years old and we have been more or less together ever since. He is absolutely honest and decent in every sense of the word and we know each other inside out."

As Jack and Raleigh now excitedly stepped on board the ship, they encountered dozens of stewards, in starched white uniforms, rushing through the corridors with telegrams and bon voyage fruit baskets. A steward, carefully avoiding the aft quarters, where passengers in steerage rode, guided the explorers to the first-class cabins, in the center of the ship, far from the rattling of the propellers. The conditions bore little resemblance to those that had prevailed when Fawcett made his first South American voyage, two decades earlier, or when Charles Dickens, crossing the Atlantic in 1842, described his cabin as an "utterly impracticable, thoroughly hopeless and profoundly preposterous box." (The dining room, Dickens added, resembled a "hearse with windows.") Now everything was designed to accommodate the new breed of tourists—"mere travelers," as Fawcett dismissed them, who had little notion of the "places which today exact a degree of endurance and a toll of life, with the physique necessary to face dangers." The first-class quarters had beds and running water; portholes allowed in sunlight and fresh air, and electric fans circulated overhead. The ship's brochure touted the *Vauban*'s "perfect ventilation secured by modern appliances," which helped to "counteract the impression that a voyage to and through the tropics is necessarily attended with discomfort."

Fawcett, like many other Victorian explorers, was a professional dabbler who, in addition to being a self-styled geographer and archaeologist, was a talented artist (his ink drawings had been displayed at the Royal Academy) and shipbuilder (he had patented the "ichthoid curve," which added knots to a vessel's speed). Despite his interest in the sea, he wrote to his wife, Nina, who was his staunchest supporter and served as his spokesperson whenever he was away, that he found the SS *Vauban* and the voyage "rather tiresome": all he wanted was to be in the jungle.

Jack and Raleigh, meanwhile, were eager to explore the ship's luxurious interior. Around one corner was a lounge with vaulted ceilings and marble columns. Around another was a dining room with white-linened tables and with waiters, in black tie, who served roasted rack of lamb and wine from decanters as an orchestra played. The ship even had a gymnasium where the young men could train for their mission.

Jack and Raleigh were no longer two anonymous kids: they were, as the newspapers hailed them, "brave," "ramrod Englishmen," each of whom resembled Sir Lancelot. They met dignitaries, who wanted them to sit at their tables, and women smoking long cigarettes who offered what Colonel Fawcett called "looks of unblushing boldness." By all accounts, Jack was uncertain how to act around women: to him, it seemed, they were as mysterious and remote as Z. But Raleigh was soon flirting with a girl, surely boasting of his upcoming adventures.

Fawcett knew that for Jack and Raleigh the expedition was still no more than a feat of imagination. In New York, the young men had relished the constant fanfare: the nights in the Waldorf-Astoria Hotel, where, on their final evening, dignitaries and scientists from around the city had gathered in the Gold Room to throw them a "Godspeed" party; the toasts at the Camp Fire Club and at the National Arts Club; the stopover at Ellis Island (an immigration official had noted that no one in the party was an "atheist," a "polygamist," an "anarchist," or "deformed"); and the motion-picture palaces, which Jack had haunted day and night.

Whereas Fawcett had built up his stamina over years of exploration, Jack and Raleigh would have to do it all at once. But Fawcett had no doubt they would succeed. In his journals, he wrote that "Jack has the makings of the right sort," and predicted, "He is young enough to adapt himself to anything, and a few months on the trail will toughen him sufficiently. If he takes after me, he will not contract the various ills and diseases . . . and in an emergency I think his courage will stand." Fawcett expressed the same confidence in Raleigh, who looked up to Jack almost as intensely as Jack did to his father. "Raleigh will follow him anywhere," he observed.

The ship's crew began to yell, "All ashore that's going ashore." The captain's whistle reverberated across the port, and the boat creaked and heaved as it receded from the docks. Fawcett could see the skyline of Manhattan, with the Metropolitan Life Insurance Tower, once the tallest on the planet, and the Woolworth Building, which had now surpassed it—the metropolis blazing with lights, as if someone had gathered up all the stars. With Jack and Raleigh at his side, Fawcett shouted to the reporters on the pier, "We shall return, and we shall bring back what we seek!"

THE VANISHING

How easily the Amazon can deceive.

It begins as barely a rivulet, this, the mightiest river in the world, mightier than the Nile and the Ganges, mightier than the Mississippi and all the rivers in China. Over eighteen thousand feet high in the Andes, amid snow and clouds, it emerges through a rocky seam—a trickle of crystal water. Here it is indistinguishable from so many other streams coursing through the Andes, some cascading down the western face toward the Pacific, sixty miles away, others, like this one, rolling down the eastern facade on a seemingly impossible journey toward the Atlantic Ocean—a distance farther than New York City to Paris. At this altitude, the air is too cold for jungle or many predators. And yet it is in this place that the Amazon is born, nourished by melting snows and rain, and pulled by gravity over cliffs.

From its source, the river descends sharply. As it gathers speed, it is joined by hundreds of other rivulets, most of them so small they remain nameless. Seven thousand feet down, the water enters a valley with the first glimmers of green. Soon larger streams converge upon it. Churning toward the plains below, the river has three thousand more miles to go to reach the ocean. It is unstoppable. So, too, is the jungle, which, owing to equatorial heat and heavy rainfalls, gradually engulfs the riverbanks. Spreading toward the horizon, this wilderness contains the greatest variety of species in the world. And, for the first time, the river becomes recognizable—it *is* the Amazon.

Still, the river is not what it seems. Curling eastward, it enters an enormous region shaped like a shallow bowl, and because the Amazon rests at the bottom of this basin, nearly 40 percent of the waters from South America—from rivers as far as Colombia, Venezuela, Bolivia, and Ecuador—drain into it. And so the Amazon becomes even mightier. Three hundred feet deep in places, it no longer needs to rush, conquering at its own pace. It meanders past the Rio Negro and the Rio Madeira; past the Tapajós and the Xingu, two of the biggest southern tributaries; past Marajó, an island larger than Switzerland, until finally, after traversing four thousand miles and collecting water from a thousand tributaries, the Amazon reaches its two-hundred-mile-wide mouth and gushes into the Atlantic Ocean. What began as a trickle now expels fifty-seven million gallons of water every second—a discharge sixty times that of the Nile. The Amazon's fresh waters push so far out to sea that, in 1500, Vicente Pinzón, a Spanish commander who had earlier accompanied Columbus, discovered the river while sailing miles off the coast of Brazil. He called it Mar Dulce, or Sweet Sea.

It is difficult to explore this region under any circumstances, but in November the onset of the rainy season renders it virtually impassable. Waves—including the fifteen-mile-an-hour monthly tidal bore known as *pororoca*, or "big roar"—crash against the shore. At Belém, the Amazon frequently rises twelve feet; at Iquitos, twenty feet; at Óbidos, thirty-five feet. The Madeira, the Amazon's longest tributary, can swell even more, rising over sixty-five feet. After months of inundation, many of these and other rivers explode over their banks, cascading through the forest, uprooting plants and rocks, and transforming the southern basin almost into an inland sea, which it was millions of years ago. Then the sun comes out and scorches the region. The ground cracks as if from an earthquake. Swamps evaporate, leaving piranhas stranded in desiccated pools, eating one another's flesh. Bogs turn into meadows; islands become hills.

This is how the dry season has arrived in the southern basin of the Amazon for as long as almost anyone can remember. And so it was in June of 1996, when an expedition of Brazilian scientists and adventurers headed into the jungle. They were searching for signs of Colonel Percy Fawcett, who had vanished, along with his son Jack and Raleigh Rimell, more than seventy years earlier.

The expedition was led by a forty-two-year-old Brazilian banker named James Lynch. After a reporter mentioned to him the story of Fawcett, he had read everything he could on the subject. He learned that the colonel's disappearance in 1925 had shocked the world—"among the most celebrated vanishing acts of modern times," as one observer called it. For five months, Fawcett had sent dispatches, which were carried through the jungle, crumpled and stained, by Indian runners and, in what seemed like a feat of magic, tapped out on telegraph machines and printed on virtually every continent; in an early example of the all-consuming modern news story, Africans, Asians, Europeans, Australians, and Americans were riveted by the same distant event. The expedition, one newspaper wrote, "captured the imagination of every child who ever dreamed of undiscovered lands."

Then the dispatches ceased. Lynch read how Fawcett had warned that he might be out of contact for months, but a year passed, then two, and the public fascination grew. Were Fawcett and the two young men being held hostage by Indians? Had they starved to death? Were they too entranced by Z to return? Debates raged in salons and speakeasies; cables were exchanged at the highest levels of governments. Radio plays, novels (Evelyn Waugh's *A Handful of Dust* is believed to have been influenced by Fawcett's saga), poems, documentaries, movies, stamps, children's stories, comic books, ballads, stage plays, graphic novels, and museum exhibits were devoted to the affair. In 1933 a travel writer exclaimed,

"Enough legend has grown up round the subject to form a new and separate branch of folk-lore." Fawcett had earned his place in the annals of exploration not for what he revealed about the world but for what he concealed. He had vowed to make "the great discovery of the century"— instead, he had given birth to "the greatest exploration mystery of the twentieth century."

Lynch also learned, to his amazement, that scores of scientists, explorers, and adventurers had plunged into the wilderness, determined to recover the Fawcett party, alive or dead, and to return with proof of Z. In February 1955, the *New York Times* claimed that Fawcett's disappearance had set off more searches "than those launched through the centuries to find the fabulous El Dorado." Some parties were wiped out by starvation and disease, or retreated in despair; others were murdered by tribesmen. Then there were those adventurers who had gone to find Fawcett and, instead, disappeared along with him in the forests that travelers had long ago christened the "green hell." Because so many seekers went without fanfare, there are no reliable statistics on the numbers who died. One recent estimate, however, put the total as high as a hundred.

Lynch seemed resistant to flights of fancy. A tall, slender man, with blue eyes and pale skin that burned in the sun, he worked at Chase Bank in São Paulo. He was married with two children. But, when he was thirty, he had become restless and began to disappear for days into the Amazon, trekking through the jungle. He soon entered several grueling adventure contests: once, he hiked for seventy-two hours without sleep and traversed a canyon by shimmying across a rope. "The idea is to drain yourself physically and mentally and see how you respond under such circumstances," Lynch said, adding, "Some people would break, but I always found it slightly exhilarating."

Lynch was more than an adventurer. Drawn to quests that were intellectual as well as physical, he hoped to illuminate some little-known aspect of the world, and he often spent months in the library researching a topic. He had, for instance, ventured to the source of the Amazon and had found a colony of Mennonites living in the Bolivian desert. But he had never encountered a case like that of Colonel Fawcett.

Not only had previous search parties failed to discover the party's fate—each disappearance becoming a conundrum unto itself—but no one had unraveled what Lynch considered the biggest enigma of all: Z. Indeed, Lynch found out that unlike other lost explorers—such as Amelia Earhart, who disappeared in 1937 while trying to fly around the globe—Fawcett had made it all but impossible to trace him. He had kept his route so secret that even his wife, Nina, confessed that he had concealed crucial details from her. Lynch dug up old newspaper accounts, but they provided few tangible clues. Then he found a dog-eared copy of *Exploration Fawcett*, a collection of some of the explorer's writings edited by his surviving son, Brian, and published in 1953. (Ernest Hemingway had kept a copy of the book on his shelf.) The book appeared to contain one of the few hints of the colonel's final course, quoting Fawcett as saying, "Our route will be from Dead Horse Camp, 11°43' south and 54°35' west, where my horse died in 1921." Although the coordinates were only a starting point, Lynch plugged them into his Global Positioning System. It pinpointed a spot in the southern basin of the Amazon in Mato Grosso—its name means "thick forest"—a Brazilian state bigger than France and Great Britain combined. To reach Dead Horse Camp would require traversing some of the Amazon's most intractable jungle; it would also entail entering lands controlled by indigenous tribes, which had secluded themselves in the dense forest and fiercely guarded their territory.

The challenge seemed insurmountable. But, as Lynch pored over financial spreadsheets at work, he wondered: What if there really is a Z? What if the jungle had concealed such a place? Even today, the Brazilian government estimates that there are more than sixty Indian tribes that have never been contacted by outsiders. "These forests are . . . almost the only place on earth where indigenous people can survive in isolation from the rest of mankind," John Hemming, the distinguished historian of Brazilian Indians and a former director of the Royal Geographical Society, wrote.

Sydney Possuelo, who was in charge of the Brazilian department set up to protect Indian tribes, has said of these groups, "No one knows for sure who they are, where they are, how many they are, and what languages they speak." In 2006, members of a nomadic tribe called Nukak-Makú emerged from the Amazon in Colombia and announced that they were ready to join the modern world, though they were unaware that Colombia was a country and asked if the planes overhead were on an invisible road.

One night Lynch, unable to sleep, went into his study, which was cluttered with maps and relics from his previous expeditions. Amid his papers on Fawcett, he came across the colonel's warning to his son: "If with all my experience we can't make it, there's not much hope for others." Rather than deter Lynch, the words only compelled him. "I have to go," he told his wife.

He soon secured a partner, Rene Delmotte, a Brazilian engineer whom he had met during an adventure competition. For months, the two men studied satellite images of the Amazon, honing their trajectory. Lynch obtained the best equipment: turbocharged jeeps with puncture-resistant tires, walkie-talkies, shortwave radios, and generators. Like Fawcett, Lynch had experience designing boats, and with a shipbuilder he constructed two twenty-five-foot aluminum vessels that would be shallow enough to pass through swamps. He also put together a medical kit that contained dozens of antidotes for snake poisons.

He chose his party with equal care. He recruited two mechanics, who could repair all the equipment, and two veteran off-road drivers. He also enlisted Dr. Daniel Muñoz, an acclaimed forensic anthropologist who, in 1985, had helped to identify the remains of Josef Mengele, the Nazi fugitive, and who could help confirm the origins of any object they might find from Fawcett's party: a belt buckle, a bone fragment, a bullet.

Although Fawcett had warned that large expeditions have "only one and all come to grief," the party soon grew to include sixteen men. Still, there was one more person who wanted to go: Lynch's sixteen-year-old son, James, Jr. Athletic and more muscular than his father, with bushy brown hair and large brown eyes, he had gone on a previous expedition and acquitted himself well. And so Lynch agreed, like Fawcett, to take his son with him.

The team assembled in Cuiabá, the capital of Mato Grosso, along the southern edge of the Amazon basin. Lynch handed out T-shirts that he had made up with a picture of footprints leading into the jungle. In England, the *Daily Mail* published a story about the expedition under the headline "Are We About to Solve the Enduring Mystery of Colonel Percy Fawcett?" For days, the group drove through the Amazon basin, traversing unpaved roads scarred with ruts and brambles. The forest grew thicker, and James, Jr., pressed his face against the window. Wiping steam from the glass, he could see the leafy crowns of trees unfurling overhead, before breaking apart, as shafts of sunlight poured into the forest, the yellow wings of butterflies and macaws suddenly visible. Once, he spotted a six-foot snake, half-burrowed in mud, with a deep depression between its eyes. "*Jararaca*," his father said. It was a pit viper, one of the most venomous snakes in the Americas. (A *jararaca* bite will cause a person to bleed from the eyes and become, as a biologist put it, "a corpse piece by piece.") Lynch swerved around the snake, while the roar of the engine sent other animals, including howler monkeys, scattering into the treetops; only the mosquitoes seemed to remain, hovering over the vehicles like sentries.

After stopping several times to camp, the expedition followed the trail to a clearing along the Xingu River, where Lynch tried to get a reading on his GPS.

"What is it?" one of his colleagues asked.

Lynch stared at the coordinates on the screen. "We're not far from where Fawcett was last seen," he said.

A net of vines and lianas covered the trails extending from the clearing, and Lynch decided that the expedition would have to proceed by boat. He instructed several members to turn back with some of the heaviest gear; once he found a place where a bush plane could land, he would radio in the coordinates, so that the equipment could be delivered by air.

The remaining team members, including James, Jr., slipped the two boats into the water and began their journey down the Xingu. The currents carried them quickly, past spiny ferns and *buriti* palms, creepers and myrtles—an endless mesh that rose on either side of them. Shortly before sunset, Lynch was going around another bend, when he thought he spotted something on the distant bank. He lifted the brim of his hat. In a break amid the branches, he could see several pairs of eyes staring at him. He told his men to cut the engines; no one made a sound. As the boats drifted onto the shore, scraping against the sand, Lynch and his men leaped out. At the same time, Indians—naked, their ears pierced with dazzling macaw feathers—emerged from the forest. Eventually, a powerfully built man, his eyes encircled in black paint, stepped forward. According to some of the Indians who spoke broken Portuguese and served as translators, he was the chief of the Kuikuro tribe. Lynch told his men to get out their gifts, which included beads, candy, and matches. The chief seemed welcoming, and he granted the expedition permission to camp by the Kuikuro village and to land a propeller plane in a nearby clearing.

That night, as James, Jr., tried to sleep, he wondered if Jack Fawcett had lain in a similar spot and seen such wondrous things. The sun woke him the next morning at dawn, and he poked his head in his father's tent. "Happy birthday, Dad," he said. Lynch had forgotten that it was his birthday. He was forty-two years old.

Several Kuikuros invited Lynch and his son to a nearby lagoon later that day, where they bathed alongside hundred-pound turtles. Lynch heard the sound of a plane landing with the rest of his men and equipment. The expedition was finally coming together.

Moments later, a Kuikuro came running down the path, yelling in his native language. The Kuikuros rushed out of the water. "What is it?" Lynch asked in Portuguese.

"Trouble," a Kuikuro replied.

The Indians began to run toward the village, and Lynch and his son followed, branches ricocheting in their faces. When they arrived, a member of their expedition approached them. "What's happening?" Lynch asked.

"They're surrounding our camp."

Lynch could see more than two dozen Indian men, presumably from neighboring tribes, rushing toward them. They, too, had heard the sound of the arriving plane. Many wore black and red paint slashed across their naked bodies. They carried bows with six-foot arrows, antique rifles, and spears. Five of Lynch's men darted toward the plane. The pilot was still in the cockpit, and the five jumped into the cabin, though it was designed for only four passengers. They shouted for the pilot to take off, but he didn't seem to realize what was happening. Then he looked out the window and saw several Indians hurrying toward him, aiming their bows and arrows. As the pilot started the engine, the Indians grabbed onto the wings, trying to keep the plane grounded. The pilot, concerned that the plane was dangerously heavy, threw whatever he could find out the window—clothes and papers, which twirled in the propellers' thrust. The plane rumbled down the makeshift runway, bouncing and roaring and swerving between trees. Just before the wheels lifted off, the last of the Indians let go.

Lynch watched the plane disappear, red dust from its wake swirling around him. A young Indian, whose body was covered in paint and who seemed to be leading the assault, stepped toward Lynch, waving a *borduna*, a four-foot-long club that warriors used to smash their enemies' heads. He herded Lynch and the eleven remaining members of his team into small boats. "Where are you taking us?" Lynch asked.

"You are our prisoners for life," the young man responded.

James, Jr., fingered the cross around his neck. Lynch had always believed that there was no adventure until, as he put it, "shit happens." But this was something he had never anticipated. He had no backup plan, no experience to call upon. He didn't even have a weapon.

He squeezed his son's hand. "Whatever happens," Lynch whispered, "don't do anything unless I tell you."

The boats turned off the major river and down a narrow stream. As they floated farther into the jungle, Lynch surveyed the surroundings—the crystal clear water filled with rainbow-colored fish, the increasingly dense thicket of vegetation. It was, he thought, the most beautiful place he had ever seen.

———•••———

THE SEARCH
BEGINS

E very quest, we are led to believe, has a romantic origin. Yet, even now, I can't provide a good one for mine.

Let me be clear: I am not an explorer or an adventurer. I don't climb mountains or hunt. I don't even like to camp. I stand less than five feet nine inches tall and am nearly forty years old, with a blossoming waistline and thinning black hair. I suffer from keratoconus—a degenerative eye condition that makes it hard for me to see at night. I have a terrible sense of direction and tend to forget where I am on the subway and miss my stop in Brooklyn. I like newspapers, take-out food, sports highlights (recorded on TiVo), and the air-conditioning on high. Given a choice each day between climbing the two flights of stairs to my apartment and riding the elevator, I invariably take the elevator.

But when I'm working on a story things are different. Ever since I was young, I've been drawn to mystery and adventure tales, ones that had what Rider Haggard called "the grip." The first stories I remember being told were about my grandfather Monya. In his seventies at the time, and sick with Parkinson's disease, he would sit trembling on our porch in

Westport, Connecticut, looking vacantly toward the horizon. My grand-mother, meanwhile, would recount memories of his adventures. She told me that he had been a Russian furrier and a freelance *National Geographic* photographer who, in the 1920s, was one of the few Western cameramen allowed into various parts of China and Tibet. (Some relatives suspect that he was a spy, though we have never found any evidence to support such a theory.) My grandmother recalled how, not long before their wedding, Monya went to India to purchase some prized furs. Weeks went by with-out word from him. Finally, a crumpled envelope arrived in the mail. There was nothing inside but a smudged photograph: it showed Monya lying contorted and pale under a mosquito net, racked with malaria. He eventually returned, but, because he was still convalescing, the wedding took place at a hospital. "I knew then I was in for it," my grandmother said. She told me that Monya became a professional motorcycle racer, and when I gave her a skeptical look she unwrapped a handkerchief, revealing one of his gold medals. Once, while in Afghanistan collecting furs, he was driving through the Khyber Pass on a motorcycle with a friend in a sidecar when his brakes failed. "As the motorcycle was spinning out of control, your grandfather said goodbye to his friend," my grandmother recalled. "Then Monya spotted some men doing construction on the road; beside them was a big mound of dirt, and he steered right for it. Your grandfather and his friend were catapulted into it. They broke some bones, nothing worse. Of course, that never stopped your grandfather from riding again."

For me, the most amazing part of these adventures was the figure at the center of them. I had known my grandfather only as an old man who could barely walk. The more my grandmother told me about him, the hungrier I became for details that might help me understand him; still, there was an element about him that seemed to elude even my grand-mother. "That's just Monya," she'd say, with a wave of her hand.

When I became a reporter, I was drawn to stories that put you in "the grip." In the 1990s, I worked as a congressional correspondent, but I kept wandering off my beat to investigate stories about con men, mobsters, and spies. While most of my articles seem unrelated, they typically have one common thread: obsession. They are about ordinary people driven to do extraordinary things—things that most of us would never dare—who get some germ of an idea in their heads that metastasizes until it consumes them.

I have always thought that my interest in these people is merely professional: they provide the best copy. But at times I wonder whether I'm more similar to them than I care to believe. Reporting involves an endless quest to ferret out details, in the hopes of discovering some hidden truth. To my wife's chagrin, when I work on stories, I tend to lose sight of everything else. I forget to pay bills or to shave. I don't change my clothes as often as I should. I even take risks that I never would otherwise: crawling hundreds of feet beneath the streets of Manhattan with tunnel diggers known as sandhogs or riding in a skiff with a giant-squid hunter during a violent storm. After I returned from the boat trip, my mother said, "You know, you remind me of your grandfather."

In 2004, while researching a story on the mysterious death of a Conan Doyle and Sherlock Holmes expert, I stumbled upon a reference to Fawcett's role in inspiring *The Lost World*. As I read more about him, I became intrigued by the fantastical notion of Z: that a sophisticated civilization with monumental architecture could have existed in the Amazon. Like others, I suspect, my only impression of the Amazon was of scattered tribes living in the Stone Age—a view that derived not only from adventure tales and Hollywood movies but also from scholarly accounts.

Environmentalists have often portrayed the Amazon as a "virgin forest," which, until recent incursions by loggers and trespassers, was all but unspoiled by human hands. Moreover, many archaeologists and geographers argue that conditions in the Amazon, like those in the Arctic, had made it impossible to develop the large populations necessary for a complex society, with divisions of labor and political hierarchies such as chiefdoms and kingdoms. Betty Meggers of the Smithsonian Institution is perhaps the most influential modern archaeologist of the Amazon. In 1971, she famously summed up the region as a "counterfeit paradise," a place that, for all its fauna and flora, is inimical to human life. Rains and floods, as well as the pounding sun, leach vital nutrients from the soil and make large-scale agriculture impossible. In such a brutal landscape, she and other scientists contend, only small nomadic tribes could survive. Because the land had provided so little nutrition, Meggers wrote, even when tribes had managed to overcome attrition from starvation and diseases, they still had to come up with "cultural substitutes" to control their populations—including killing their own. Some tribes committed infanticide, abandoned their sick in the woods, or engaged in blood revenge and warfare. In the 1970s, Claudio Villas Boas, who was one of the great defenders of Amazonian Indians, told a reporter, "This is the jungle and to kill a deformed child—to abandon the man without family—can be essential for the survival of the tribe. It's only now that the jungle is vanishing, and its laws are losing their meaning, that we are shocked."

As Charles Mann notes in his book *1491*, the anthropologist Allan R. Holmberg helped to crystallize the popular and scientific view of Amazonian Indians as primitives. After studying members of the Sirionó tribe in Bolivia in the early 1940s, Holmberg described them as among "the most culturally backward peoples of the world," a society so consumed by the quest for food that it had developed no art, religion, clothes, domesticated animals, solid shelter, commerce, roads, or even the ability to count beyond three. "No records of time are kept," Holmberg said, "and no type of calendar exists." The Sirionó didn't even have a "concept of romantic" love. They were, he concluded, "man in the raw state of nature." According to Meggers, a more sophisticated civilization from the Andes had migrated down to Marajó Island, at the mouth of the Amazon, only to slowly unravel and die out. For civilization, the Amazon was, in short, a death trap.

While looking into Z, I discovered that a group of revisionist anthropologists and archaeologists have increasingly begun to challenge these long-standing views, believing that an advanced civilization could have in fact emerged in the Amazon. In essence, they argue that the traditionalists have underestimated the power of cultures and societies to transform and

transcend their natural environments, much the way humans are now creating stations in outer space and growing crops in the Israeli desert. Some
contend that the traditionalists' ideas still carry a taint of the racist views of
Native Americans, which had once infused earlier reductive theories of
environmental determinism. The traditionalists, in turn, charge that the
revisionists are an example of political correctness run amok, and that they
perpetuate a long history of projecting onto the Amazon an imaginary
landscape, a fantasy of the Western mind. At stake in the debate is a fundamental understanding of human nature and the ancient world, and the
feud has pitted scholars viciously against each other. When I called Meggers at the Smithsonian Institution, she dismissed the possibility of anyone
discovering a lost civilization in the Amazon. Too many archaeologists,
she said, are "still chasing El Dorado."

One acclaimed archaeologist from the University of Florida, in particular, disputes the conventional interpretation of the Amazon as a counterfeit paradise. His name is Michael Heckenberger, and he works in the
Xingu region where Fawcett is believed to have vanished. Several anthropologists told me that he was the person I should talk to, but warned that
he rarely emerges from the jungle and avoids any distractions from his
work. James Petersen, who in 2005 was head of the anthropology department at the University of Vermont and had trained Heckenberger, told
me, "Mike is absolutely brilliant and on the cutting edge of archaeology in
the Amazon, but I'm afraid you're barking up the wrong tree. Look, the
guy was the best man at my wedding and I can't get him to respond to any
of my communications."

With the University of Florida's help, I eventually succeeded in
reaching Heckenberger on his satellite phone. Through static and what
sounded like the jungle in the background, he said that he was going to be
staying in the Kuikuro village in the Xingu and, to my surprise, would be
willing to meet me if I made it that far. Only later, as I began to piece together more of the story of Z, did I discover that this was the very place
where James Lynch and his men had been kidnapped.

. . .

"YOU'RE GOING TO the Amazon to try to find someone who disappeared two hundred years ago?" my wife, Kyra, asked. It was a January night in 2005, and she was standing in the kitchen of our apartment, serving cold sesame noodles from Hunan Delight.

"It was only eighty years ago."

"So you're going to look for someone who vanished *eighty* years ago?"

"That's the basic idea."

"How will you even know where to look?"

"I haven't quite figured that part out yet." My wife, who is a producer at *60 Minutes* and notably sensible, put the plates on the table, waiting for me to elaborate. "It's not like I'll be the first to go," I added. "Hundreds of others have done it."

"And what happened to them?"

I took a bite of the noodles, hesitating. "Many of them disappeared."

She looked at me for a long moment. "I hope you know what you're doing."

I promised her that I would not rush into the Xingu, at least until I knew where to begin my route. Most recent expeditions had relied on the coordinates for Dead Horse Camp contained in *Exploration Fawcett*, but, given the colonel's elaborate subterfuge, it seemed strange that the camp would be that easy to find. While Fawcett had taken meticulous notes about his expeditions, his most sensitive papers were believed to have been either lost or kept private by his family. Some of Fawcett's correspondence and the diaries of members of his expeditions, however, had ended up in British archives. And so, before plunging into the jungle, I set out to England to see if I could uncover more about Fawcett's zealously guarded route and the man who, in 1925, had seemingly vanished from the earth.

4

BURIED

TREASURE

Percy Harrison Fawcett had rarely, if ever, felt so alive.

It was 1888, and he was a twenty-one-year-old lieutenant in the Royal Artillery. He had just received a month's leave from his garrison in the British colony of Ceylon and was decked out in a crisp white uniform with gold buttons and a spiked helmet strapped under his chin. Even with a rifle and a sword, though, he looked like a boy—"the callowest" of young officers, as he called himself.

He went into his bungalow at Fort Frederick, which overlooked the shimmering blue harbor in Trincomalee. Fawcett, who was an inveterate dog lover, shared his room with seven fox terriers, which, in those days, often followed an officer into battle. He searched among the local artifacts cluttering his quarters for a letter he had stashed. There it was, with strange curling characters scrawled across the front in sepia ink. Fawcett had received the note from a colonial administrator, who had been given it by a village headman for whom he had done a favor. As Fawcett later wrote in his journal, a message, in English, was attached to the mysterious script and said that in the city of Badulla, in the interior of the island, was a plain covered at one end with rocks. In Sinhalese, the spot was sometimes called Galla-pita-Galla—"Rock upon Rock." The message went on:

> Beneath these rocks is a cave, once easy to enter, but now difficult of approach as the entrance is obscured by stones, jungle and long grass. Leopards are sometimes found there. In that cave is a treasure . . . [of] uncut jewels and gold to an extent greater than that possessed of many kings.

Although Ceylon (today Sri Lanka) was renowned as "the jewel box of the Indian Ocean," the colonial administrator had placed little credence in such an extravagant tale and passed the documents to Fawcett, who he thought might find them interesting. Fawcett had no idea what to make of them—they might well be poppycock. But, unlike most of the aristocratic officer corps, he had little money. "As an impecunious Artillery lieutenant," he wrote, "the idea of treasure was too attractive to abandon." It was also a chance to escape from the base and its white ruling caste, which mirrored upper-class English society—a society that, beneath its veneer of social respectability, had always contained for Fawcett a somewhat Dickensian horror.

His father, Captain Edward Boyd Fawcett, was a Victorian aristocrat who had been a member of the Prince of Wales's inner circle and one of the empire's great batsmen in cricket. But as a young man he had degenerated into alcoholism—his nickname was Bulb, because his nose had become so bulbous from liquor—and, in addition to philandering, he squandered the family's wealth. Years later, a relative, straining to describe him in the best light, wrote that Captain Fawcett "possessed great abilities which found no true application—a good man gone wrong . . . A Balliol scholar and fine athlete . . . yachtsman, charmer and wit, equerry to the Prince of Wales (later to succeed Queen Victoria as Edward VII), he dissipated two substantial fortunes at court, neglected his wife and children . . .

and, in consequence of his dissolute ways and addiction to drink at the end of his short life, died of consumption aged forty-five."

Percy's mother, Myra Elizabeth, provided little refuge from this "disturbed" environment. "Her unhappy married life caused her much frustration and embitterment, inclining her to caprice and injustice, particularly towards her children," the family member wrote. Percy later confided to Conan Doyle, with whom he corresponded, that his mother was all but "hateful." Still, Percy tried to protect her reputation, along with his father's, by alluding to them only obliquely in *Exploration Fawcett*: "Perhaps it was all for the best that my childhood . . . was so devoid of parental affection that it turned me in upon myself."

With what money they had left, Fawcett's parents sent him to Britain's elite public schools—including Westminster—which were notorious for their harsh methods. Though Fawcett insisted that his frequent canings "did nothing to alter my outlook," he was forced to conform to the Victorian notion of a gentleman. Dress was considered an unmistakable index of character, and he often wore a black frock coat and a waistcoat and, on formal occasions, tails and a top hat; immaculate gloves, prepared with stretcher and powder machines, were so essential that some men went through six pairs in a day. Years later, Fawcett complained that "the memorable horror of [such garments] still lingered from drab days at Westminster School."

Reclusive, combative, and hypersensitive, Fawcett had to learn to converse about works of art (though never to flaunt his knowledge), to waltz without reversing himself, and to be unerringly proper in the presence of the opposite sex. Victorian society, fearful that industrialization was eroding Christian values, was obsessed with mastery over bodily instincts. There were crusades against obscene literature and "masturbatory disease," and abstinence pamphlets disseminated in the countryside instructing mothers to "keep a watchful eye on the hayfields." Doctors recommended "spiked penile rings" to restrain uncontrolled urges. Such fervor contributed to Fawcett's view of life as a never-ending war against the physical forces surrounding him. In later writings, he warned of "craving for sensual excitement" and "vices and desires" that are too often "concealed."

Gentlemanliness, though, was about more than propriety. Fawcett was expected to be, as one historian wrote of the Victorian gentleman, "a natural leader of men . . . fearless in war." Sports were considered the ultimate training for young men who would soon prove their mettle on distant battlefields. Fawcett became, like his father, a top-notch cricket player. Local newspaper accounts repeatedly hailed his "brilliant" play. Tall and lean, with remarkable hand-eye coordination, he was a natural athlete, but spectators noticed an almost maniacal determination about his style of play. One observer said that Fawcett invariably showed the bowlers that "it takes something more than the ordinary to dislodge him when once set." When he took up rugby and boxing, he displayed the same stubborn ferocity; in one rugby match, he plowed through his opponents, even after his front teeth had been knocked out.

Already uncommonly tough, Fawcett was made even more so when he was dispatched, at the age of seventeen, to the Royal Military Academy at Woolwich, or "the Shop," as it was known. Although Fawcett had no desire to be a soldier, his mother apparently forced him to go because she liked the splendid uniforms. The coldness of the Shop supplanted the coldness of his home. "Snookers"—new cadets like Fawcett—underwent hours of drills, and if they violated the code of a "gentleman cadet" they were flogged. Older cadets often made the younger ones "look out for squalls," which meant sticking their naked arms and legs out an open window in the cold for hours. Or snookers were ordered to stand on two stacked stools balanced on top of a table as the bottom legs were kicked out from under them. Or their skin was pressed against a scalding poker. "The fashion of torture was often ingenious, and sometimes worthy of the most savage races," a historian of the academy stated.

By the time Fawcett graduated, almost two years later, he had been taught, as a contemporary put it, "to regard the risk of death as the most piquant sauce to life." More important, he was trained to be an apostle of Western civilization: to go forth and convert the world to capitalism and Christianity, to transform pastures into plantations and huts into hotels, to introduce to those living in the Stone Age the marvels of the steam engine and locomotive, and to ensure that the sun never set on the British Empire.

NOW, AS FAWCETT slipped away from the secluded base in Ceylon with his treasure map in hand, he suddenly found himself amid verdant forests and crystalline beaches and mountains, and people dressed in colors that he had never seen before, not funereal blacks and whites like in London, but purples and yellows and rubies, all flashing and radiating and pulsating—a vista so astonishing that even the arch cynic Mark Twain, who visited the island around the same time period, remarked, "Dear me, it is beautiful!"

Fawcett hopped a ride on a cramped sailing vessel that, alongside the British battleships, was only a speck of wood and canvas. As the boat left the inlet, he could see Fort Frederick high on the bluff, its outer wall pocked with cannon holes from the late eighteenth century, when the British had tried to seize the promontory from the Dutch, who had previously seized it from the Portuguese. After traveling some eighty miles down the country's eastern seaboard, the boat pulled in to port at Batticaloa, where canoes circulated around incoming ships. Sinhalese traders, shouting above the splash of the oars, would offer precious stones, especially to a sahib who, wearing a top hat and with a fob watch dangling from his vest, no doubt had pockets filled with sterling. Upon disembarking, Fawcett would have been surrounded by more merchants: some Sinhalese, some Tamils, some Muslims, all crowded in the bazaar, hawking fresh produce. The air was suffused with the aroma of dried tea leaves, the sweet scent of vanilla and cacao, and something more pungent—dried fish, only not with the usual rancid odor of the sea but laden with curry. And there were people: astrologers, peddlers, dhobis, jaggery sellers, goldsmiths, tom-tom beaters, and beggars. To reach Badulla, about a hundred miles inland, Fawcett took a bullock cart, which rattled and groaned as the driver's whip lashed against the bull's flanks, prodding the beast up the mountain road, past rice fields and tea plantations. In Badulla, Fawcett asked a British plantation owner if he had heard of a place called Galla-pita-Galla.

"I'm afraid I can't tell you anything," Fawcett recalled him saying. "There's a ruin up there they call the 'King's Bath,' which may once have been a tank [reservoir] or something, but as for rocks—why, dammit, it's all rocks!" He recommended that Fawcett talk to a local headman named Jumna Das, a descendant of the Kandyan kings who ruled the country until 1815. "If anyone can tell you where Galla-pita-Galla is, it's him," the Englishman said.

That evening, Fawcett found Jumna Das, who was tall and elderly, with an elegant white beard. Das explained that the treasure of the Kandyan kings was rumored to have been buried in this region. There was no doubt, Das went on, that archaeological remains and mineral deposits lay around the foothills to the southeast of Badulla, perhaps near Galla-pita-Galla.

Fawcett was unable to locate the treasure, but the prospect of the jewels still glimmered in his mind. "Did the hound find its greatest pleasure in the chase or in the killing of its quarry?" he wondered. Later, he set out again with a map. This time, with the help of a team of hired laborers, he discovered a spot that seemed to resemble the cave described in the note. For hours, the men dug as mounds of earth formed around them, but all they uncovered were shards of pottery and a white cobra, which sent the workers scattering in terror.

Fawcett, despite his failure, relished his flight from everything he knew. "Ceylon is a very old country, and ancient peoples had more wisdom than we of today know," Das told Fawcett.

That spring, after reluctantly returning to Fort Frederick, Fawcett learned that Archduke Franz Ferdinand, a nephew of the Austro-Hungarian emperor, was planning to visit Ceylon. A gala party was announced in Ferdinand's honor, and many of the ruling elite, including Fawcett, turned out. The men wore long black dress coats and white silk cravats, the women billowing bustle skirts, with corsets pulled so tight they could barely breathe. Fawcett, who would have worn his most ceremonial dress, was a commanding and charismatic presence.

"He obviously did exert some fascination on women," a relative observed. Once, at a charity event, a reporter noted that "the way the ladies obeyed him was a sight for a king." Fawcett did not meet Ferdinand, but he spotted a more alluring figure, a girl who seemed no more than seventeen or eighteen, her skin pale, her long brown hair pinned atop her head, highlighting her exquisite features. Her name was Nina Agnes Paterson, and she was the daughter of a colonial magistrate.

Although Fawcett never acknowledged it, he must have felt some of the desires that so terrified him. (Among his papers he had kept a fortune-teller's warning: "Your greatest dangers come through women, who are greatly attracted to you, and to whom you are greatly attracted, yet they more often bring you sorrow and boundless troubles than anything else.") Not permitted by custom to approach Nina and ask her to dance, he had to find someone to officially present him, which he did.

Despite being bubbly and flighty, Nina was highly cultured. She spoke German and French, and had been tutored in geography, religious studies, and Shakespeare. She also shared some of Fawcett's brashness (she advocated women's rights) and independent curiosity (she liked to explore the island and read Buddhist texts).

The next day Fawcett wrote to his mother to tell her that he had met the ideal woman, "the only one I want to marry." Nina lived with her family on the opposite end of the island, in Galle, in a large house filled with servants, and Fawcett made pilgrimages to court her. He began to call her "Cheeky," in part, one family member said, because "she always had to have the last word"; she, in turn, called him "Puggy," because of his tenac-

ity. "I was very happy and I had nothing but admiration for Percy's character: an austere, serious and generous man," Nina later told a reporter.

On October 29, 1890, two years after they met, Fawcett proposed.
"My life would have no meaning without you," he told her. Nina agreed
immediately, and her family held a party to celebrate. But, according to
relatives, some members of Fawcett's family opposed the engagement and
lied to Fawcett, telling him that Nina was not the lady he thought she
was—in other words, that she was not a virgin. It is unclear why the family objected to the marriage and leveled such an allegation, but Fawcett's
mother appears to have been at the center of the machinations. In a letter
years later to Conan Doyle, Fawcett implied that his mother had been "a
silly old thing and an ugly old thing for being so hateful" to Nina, and that
she had "a good deal to make up for." At the time, though, Fawcett's fury
was unleashed not at his mother but at Nina. He wrote her a letter, saying,
"You are not the pure young girl I thought you to be." He then termi-
nated their engagement.

For years, they had no more contact. Fawcett remained at the fort,
where, high on the cliffs, he could see a pillar dedicated to a Dutch maiden
who, in 1687, had leaped to her death after her fiancé deserted her. Nina,
meanwhile, returned to Great Britain. "It took me a long time to recover
from this blow," she later told a reporter, though concealing the true reason for Fawcett's decision. Eventually, she met a captain in the Army
named Herbert Christie Prichard, who was either unaware of the charge
against her or unwilling to cast her out. In the summer of 1897, the two
wed. But five months later he collapsed from a cerebral embolism. As
Nina put it, "Destiny cruelly struck me again for the second time." Moments before he died, Prichard reputedly told her, "Go . . . and marry
Fawcett! He is the real man for you." By then, Fawcett had discovered his
family's deception and, according to one relative, wrote to Nina and
"begged her to take him back."

"I thought I had no love left for him," Nina confessed. "I thought that he had killed the passion I had for him with his brutish behavior." But, when they met again, she could not bring herself to rebuff him: "We looked at each other and, invincibly this time, happiness jumped all over us. We had found each other again!"

On January 31, 1901, nine days after Queen Victoria died, ending a reign that lasted almost sixty-four years, Nina Paterson and Percy Harrison Fawcett were finally married, and eventually settled at the military garrison in Ceylon. In May 1903, their first child, Jack, was born. He looked like his father, only with his mother's fairer skin and finer features. "A particularly beautiful boy," Fawcett wrote. Jack seemed preternaturally gifted, at least to his parents. "He ran about at seven months old and talked freely at a year old," Fawcett boasted. "He was and is, physically and intellectually, far ahead."

Although Ceylon had become for his wife and son "an earthly paradise," Fawcett began to chafe at the confines of Victorian society. He was too much of a loner, too ambitious and headstrong ("audacious to the point of rashness," as one observer put it), too intellectually curious to fit within the officer corps. While his wife had dispelled some of his moodiness, he remained, as he put it, a "lone wolf," determined to "seek paths of my own rather than take the well-trodden ways."

These paths led him to one of the most unconventional figures to emerge in the Victorian era: Helena Petrovna Blavatsky, or, as she was usually called, Madame Blavatsky. For a moment during the late nineteenth century, Blavatsky, who claimed to be psychic, seemed on the threshold of founding a lasting religious movement. Marion Meade, one of her most dispassionate biographers, wrote that during her lifetime people across the globe furiously debated whether she was "a genius, a consummate fraud, or simply a lunatic. By that time, an excellent case could have been made for any of the three." Born in Russia in 1831, Blavatsky was short and fat, with bulging eyes and folds of skin falling from her multiple chins. Her face was so broad that some people suspected she was a man. She professed to be a virgin (in fact, she had two husbands and an illegitimate son) and an apostle of asceticism (she smoked up to two hundred cigarettes a day and swore like a soldier). Meade wrote, "She weighed more than other people, ate more, smoked more, swore more, and visualized heaven and earth in terms that dwarfed any previous conception." The poet William Butler Yeats, who fell under her spell, described her as "the most human person alive."

As she traveled to America and Europe in the 1870s and 1880s, she gathered followers who were mesmerized by her odd charms and Gothic appetites and, what's more, by her powers to seemingly levitate objects and speak with the dead. The rise of science in the nineteenth century had had a paradoxical effect: while it undermined faith in Christianity and the literal word of the Bible, it also created an enormous void for someone to explain the mysteries of the universe that lay beyond microbes and evolution and capitalist greed. George Bernard Shaw wrote that perhaps never before had so many people been "addicted to table-rapping, materialization séances, clairvoyance, palmistry, crystal-gazing and the like."

The new powers of science to harness invisible forces often made these beliefs seem more credible, not less. If phonographs could capture human voices, and if telegraphs could send messages from one continent to the other, then why couldn't science eventually peel back the Other World? In 1882, some of England's most distinguished scientists formed the Society for Psychical Research. Members soon included a prime minister and Nobel Prize laureates, as well as Alfred Tennyson, Sigmund Freud, and Alfred Russel Wallace, who, along with Darwin, developed the theory of evolution. Conan Doyle, who in Sherlock Holmes had created the embodiment of the rationalist mind, spent years trying to confirm the existence of fairies and sprites. "I suppose I am Sherlock Holmes, if anybody is, and I say that the case for spiritualism is absolutely proved," Conan Doyle once declared.

While Madame Blavatsky continued to practice the arts of a medium, she gradually turned her attention to more ambitious psychic frontiers. Claiming that she was a conduit for a brotherhood of reincarnated Tibetan mahatmas, she tried to give birth to a new religion called Theosophy, or "wisdom of the gods." It drew heavily on occult teachings and Eastern religions, particularly Buddhism, and for many Westerners it came to represent a kind of counterculture, replete with vegetarianism. As the historian Janet Oppenheim noted in *The Other World*, "For those who wanted to rebel dramatically against the constraints of the Victorian ethos—however they perceived that elusive entity—the flavor of heresy must have been particularly alluring when concocted by so unabashed an outsider as H. P. Blavatsky."

Some Theosophists, taking their heresy even further, became Buddhists and aligned themselves with religious leaders in India and Ceylon who opposed colonial rule. Among these Theosophists was Fawcett's older brother, Edward, to whom Percy had always looked up. A hulking mountain climber who wore a gold monocle, Edward, who had been a child prodigy and published an epic poem at the age of thirteen, helped Blavatsky research and write her 1893 magnum opus, *The Secret Doctrine*. In 1890, he traveled to Ceylon, where Percy was stationed, to take the Pansil, or five precepts of Buddhism, which includes vows not to kill, drink liquor, or commit adultery. An Indian newspaper carried an account of the ceremony under the headline "Conversion of an Englishman to Buddhism":

> The ceremony commenced at about 8:30 p.m., in the *sanctum sanctorum* of the Buddhist Hall, where the High Priest Sumangala examined the candidate. Satisfied with the views of Mr. Fawcett, the High Priest . . . said that it gave him the greatest pleasure to introduce Mr. Fawcett, an educated Englishman . . . Mr. Fawcett then stood up and begged the High Priest to give him the "Pansil." The High Priest assented, and the "Pansil" was given, Mr. Fawcett repeating it after the High Priest. At the last line of the "Five Precepts" the English Buddhist was cheered vociferously by his co-religionists present.

On another occasion, according to family members, Percy Fawcett, apparently inspired by his brother, took the Pansil as well—an act that, for a colonial military officer who was supposed to be suppressing Buddhists and promoting Christianity on the island, was more seditious. In *The Victorians*, the British novelist and historian A. N. Wilson noted, "At the very time in history when the white races were imposing Imperialism on Egypt and Asia, there is something gloriously subversive about those Westerners who succumbed to the Wisdom of the East, in however garbled or preposterous a form." Other scholars point out that nineteenth and early twentieth century Europeans—even the most benignly motivated—exoticized the East, which only helped to legitimize imperialism. At least in Fawcett's mind, what he had been taught his whole life about the superiority of Western civilization clashed with what he experienced beyond its shores. "I transgressed again and again the awful laws of traditional behavior, but in doing so learned a great deal," he said. Over the years, his attempt to reconcile these opposing forces, to balance his moral absolutism and cultural relativism, would force him into bizarre contradictions and greater heresies.

Now, though, the tension merely fueled his fascination with explorers like Richard Francis Burton and David Livingstone, who had been esteemed by Victorian society, even worshipped by it, and yet were able to live outside it. Fawcett devoured accounts of their adventures in the penny presses, which were being churned out by new steam-powered printing machines. In 1853, Burton, disguised as a Muslim pilgrim, had managed to sneak into Mecca. Four years later, in the race to find the source of the Nile, John Speke had gone nearly blind from an infection and almost deaf from stabbing a beetle that was boring into his ear canal. In the late 1860s, the missionary David Livingstone, also searching for the Nile's source, vanished into the heart of Africa, and in January 1871, Henry Morton Stanley set out to find him, vowing, "No living man . . . shall stop me. Only death can prevent me." Incredibly, ten months later, Stanley succeeded, famously greeting him, "Dr. Livingstone, I presume?" Livingstone, intent on continuing his search, refused to return with him.

Suffering from a clot in his artery, disoriented, bleeding internally, and hungry, he died in northeast Zambia in 1873; in his last moments, he had been kneeling in prayer. His heart, as he requested, was buried there, while the rest of his body was carried by his followers across the continent, borne aloft as if he were a saint, and transported back to England, where throngs of people paid tribute to him at Westminster Abbey.

Fawcett later became friendly with the novelist who most vividly conjured up this world of the Victorian adventurer-savant: Sir Henry Rider Haggard. In 1885, Haggard published *King Solomon's Mines*, which was advertised as "THE MOST AMAZING BOOK EVER WRITTEN." Like many quest novels, it was patterned on folktales and myths, such as that of the Holy Grail. The hero is the iconic Allan Quatermain, a no-nonsense elephant hunter who searches for a hidden cache of diamonds in Africa with a map traced in blood. V. S. Pritchett noted that, whereas "E. M. Forster once spoke of the novelist sending down a bucket into the unconscious," Haggard "installed a suction pump. He drained the whole reservoir of the public's secret desires."

Yet Fawcett did not have to look so far to see his desires spilled on the page. After abandoning Theosophy, Fawcett's older brother, Edward, remade himself into a popular adventure novelist who for a time was hailed as the English answer to Jules Verne. In 1894, he published *Swallowed by an Earthquake*, which tells the story of a group of friends who are plunged into a subterranean world where they discover dinosaurs and a tribe of "wild-man that eats men."

It was Edward's next novel, however, that most acutely reflected his younger brother's private fantasies—and, in many ways, chillingly foretold Percy's future. Called *The Secret of the Desert* and published in 1895, the novel appeared with a blood-red cover that was engraved with a picture of an explorer wearing a pith helmet who was dangling from a rope over a palace wall. The tale centers on an amateur cartographer and archaeologist named Arthur Manners—the very personification of the Victorian sensibility. With funding from a scientific body, Manners, the "most venturesome of travellers," abandons the quaint British countryside to explore the perilous region of central Arabia. Insisting on going alone ("possibly thinking that it would be just as well to enjoy what celebrity might be in store for him unshared"), Manners wanders into the depths of the Great Red Desert in search of unknown tribes and archaeological ruins. After two years elapse without any word from him, many in England fear that he has starved or been taken hostage by a tribe. Three of Manners's colleagues launch a rescue mission, using an armor-plated vehicle that one of them has constructed—a futuristic contraption that, like Verne's submarine in *20,000 Leagues Under the Sea*, reflects both the progress and the terrifying capabilities of European civilization. The expedition picks up reports that Manners headed in the direction of the fabled Oasis of Gazelles, which is said to contain "strange ruins, relics of some race once no doubt of great renown, but now wholly forgotten." Anyone who has attempted to reach it has either vanished or been killed. As Manners's friends make toward it, they run out of water and fear that "we would-be rescuers are ourselves lost men." Then they spot a shimmering pool—the Oasis of Gazelles. And beside it are the ruins of a temple laden with treasure. "I was overcome with admiration for the forgotten race that had reared this astounding fabric," the narrator says.

The explorers discover that Manners is being held prisoner inside the temple and spirit him away in the high-speed tank. Without time to bring any artifacts to prove to the world their discovery, they must rely on Manners to persuade the "skeptics." But a member of the expedition, planning to return and excavate the ruins before anyone else, says of Manners, "He won't, I hope, be very particular about mentioning the exact latitude and longitude."

ONE DAY FAWCETT set out from Fort Frederick, trekking inland through a morass of vines and brambles. "Everywhere about me there was sound—the sound of the wild," he wrote of Ceylon's jungle. After hours, he came upon what he was looking for: a half-buried wall carved with hundreds of images of elephants. It was a remnant of an ancient temple, and all around it Fawcett could see adjoining ruins: stone pillars and palace archways and dagobas. They were part of Anuradhapura, a city that had been built more than two thousand years earlier. Now, as a contemporary of Fawcett's put it, "the city has vanished like a dream . . . Where are the hands which reared it, the men who sought its shelter in the burning heat of noon?" Later, Fawcett wrote a friend that the "old Ceylon is buried under forest and mould . . . There are bricks and vanishing dagobas and inexplicable mounds, pits, and inscriptions."

Fawcett was no longer a boy; he was in his thirties, and he could not bear to spend the rest of his life sequestered in one military garrison after another, entombed in his imagination. He wanted to become what Joseph Conrad had dubbed "a geography militant," someone who, "bearing in his breast a spark of the sacred fire," discovered along the secret latitudes and longitudes of the earth the mysteries of mankind. And he knew that there was only one place for him to go: the Royal Geographical Society, in London. It had launched Livingstone and Speke and Burton and given birth to the Victorian age of discovery. And Fawcett had no doubt that it would help him realize what he called "my Destiny."

BLANK SPOTS
ON THE MAP

H ere you go, the *Royal* Geographical Society," the taxi driver said, as the cab let me out in front of the entrance, across from Hyde Park, on a February morning in 2005. The building resembled an extravagant manor, which it had been before the Society, in need of a larger space, purchased it in 1912. Three stories high, it had redbrick walls, sash windows, Dutch pilasters, and an overhanging copper roof that came together, along with several chimneys, at various jumbled points, like a child's vision of a castle. Along the outer wall were life-size statues of Livingstone, with his trademark cap and walking stick, and of Ernest Shackleton, the Antarctic explorer, bundled in scarves and wearing boots. At the entrance, I asked a guard for the location of the archives, which I hoped would shed further light on Fawcett's career as an explorer, and on his last voyage.

When I had first called John Hemming, a former director of the Royal Geographical Society and a historian of the Brazilian Indians, to ask about the Amazon explorer, he said, "You're not one of those Fawcett lunatics, are you?" The Society had apparently become wary of people who were consumed by Fawcett's fate. Despite the passage of time and the diminished likelihood of finding him, some people seemed to grow more rather than less fanatical. For decades, they had pestered the Society for information, concocting their own bizarre theories, before setting out into the wilderness to effectively commit suicide. They were often called the "Fawcett freaks." One person who went in search of Fawcett in 1995 wrote in an unpublished article that his fascination had mutated into a "virus" and that, when he called upon the Society for help, an "exasperated" staff person said of Fawcett hunters, "I think they're mad. These people are completely obsessed." I felt slightly foolish descending upon the Society to request all of Fawcett's papers, but the Society's archives, which contain Charles Darwin's sextant and Livingstone's original maps, had been opened to the general public only in the previous few months, and could prove invaluable.

A guard at the front desk gave me a card authorizing me to enter the building, and I walked down a cavernous marble corridor, passing an old smoking lounge and a walnut-paneled map room where explorers like Fawcett had once gathered. In recent years, the Society had added a modern glass pavilion, but the renovation could not dispel the anachronistic air that hung over the institution.

Yet in Fawcett's day the Society was helping to engineer one of the most incredible feats of humankind: the mapping of the world. Perhaps no deed, not the building of the Brooklyn Bridge or the Panama Canal, rivals its scope or human toll. The endeavor, from the time the ancient Greeks laid out the main principles of sophisticated cartography, took hundreds of years, cost millions of dollars, and claimed thousands of lives, and, when it was all but over, the achievement was so overwhelming that few could recall what the world looked like before, or how the feat had been accomplished.

In a corridor of the Royal Geographical Society's building, I noticed on the wall a gigantic seventeenth-century map of the globe. On the margins were sea monsters and dragons. For ages, cartographers had no means of knowing what existed on most of the earth. And more often than not these gaps were filled in with fantastical kingdoms and beasts, as if the make-believe, no matter how terrifying, were less frightening than the truly unknown.

During the Middle Ages and the Renaissance, maps depicted fowl in Asia that tore humans apart, a bird in Germany that glowed in the dark, people in India with everything from sixteen toes to dog heads, hyenas in Africa whose shadows rendered dogs mute, and a beast called a "cockatrice" that could kill with a mere puff of its breath. The most dreaded place on the map was the land of Gog and Magog, whose armies, the book of Ezekiel had warned, would one day descend from the north to wipe out the people of Israel, "like a cloud to cover the land."

At the same time, maps expressed the eternal longing for something more alluring: a terrestrial paradise. Cartographers included as central landmarks the Fountain of Youth, for which Ponce de León scoured Florida in the sixteenth century, and the Garden of Eden, which the seventh-century encyclopedist Isidore of Seville reported was filled "with every kind of wood and fruit-bearing tree, having also the tree of life."

In the twelfth century, these feverish visions were inflamed when a letter appeared in the court of the emperor of Byzantium, purportedly written by a king named Prester John. It said, "I, Prester John, who reign supreme, exceed in riches, virtue, and power all creatures who dwell under heaven. Seventy-two kings pay tribute to me." It continued, "Honey flows in our land, and milk everywhere abounds. In one of our territories no poison can do harm and no noisy frog croaks, no scorpions are there, and no serpents creep through the grass. No venomous reptiles can exist there or use their deadly power." Though the letter was likely written as an allegory, it was taken as proof of paradise on earth, which mapmakers placed in the unexplored territories of the Orient. In 1177, Pope Alexander III dispatched his personal physician to extend "to the dearest son in Christ, the famous and high king of the Indians, the holy priest, his greetings and apostolic benediction." The doctor never returned. Still, the Church and royal courts continued for centuries to send emissaries to locate this fabulous kingdom. In 1459, the learned Venetian cartographer Fra Mauro created one of the most exhaustive maps of the world. At last, Prester John's mythic kingdom was wiped from Asia. Instead, in Ethiopia, Mauro had written, *"qui il Presto Janni fa residential principal"*—"here Prester John makes his principal residence."

Even as late as 1740, it was estimated that fewer than a hundred and twenty places on the planet had been accurately mapped. Because precise portable clocks did not exist, navigators had no means of determining longitude, which is most easily measured as a function of time. Ships plowed into rocks and shoals, their captains convinced that they were hundreds of miles out to sea; thousands of men and millions of dollars' worth of cargo were squandered. In 1714, Parliament announced that "the Discovery of the Longitude is of such Consequence to Great Britain for the safety of the Navy and Merchant-Ships as well as for the improvement of Trade" that it was offering a twenty-thousand-pound prize—the equivalent today of twelve million dollars—for a "Practical and Useful" solution. Some of the greatest scientific minds tried to solve the problem. Most hoped to use the position of the moon and stars to fix time, but in 1773 John Harrison was recognized as the winner with his more feasible solution: a three-pound, diamond-and-ruby-laden chronometer.

Despite its success, Harrison's clock could not overcome the main problem that had bedeviled mapmakers: distance. Europeans had not yet traveled to the farthest ends of the earth—the North and South Poles. Nor had they surveyed much of the interior of Africa, Australia, or South America. Cartographers scrawled across these areas on the map a single haunting word: "Unexplored."

Finally, in the nineteenth century, as the British Empire was increasingly expanding, several English scientists, admirals, and merchants believed that an institution was needed to create a map of the world based on observation rather than on imagination, an organization that detailed both the contours of the earth and everything that lay within them. And so, in 1830, the Royal Geographical Society of London was born. According to its mission statement, the Society would "collect, digest and print . . . new interesting facts and discoveries"; build a repository of "the best books on geography" and "a complete collection of maps"; assemble the most sophisticated surveying equipment; and help launch explorers on their travels. All this was part of its mandate to chart every nook and cranny of the earth. "There was not a square foot of the planet's surface to which Fellows of this Society should not at least try to go," a later president of the institution vowed. "That is our business. That is what we are out for." While the Society would serve as a handmaiden of the British Empire, what it was out for represented a departure from the previous age of discovery, when conquistadores, like Columbus, were dispatched strictly in pursuit of God, gold, and glory. In contrast, the Royal Geographical Society wanted to explore for the sake of exploration—in the name of the newest god, Science.

Within weeks of its unveiling, the Society had attracted nearly five hundred members. "[It] was composed almost entirely of men of high social standing," a secretary of the institution later remarked, adding, "It may thus be regarded as having been to some extent a Society Institution to which everybody who was anybody was expected to belong." The original list of members included acclaimed geologists, hydrographers, natural philosophers, astronomers, and military officers, as well as dukes, earls, and knights. Darwin became a member in 1838, as did one of his sons, Leonard, who in 1908 was elected president of the Society.

As the Society launched more and more expeditions around the world, it drew into its ranks not just adventurers, scholars, and dignitaries but also eccentrics. The Industrial Revolution, in addition to producing appalling conditions for the lower classes, had engendered unprecedented wealth for members of the middle and upper classes in Britain, who could suddenly afford to make leisurely pursuits such as travel a full-time hobby. Hence the rise of the amateur in Victorian society. The Royal Geographical Society became a haven for such people, along with a few poorer members, like Livingstone, whose exploits it helped to finance. Many of its members were odd even by Victorian standards. Richard Burton espoused atheism and defended polygamy so fervently that, while he was off exploring, his wife inserted into one of his manuscripts the following disclaimer: "I protest vehemently against his religious and moral sentiments, which belie a good and chivalrous life."

Not surprisingly, such members produced a fractious body. Burton recalled how at a meeting attended by his wife and family he grew so agitated after an opponent had "spoken falsely" that he waved his map pointer at members of the audience, who "looked as if a tiger was going to spring in amongst them, or that I was going to use the stick like a spear upon my adversary, who stood up from the benches. To make the scene more lively, my wife's brothers and sisters were struggling in the corner to hold down their father, an old man, who had never been used to public speaking, and who slowly rose up in speechless indignation at hearing me accused of making a misstatement." Years later, another member conceded, "Explorers are not, perhaps, the most promising people with whom to build a society. Indeed, some might say that explorers become explorers precisely because they have a streak of unsociability and a need to remove themselves at regular intervals as far as possible from their fellow men."

Debates raged within the Society over the course of rivers and mountains, the boundaries of cities and towns, and the size of the oceans. No less intense were the disputes over who deserved recognition, and the subsequent fame and fortune, for making a discovery. And the discussions often involved the most fundamental questions of morality and human existence: Were newly discovered tribes savages or civilized? Should they be converted to Christianity? Did all of humanity stem from one ancient civilization or from many? The struggle to answer such questions frequently pitted the so-called "armchair" geographers and theoreticians, who pored over incoming data, against the rough-and-tumble explorers, who worked in the field. One official of the Society reprimanded an African explorer for his suppositions, telling him, "What you can do, is state accurately what you *saw*, leaving it to stay-at-home men of science to collate the data of very many travelers, in order to form a theory." The explorer Speke, in turn, denounced those geographers "who sit in carpet slippers, and criticise those who labour in the field."

Perhaps the most vicious feud was over the source of the Nile. After Speke claimed in 1858 that he had discovered the river's origin, at a lake he christened Victoria, many of the Society's members, led by his former traveling companion Burton, refused to believe him. Speke said of Burton, "B is one of those men who never can be wrong, and will never acknowledge an error." In September of 1864, the two men, who had once nursed each other back from death on an expedition, were supposed to square off in a public meeting. The London *Times* called it a "gladiatorial exhibition." But, as the meeting was about to begin, the gatherers were informed that Speke would not be coming: he had gone hunting the previous day, and was found dead of a self-inflicted gunshot wound. "By God, he's killed himself!" Burton reportedly exclaimed, staggering on the stage; later, Burton was seen in tears, reciting his onetime companion's name over and over. Although it was never known for certain if the shooting was intentional, many suspected, like Burton, that the protracted feud had caused the man who had conquered the desert to take his own life. A decade later, Speke's claim to having discovered the Nile's source would be proved correct.

During the Society's early years, no member personified the organization's eccentricities or audacious mission more than Sir Francis Galton. A cousin of Charles Darwin's, he had been a child prodigy who, by the age of four, could read and recite Latin. He went on to concoct myriad inventions. They included a ventilating top hat; a machine called a Gumption-Reviver, which periodically wet his head to keep him awake during endless study; underwater goggles; and a rotating-vane steam engine. Suffering from periodic nervous breakdowns—"sprained brain," as he called it—he had a compulsion to measure and count virtually everything. He quantified the sensitivity of animal hearing, using a walking stick that could make an inconspicuous whistle; the efficacy of prayer; the average age of death in each profession (lawyers: 66.51; doctors: 67.04); the exact amount of rope needed to break a criminal's neck while avoiding decapitation; and levels of boredom (at meetings of the Royal Geographical Society he would count the rate of fidgets among each member of the audience). Notoriously, Galton, who like so many of his colleagues was a profound racist, tried to measure levels of intelligence in people and later became known as the father of eugenics.

In another age, Galton's monomania with quantification might have made him a freak. But, as the evolutionary biologist Stephen Jay Gould once observed, "no man expressed his era's fascination with numbers so well as Darwin's celebrated cousin." And there was no place that shared his fascination more than the Royal Geographical Society. In the 1850s, Galton, who had inherited enough money to enable him to avoid the burden of a conventional career, became a member of the Society and, with its endorsement and guidance, explored southern Africa. "A passion for travel seized me," he wrote, "as if I had been a migratory bird." He mapped and documented everything that he could: latitudes and longitudes, topography, animals, climate, tribes. Returning to great fanfare, he received the Royal Geographical Society's gold medal, the field's most prestigious honor. In 1854, Galton was elected to the Society's governing body, on which, for the next four decades, he served in varying capacities, including honorary secretary and vice president. Together, Galton and this collection of men—they were all men until a divisive vote at the end of the nineteenth century admitted twenty-one women—began to attack, as Joseph Conrad put it of such militant geographers, "from north and south and east and west, conquering a bit of truth here and a bit of truth there, and sometimes swallowed up by the mystery their hearts were so persistently set on unveiling."

"WHAT MATERIALS are you looking for?" one of the archivists asked me.

I had gone down into the small reading room in the basement.

Bookshelves, illuminated under fluorescent lights, were crammed with travel guides, atlases, and bound copies of the *Proceedings of the Royal Geographical Society*. Most of the Society's collection of more than two million maps, artifacts, photographs, and expedition reports had been moved in recent years from what had been called "Dickensian conditions" to climate-controlled catacombs, and I could see staff flitting in and out of them through a side door.

When I told the archivist that I was looking for Fawcett's papers, she gave me a quizzical look. "What is it?" I asked.

"Well, let's just say many people who are interested in Fawcett are a little . . ." Her voice trailed off as she disappeared into the catacombs. While I was waiting, I skimmed through several accounts of expeditions backed by the Society. One described an 1844 expedition led by Charles Sturt and his second-in-command, James Poole, which searched the Australian desert for a legendary inland sea. "So great is the heat that . . . our hair has ceased to grow, our nails have become brittle as glass," Sturt wrote in his diary. "The scurvy shows itself upon us all. We are attacked by violent headaches, pains in the limbs, swollen and ulcerated gums. Mr. Poole became worse and worse: ultimately the skin over his muscles became black, and he lost the use of his lower extremities. On the 14th he suddenly expired." The inland sea never existed, and these accounts made me aware of how much of the discovery of the world was based on failure rather than on success—on tactical errors and pipe dreams. The Society may have conquered the world, but not before the world had conquered its members. Among the Society's long list of those who were sacrificed, Fawcett filled a distinct category: neither alive nor dead—or, as one writer dubbed him, "the living dead."

The archivist soon emerged from the stacks carrying a half-dozen mottled folders. As she placed them on the table, they released purplish dust. "You'll have to put these on," she said, handing me a pair of white gloves. After I slipped them over my fingers, I opened the first folder: yellowed, crumbling letters spilled out. On many of the pages were impossibly small, slanting words that ran together, as if written in code. It was Fawcett's handwriting. I took one of the pages and spread it in front of me. The letter was dated 1915 and began "Dear Reeves." The name was familiar, and I opened one of the books on the Royal Geographical Society and scanned its index. Edward Ayearst Reeves had been the map curator of the institution from 1900 to 1933.

The folders contained more than two decades of correspondence between Fawcett and officials at the Society. Many of the letters were addressed to Reeves or to Sir John Scott Keltie, who was the RGS secretary from 1892 to 1915 and later its vice president. There were also scores of letters from Nina, government officials, explorers, and friends concerning Fawcett's disappearance. I knew it would take me days, if not weeks, to go through everything, and yet I felt delight. Here was a road map to Fawcett's life as well as to his death.

I held one of the letters up to the light. It was dated December 14, 1921. It said, "There is very little doubt that the forests cover traces of a lost civilization of a most unsuspected and surprising character."

I opened my reporter's pad and started to take notes. One of the letters mentioned that Fawcett had received "a diploma" from the RGS. I had never seen any reference to the Society having given out diplomas, and I asked the archivist why Fawcett had been awarded one.

"He must have enrolled in one of the Society's training programs," she said. She walked over to a bookshelf and began to riffle through journals. "Yes, right here. He apparently took a course and graduated around 1901."

"You mean he actually went to school to become an explorer?"

"I guess you could call it that."

6

THE DISCIPLE

Fawcett didn't want to be late. It was February 4, 1900, and all he had to do was get from his hotel in Redhill, Surrey, to No. 1 Savile Row, in the Mayfair district of London, but nothing in the city moved— or, more accurately, everything seemed to be moving. Billboard men. Butcher boys. Clerks. Horse-drawn omnibuses. And that strange beast which was invading the streets, scaring the horses and pedestrians, breaking down on every curb: the automobile. The law had originally required drivers to proceed at no more than two miles per hour with a footman walking ahead waving a red flag, but in 1896 the speed limit had been raised to fourteen miles per hour. And everywhere Fawcett turned the new and the old seemed to be at war: electric lights, scattered on the fancier granite streets, and gas lamps, lodged on most cobblestoned corners, glowing in the fog; the Tube bolting through the earth like one of Edward Fawcett's science-fiction inventions, and bicycles, only a few years earlier the smartest thing on the footpaths and now already fusty. Even the smells seemed at odds: the traditional stench of horse dung and the newer whiff of petrol. It was as if Fawcett were glimpsing the past and the future at once.

Since he had left England for Ceylon fourteen years earlier, London seemed to have become more crowded, more dirty, more modern, more rich, more poor, more everything. With over four and a half million people, London was the biggest city in the world, larger than Paris or New York. Flower girls yelled, "All a growin' and all a blowin'!" Newspaper boys cried, " 'Orrible murder!"

As Fawcett pushed his way through the crowds, he no doubt struggled to keep his clothes free of the soot from coal furnaces that had mixed with fog to form London's own species of grime, a tenacious black mixture that penetrated everything; even the keyholes on houses had to be sheathed with metal plates. Then there was the horse manure—"the London mud," as it was politely called—which, though swept up by street urchins and sold door-to-door as garden fertilizer, was virtually everywhere Fawcett stepped.

Fawcett turned onto an elegant street in Burlington Gardens, away from brothels and blacking factories. On the corner was a handsome stone house with a portico. It was No. 1 Savile Row. And Fawcett could see the bold sign: ROYAL GEOGRAPHICAL SOCIETY.

As Fawcett entered the three-story house—the Society had not yet moved near to Hyde Park—he was aware that he was stepping into an enchanting place. Over the front door was a half window in the shape of a hemispherical lantern; each pane represented the parallels and meridians of a globe. Fawcett would have walked past the office of the chief clerk and his two assistants, past a stairwell that led to a council room, until he arrived at a glass-roofed chamber. Sunlight filtered in, illuminating, through dusty shafts, globes and chart tables. It was the map room, and usually sitting at the far end, on a dais, was the man Fawcett was looking for: Edward Ayearst Reeves.

In his late thirties, with a receding hairline, beakish nose, and neatly trimmed mustache, Reeves was not only the map curator but also the chief instructor of surveying—and the person primarily charged with turning Fawcett into a gentleman explorer. A skilled draftsman, Reeves had started working at the Society in 1878, at the age of sixteen, as an assistant to the previous curator, and he never seemed to forget that sense of awe that newcomers felt upon arrival. "How well I remember it all," he wrote in his autobiography, *The Recollections of a Geographer.* "With what pride, and yet with what fear and trembling I first entered the precinct of this wonderful place of which I had read in books, and from which explorers had been sent out to all parts of the world and returned to tell of their marvelous discovery and heroic adventures." Unlike many of the bellicose, wild-eyed members of the Society, Reeves had a warm, gentle manner. "He had an innate capacity for teaching," a colleague said. "He knew exactly how to put a point so that the most obtuse student could grasp it."

Fawcett and Reeves eventually went up to the third floor, where the classes were held. Francis Galton had advised each recruit that he would soon find himself admitted into "the society of men with whose names he had long been familiar, and whom he had reverenced as his heroes." Taking the surveying course about the same time as Fawcett was Charles Lindsay Temple, who could regale his colleagues with stories of his time in the Civil Service in Brazil; Lieutenant T. Dannreuther, who was obsessed with collecting rare butterflies and insects; and Arthur Edward Seymour Laughton, who was gunned down by Mexican bandits in 1913, at the age of thirty-eight.

Reeves got down to business. If Fawcett and the other students heeded his instructions, they could become the next generation of great explorers. Reeves would teach them what cartographers had not been able to do for most of history: fix their position anywhere. "If you could blindfold a man, and take him to any spot on the earth's surface, say somewhere in the middle of Africa, and then remove the bandage from his eyes, he could [if properly trained] show you on a map, in a short time, the exact spot upon which he stands," Reeves said. Moreover, if Fawcett and his colleagues dared to climb the highest peaks and penetrate the deepest forest, they could chart the world's remaining undiscovered realms.

Reeves displayed a series of strange objects. One looked like a telescope attached to a circular metal wheel, with various screws and chambers. Reeves explained that it was a theodolite, which could determine the angle between the horizon and celestial bodies. He demonstrated more tools—artificial horizons, aneroids, and sextants—and then led Fawcett and the others up to the roof of the building, to test the equipment. The fog often made it hard to observe the sun or the stars, but now they could see well enough. Latitude, Reeves said, could be found by measuring the angle of the noon sun above the horizon or the height of the North Star, and each of the students tried to use the devices to fix his position, an extremely difficult task for a beginner. As Fawcett took his turn, Reeves watched in astonishment. "He was extremely quick at learning anything new," Reeves recalled. "And, although he never used a sextant and artificial horizon before for star observation, I remember the first night he tried he brought the stars down into the artificial horizon, and took excellent altitude right away without any difficulty. Anyone who has attempted this will know that as a rule it is only done after considerable practice."

Fawcett was taught not just how to survey but how to see—to record and classify everything around him, in what the Greeks called an *autopsis*. There were two principal manuals to help him. One was *Art of Travel*, written by Francis Galton for a general audience. The other was *Hints to Travellers*, which had been edited by Galton and served as the Society's unofficial bible. (Fawcett brought a copy with him even on his final trip.) The 1893 edition stated, "It is a loss, both to himself and others, when a traveller does not observe." The manual continued, "Remember that the first and best instruments are the traveller's own eyes. Use them constantly, and record your observation on the spot, keeping for the purpose a note-book with numbered pages and a map . . . Put down, as they occur, all important objects; streams, their volume, colour; mountain ranges, their character and apparent structure and glaciation, the colour and forms of the landscape, prevalent winds, climate . . . In short, describe to yourself at the time all you see." (The need to record every observation was so ingrained that during Robert Falcon Scott's race to the South Pole he continued to make notations even as he and all his men were dying. Among the last words scribbled in his diary were "Had we lived, I should have had a tale to tell of the hardihood, endurance, and courage of my companions which would have stirred the heart of every Englishman. These rough notes and our dead bodies must tell the tale.")

To hone the aspiring explorers' powers of observation, the manuals, in conjunction with seminars provided by the Society, offered basic instructions on botany, geology, and meteorology. Students were also initiated into the fledgling field of anthropology, what was then often called the "science of savages." Despite the Victorians' dizzying contact with alien cultures, the field was still composed almost entirely of amateurs and enthusiasts. (In 1896, Great Britain had only one university professor of anthropology.) Just as Fawcett had been taught to see the contours of the earth, he was now taught how to observe the Other—what *Hints to Travellers* referred to as "savages, barbarians, or the lower civilised nations." The manual warned each student against "the prejudices with which his European mode of thought has been surrounded," even as it noted that "it is established that some races are inferior to others in volume and complexity of brain, Australians and Africans being in this respect below Europeans."

As with mapping the world, there were "tools" for taking the measure of man: tapelines and calipers for calculating body proportions; dynamometers for assessing muscle strength and spring balances to determine weight; plaster of Paris for making impressions; and a craniometer to gauge the size of a skull. "Where practicable, native skeletons, and especially skulls, should be sent home for accurate examination," the manual said. Of course, this could be tricky: "It is hardly safe to risk the displeasure of the natives at the removal of the dead." It was deemed unknown how "emotions are differently expressed by different races, so that it is worth while to notice particularly if their smiling, laughing, frowning, weeping, blushing, &c, differ perceptibly from ours."

Fawcett and his classmates were also schooled in the fundamentals of mounting and executing an expedition—everything from how to make pillows out of mud to choosing the best pack animals. "Notwithstanding his inveterate obstinacy, the ass is an excellent and sober little beast, far too much despised by us," Galton pointed out, calculating, with his usual obsessiveness, that an ass could carry about sixty-five pounds, a horse up to a hundred pounds, and a camel up to three hundred.

Before embarking, the explorer was instructed to have each member of his expedition sign a formal agreement, like a treaty. Galton provided a sample:

> We, the undersigned, forming an expedition about to explore the interior of _____, under Mr. A., consent to place ourselves (horses and equipments) entirely and unreservedly under his orders for the above purpose, from the date hereof until our return to _____, or, on failure in this respect, to abide all consequences that may result . . .
>
> We severally undertake to use our best endeavors to promote the harmony of the party, and the success of the expedition. In witness whereof we sign our names.
>
> (Here follow the signatures.)

The students were warned that they should not lord it over their men and must constantly be on the lookout for cliques, dissent, and mutiny. "Promote merriment, singing, fiddling, with all your powers," Galton advised. Care must also be taken with native helpers: "A frank, joking, but determined manner, joined with an air of showing more confidence to the savage than you really feel, is the best."

Disease and injury could devastate a party, and Fawcett received some basic medical tips. He learned, for instance, how to remove a decaying tooth by "constantly pushing and pulling." If he ingested poison, he was taught to immediately make himself throw up: "Use soap-suds or gunpowder if proper emetics are not at hand." For a venomous snakebite, Fawcett would have to ignite gunpowder in the wound or cut away the infected flesh with a knife. "Afterwards burn out [the area around the bite] with the end of your iron ramrod, heated as near a white heat as you can readily get," Galton advised. "The arteries lie deep, and as much flesh may, without much danger, be cut or burnt into, as the fingers can pinch up. The next step is to use the utmost energy, and even cruelty, to prevent the patient's giving way to that lethargy and drowsiness which is the usual effect to snake poison, and too often ends in death." The treatment for a hemorrhaging wound—say, from an arrow—was equally "barbarous": "Pour boiling grease into the wound."

Nothing, though, compared with the horrors of thirst and hunger. One trick was to "excite" saliva in the mouth. "This can be done by chewing something, as a leaf; or by keeping in the mouth a bullet or a smooth, non-absorbent stone, such as a quartz pebble," Galton explained. When starving, Fawcett was instructed to drink an animal's blood, if available. Locusts, grasshoppers, and other insects were also edible—and might save a man's life. ("To prepare them, pull off the legs and wings and roast them with a little grease in an iron dish, like coffee.")

Then there was the threat of hostile "savages" and "cannibals." When penetrating such territories, an explorer was cautioned to move under the cover of darkness, with a rifle cocked and ready. To seize a prisoner, "take your knife, put it between your teeth, and, standing over him, take the caps off your gun, and lay it down by your side. Then handcuff him, in whatever way you best can. The reason of setting to work in this way is, that a quick supple savage, while you are fumbling with your strings, and bothered with a loaded gun, might easily spring round, seize hold of it, and quite turn the tables against you."

Finally, the students were advised how to proceed if a member of their party perished. They must write down a detailed account of what had happened and have the remaining members of the expedition corroborate it. "If a man be lost, before you turn away and abandon him to his fate, call the party formally together, and ask them if they are satisfied that you have done all that was possible to save him, and record their answers," Galton stated. When a companion died, his effects must be collected for relatives and his body buried with dignity. "Choose a well-marked situation, dig a deep grave, bush it with thorns, and weight it well over with heavy stones, as a defense against animals of prey."

After more than a year of course work, Fawcett sat down, along with his classmates, for the final examination. The students had to demonstrate a mastery of surveying, which required a deep understanding of complex geometry and astronomy. Fawcett had spent hours cramming with Nina, who shared his interest in exploration and worked tirelessly to help him. If he failed, he knew that he would be back to square one—back to being a soldier. He carefully filled in each answer. When he finished, he handed his paper in to Reeves. Then he waited. Reeves informed the students of their results, and broke the news to Fawcett. He had passed—and more than that. Reeves, in his memoir, singled Fawcett out, noting that he had graduated "with great credit." Fawcett had done it; he had received the imprimatur of the Royal Geographical Society—or, as he put it, "The R.G.S. bred me as an explorer." All he needed now was a mission.

Freeze-Dried Ice Cream and Adrenaline Socks

Y ou can't just go like that," my wife said.

I looked down at the bed, where I had laid out some shorts and a pair of Adidas sneakers. "I've got a Swiss Army knife," I said.

"You're not giving me a whole lot of confidence."

The next day, at her prodding, I tried to find a place where I could purchase more suitable gear. Friends directed me to one of the many stores in Manhattan that cater to the growing number of hikers, off-road bikers, extreme-sports junkies, and weekend warriors. The store was virtually the size of an industrial warehouse, and, as I stepped inside, I was overwhelmed. There were rainbow-colored tents and banana-hued kayaks and mauve mountain bikes and neon snowboards dangling from the ceilings and walls. Whole aisles were devoted to insect repellents, freeze-dried foods, lip balms, and sunscreens. A separate section existed for footwear ("Gurus can lead you to a perfect fit!" a sign said), which didn't include an additional space for "spring loaded ratchet binding" snowshoes. There was an area for "adrenaline socks" and one for Techwick "skivvies." Racks held magazines like *Hooked on the Outdoors* and *Backpacker: The Outdoors at Your Doorstep*, which had articles titled "Survive a Bear Attack!" and "America's Last Wild Places: 31 Ways to Find Solitude, Adventure—and Yourself." Wherever I turned, there were customers, or "gear heads." It was as if the fewer the opportunities for genuine exploration, the greater the means were for anyone to attempt it, and the more baroque the ways—bungee cording, snowboarding—that people found to replicate the sensation. Exploration, however, no longer seemed aimed at some outward discovery; rather, it was directed inward, to what guidebooks and brochures called "camping and wilderness therapy" and "personal growth through adventure."

I was standing in bewilderment before a glass case filled with several watch-like contraptions when a young attendant with long, lean arms appeared from behind the counter. He had the glow of someone who had recently returned from Mount Everest.

"Can I help you with something?" he asked.

"What's that thing there?" I asked.

"Oh, that rocks." He slid open the counter door and removed the item. "It's a little computer. See? It'll give you the temperature wherever you are. And the altitude. It's also got a digital compass, clock, alarm, and chronometer. You can't beat it."

I asked how much it was, and he said about two hundred dollars, though I wouldn't regret it.

"And what's that?" I asked, pointing to another gadget.

"Pretty much the same deal. Only that one monitors your heart rate, too. Plus, it's a great logbook. It'll store all the data you want to put in about weather, distances, rates of ascent—you name it. What kind of trip you planning anyway?"

When I explained, as best I could, my intentions, he seemed enthusiastic, and I thought of one Fawcett seeker from the 1930s who had classified people based on their reactions to his plans:

> There were the Prudent, who said: "This is an extraordinarily foolish thing to do." There were the Wise, who said: "This is an ex-

traordinarily foolish thing to do; but at least you will know better next time." There were the Very Wise, who said: "This is a foolish thing to do, but not nearly so foolish as it sounds." There were the Romantic, who appeared to believe that if everyone did this sort of thing all the time the world's troubles would soon be over. There were the Envious, who thanked God they were not coming; and there were the other sort, who said with varying degrees of insincerity that they would give anything to come. There were the Correct, who asked me if I knew any of the people at the Embassy. There were the Practical, who spoke at length of inoculations and calibres . . . There were the Apprehensive, who asked me if I had made my will. There were the Men Who Had Done A Certain Amount of That Sort of Thing In Their Time, You Know, and these imparted to me elaborate stratagems for getting the better of ants and told me that monkeys made excellent eating, and so for that matter did lizards, and parrots; they all tasted rather like chicken.

The salesman seemed like the Romantic type. He asked how long I intended to go, and I said I didn't know—at least a month, probably more.

"Awesome. Awesome. That should let you get immersed in the place." He seemed to be thinking of something. Then he asked if it was true that some catfish in the Amazon, called a candiru, "you know, that *it*—"

He didn't finish his question, though he didn't have to. I had read about the almost translucent, toothpick-like creature in *Exploration Fawcett*. More feared than piranhas, it is one of the few creatures in the world to survive strictly on a diet of blood. (It is also called the "vampire fish of Brazil.") Ordinarily, it burrows in the gills of a fish and sucks its blood, but it also strikes human orifices—a vagina or an anus. It is, perhaps, most notorious for lodging in a man's penis, where it latches on irrevocably with its spines. Unless removed, it means death, and in the remote Amazon victims are reported to have been castrated in order to save them. Fawcett, who had seen a candiru that had been surgically extricated from a man's urethra, said, "Many deaths result from this fish, and the agony it can cause is excruciating."

When I told the salesman what I knew about the candiru, he seemed to transform from the Romantic into the Practical. Although there was little to protect someone from such a creature, he told me about one gizmo after another that was revolutionizing the art of camping: a tool that was a digital thermometer, a flashlight, a magnifying glass, and a whistle; compression sacks that shrank everything inside; Swiss Army knives with a computer flash drive to store photographs and music; water-purifying bottles that doubled as lanterns; portable solar-powered hot showers; kayaks that folded into the size of a duffel bag; a floating flashlight that didn't need batteries; parkas that converted into sleeping bags; poleless tents; a tablet that "destroys viruses and bacteria in 15 minutes."

The more he explained things, the more emboldened I became. I can do this, I thought, piling several of the most James Bond–like items into my basket. Finally, the salesman said, "You've never camped before, have you?"

He then helped me find the things that I'd really need, including comfortable hiking boots, a sturdy backpack, synthetic clothes, freeze-dried food, and a mosquito net. I also tossed in a handheld Global Positioning System just to be safe. "You'll never get lost again," he said.

I thanked him profusely, and when I got back to our apartment building I carried the equipment into the elevator. I hit the second-floor button. Then, as the door was about to close, I extended my hand to stop it. I got out and, hauling the stuff in my arms, walked up the stairs instead.

That night, after I put my son, Zachary, to sleep, I laid out all the things I planned to take on the trip and began to pack them. Among the items was a file I had made with copies of the most important Fawcett documents and papers. As I flipped through them, I paused at a letter that detailed something, in Brian Fawcett's words, so "hush-hush" that his father "never spoke of its objects" to anyone. After receiving his diploma from the Society, the letter said, Fawcett had been given his first assignment, in 1901, from the British government. He was to go to Morocco—not as an explorer but as a spy.

8

INTO

THE AMAZON

I t was the perfect cover. Go in as a cartographer, with maps and telescope and high-powered binoculars. Survey your target the way you
surveyed the land. Observe everything: people, places, conversations.

In his diary, Fawcett had jotted down a list of things that his British
handler—someone he called simply "James"—had asked him to assess:
"nature of trails . . . villages . . . water . . . army and organization . . . arms
and guns . . . political." Wasn't an explorer really just an infiltrator, someone who penetrated alien lands and returned with secrets? In the nineteenth century, the British government had increasingly recruited agents
from the ranks of explorers and mapmakers. It was a way not only to sneak
people into foreign territories with plausible deniability but also to tap recruits skilled in collecting the sensitive geographical and political data that
the government most coveted. British authorities transformed the Survey
of India Department into a full-time intelligence operation. Cartographers
were trained to use cover stories and code names ("Number One," "The
Pundit," "The Chief Pundit"), and, when entering lands forbidden to
Westerners, to wear elaborate disguises. In Tibet, many surveyors dressed

as Buddhist monks and employed prayer beads to measure distances (each sliding bead represented a hundred paces) and prayer wheels to conceal compasses and slips of paper for notations. They also installed trapdoors in their trunks to hide larger instruments, like sextants, and poured mercury, essential for operating an artificial horizon, into their pilgrim's begging bowls. The Royal Geographical Society was often aware of, if not complicit in, such activities—its ranks were scattered with current and former spies, including Francis Younghusband, who served as president of the Society from 1919 to 1922.

In Morocco, Fawcett was participating in an African version of what Rudyard Kipling, referring to the colonial competition for supremacy over central Asia, called "the Great Game." Scribbling in his secret scrolls, Fawcett wrote that he "chatted" with a Moroccan official who was "full of information." When venturing beyond the main desert routes, where tribes kidnapped or murdered foreign trespassers, Fawcett later noted, "some sort of Moorish disguise is considered necessary, and even then the journey is attended with very great risk." Fawcett managed to insinuate himself into the royal court to spy on the sultan himself. "The Sultan is young and weak in character," he wrote. "Personal pleasure is the first consideration, and time is passed bicycle trick riding, at which he is a considerable adept, in playing with motorcars, mechanical toys, photography, billiards, pig sticking on bicycles, feeding his menagerie." All this information Fawcett delivered to "James" and then returned to England in 1902. It was the only time Fawcett acted as an official spy, but his cunning and powers of observation caught the attention of Sir George Taubman Goldie, a British colonial administrator who in 1905 became president of the Royal Geographical Society.

In early 1906, Goldie summoned Fawcett, who, since his Morocco trip, had been stationed in several military garrisons, most recently in Ireland. Goldie was not someone to trifle with. Famous for his keen intelligence and volatile temper, he had almost single-handedly imposed the British Empire's control over Niger, in the 1880s and 1890s. He had shocked Victorian society by running off to Paris with a governess, and was an unrepentant atheist who championed Darwin's theory of evolution. "[He] was lashed into frenzies of impatience by stupidity, or incompetence," one of his biographers wrote. "Never did man suffer fools less gladly."

Fawcett was led into the RGS to see Goldie, whose blue eyes seemed to "bore holes into one," as a subordinate once put it. Goldie, who was nearly sixty, always carried in his pocket a tube of poison, which he planned to take if he ever became physically handicapped or incurably ill. As Fawcett recalled, Goldie asked him, "Do you know anything about Bolivia?"

When Fawcett said no, Goldie continued, "One usually thinks of Bolivia as a country on the roof of the world. A great deal of it is in the mountains; but beyond the mountains, to the east, lies an enormous area of tropical forest and plains." Goldie reached into his desk and pulled out a large map of Bolivia, which he spread before Fawcett like a tablecloth. "Here you are, Major—here's about as good a map of the country as I have! Look at this area! It's full of blank spaces." As Goldie traced his finger over the map, he explained that the area was so unexplored that Bolivia, Brazil, and Peru could not even agree on their borders: they were simply speculative lines sketched through mountains and jungles. In 1864, boundary disputes between Paraguay and its neighbors had erupted into one of the worst conflicts in Latin American history. (About half the Paraguayan population was killed.) Because of the extraordinary economic demand for rubber—"black gold"—which was abundant in the region, the stakes over the Amazon delimitation were equally fraught. "A major conflagration could arise out of this question of what territory belongs to whom," Goldie said.

"All this is most interesting," Fawcett interrupted. "But what has it got to do with me?"

Goldie said that the countries had established a boundary commission and were seeking an impartial observer from the Royal Geographical Society to map the borders in question—beginning with an area between

Bolivia and Brazil that comprised several hundred miles in nearly impassable terrain. The expedition would take up to two years, and there was no guarantee that its members would survive. Disease was rampant in the region, and the Indians, who had been attacked mercilessly by rubber trappers, murdered interlopers. "Would you be interested in taking it on?" Goldie asked.

Fawcett later said that he felt his heart pounding. He thought about his wife, Nina, who was pregnant again, and his son, Jack, who was almost three years old. Still, he didn't hesitate: "Destiny intended me to go, so there could be no other answer!"

THE CRAMPED, DIRTY hold of the SS *Panama* was filled with "toughs, would be toughs, and leather faced old scoundrels," as Fawcett put it. Prim in his starched white collar, Fawcett sat beside his second-in-command for the expedition, a thirty-year-old engineer and surveyor named Arthur John Chivers, whom the Royal Geographical Society had recommended. Fawcett passed the time by studying Spanish, while other passengers sipped whiskey, spit tobacco, played dice, and slept with whores. "They were all good fellows in their way," Fawcett wrote, adding, "To [Chivers] and myself it served as a useful introduction to an aspect of life we had not hitherto known, and much of our English reserve was knocked off in the process."

The ship docked in Panama, where the construction of the canal—the most audacious attempt yet by man to tame nature—was under way, and the project gave Fawcett the first inkling of what he was about to encounter: stacked on the pier were dozens of coffins. Since the canal's excavation began, in 1881, more than twenty thousand laborers had died from malaria and yellow fever.

In Panama City, Fawcett boarded a ship for Peru, then proceeded by train up the glimmering, snowcapped Andes. When the train reached around twelve thousand feet, he switched to a boat and crossed Lake Titicaca ("How strange it is to see steamers in operation up here on the roof of the world!"), before squeezing into another jaw-rattling train, which took him across the plains to La Paz, the capital of Bolivia. There he waited more than a month for the government to provide a few thousand dollars, a sum far less than he had counted on, for provisions and travel expenses, his impatience provoking a row with local officials that had to be smoothed over by the British consul. Finally, on July 4, 1906, he and Chivers were ready to go. They loaded their mules with tea, preserved milk, Edwards' Desiccated Soup, sardines in tomato sauce, lemonade effervescing powder, and kola-nut biscuits, which, according to *Hints to Travellers*, produced "a marvelous effect in sustaining strength during exertion." They also brought surveying instruments, rifles, rappelling ropes, machetes, hammocks, mosquito nets, collecting jars, fishing lines, a stereoscopic camera, a pan for sifting gold, and gifts such as beads for tribal encounters. A medical kit was stocked with gauze bandages; iodine for mosquito bites; permanganate of potash for cleaning vegetables or arrow wounds; a pencil knife for cutting out flesh poisoned from snakebites or gangrene; and opium. In his rucksack, Fawcett stuffed a copy of *Hints to Travellers* and his diary with his favorite poems to recite in the wilderness. One poem he often took was Rudyard Kipling's "The Explorer":

"Something hidden. Go and find it. Go and look
   behind the Ranges—
"Something lost behind the Ranges. Lost and waiting
   for you. Go!"

Fawcett and Chivers went over the Andes and began their descent into the jungle. Fawcett, wearing gabardine breeches, leather boots, a Stetson, and a silk scarf wrapped around his neck—his standard explorer's uniform—made his way along the edges of cliffs, which fell away hundreds of feet. Traveling in a blizzard, the men could see no more than a few yards ahead, though they heard rocks slipping from under the hooves of their pack animals and cascading into the gorges. It was hard to believe, as wind whipped around twenty-thousand-foot peaks, that they were on their way to the jungle. The altitude made them dizzy and nauseated. The animals staggered forward, out of breath, their noses bleeding from a lack of oxygen. Years later, moving through the same mountains, Fawcett would lose half a convoy of twenty-four mules. "A mule's load would often foul on jutting rocks, and knock [the animal] screaming over the precipices," he wrote.

Occasionally, Fawcett and Chivers came upon a footbridge—strung together with palmetto slats and cables—that stretched more than a hundred yards over a gorge and swung wildly in the wind, like a shredded flag. The mules, too scared to pass, had to be blindfolded. After cajoling them across, the explorers picked their way downward around boulders and cliffs, spotting the first signs of vegetation—magnolias and stunted trees. By three thousand feet, where the heat was palpable, they encountered roots and vines creeping up the mountainside. Then Fawcett, drenched in sweat, peered into a valley and saw trees shaped like spiders and parachutes and clouds of smoke; waterways threading back and forth for thousands of miles; a jungle canopy so dark it appeared almost black—Amazonia.

Fawcett and Chivers eventually abandoned their pack animals for a raft made from sticks and twine and drifted into the Amazon frontier, a collection of Dodge-like towns with mocking names, such as Hope and Beautiful Village, that had recently been carved into the jungle by settlers who had fallen under the spell of *oro negro*—"black gold." Christopher Columbus had first reported seeing Indians bouncing a ball made from the strange, sticky substance that bled from tropical trees, but it wasn't until 1896, when B. F. Goodrich manufactured the first automobile tires in the United States, that rubber madness consumed the Amazon, which held a virtual monopoly on the highest-quality latex. In 1912, Brazil alone exported more than thirty million dollars' worth of rubber, the equivalent today of nearly half a billion dollars. Rubber barons had transformed Manaus, along the Amazon River, into one of the gaudiest cities in the world. "No extravagance, however absurd, deterred them," the historian Robin

Furneaux wrote in *The Amazon*. "If one rubber baron bought a vast yacht, another would install a tame lion in his villa, and a third would water his horse on champagne." And nothing was more extravagant than the opera house, with its Italian marble, Bohemian glass, gilded balconies, crystal chandeliers, Victorian murals, and a dome bathed in the colors of the national flag. Prefabricated in Europe and costing an estimated ten million dollars in taxpayers' money, the opera house was shipped in pieces more than a thousand miles up the Amazon River, where laborers were deployed around the clock to assemble it, working at night under Brazil's first electric lightbulbs. It didn't matter that almost no one from Manaus had heard of Puccini or that more than half the members of a visiting opera troupe eventually died of yellow fever. This was the apotheosis of the rubber boom.

The prospect of fortune had enticed thousands of illiterate workers into the wilderness, where they quickly became indebted to rubber barons who had provided them with transportation, food, and equipment on credit. Wearing a miner's lamp to help him see, a trapper would hack through jungle, toiling from sunrise to sundown, searching for rubber trees, then, upon his return, hungry and feverish, would spend hours hunched over a fire, inhaling toxic smoke as he cooked the latex over a spit until it coagulated. It often took weeks to produce a single rubber ball large enough to sell. And it was rarely enough to discharge his debt. Countless trappers died of starvation, dysentery, and other diseases. The Brazilian writer Euclides da Cunha called the system "the most criminal organization of labour ever devised." He noted that the rubber trapper "actually comes to embody a gigantic contradiction: he is a man working to enslave himself!"

The first frontier town that Fawcett and Chivers came to was Rurrenabaque, in northwest Bolivia. Although it appeared in capital letters on Fawcett's map, it consisted of little more than a strip of mud with bamboo huts, and with vultures circling overhead. "My heart sank," Fawcett wrote in his journals, "and I began to realize how truly primitive this river country was."

The region was removed from any center of power or ruling authority. In 1872, Bolivia and Brazil had attempted to build a railroad through the jungle, but so many workers died from disease and from Indian attacks that the project became known as the Railroad of the Dead. It was said that one man died per tie. When Fawcett arrived, more than three decades later, the railway was under construction by a third firm; still, only five miles of track had been laid—or, as Fawcett put it, it ran "from 'nowhere' to 'nowhere.' " Because the Amazon frontier was so isolated, it was governed by its own laws and, as one observer put it, made the American West seem by comparison "as proper as a prayer meeting." When a British traveler passed through the region in 1911, he reported one resident telling him, "Government? What is that? We know no government here!" The area was a haven for bandits, fugitives, and fortune hunters who carried guns on each hip, lassoed jaguars out of boredom, and killed without hesitation.

As Fawcett and Chivers descended deeper into this world, they reached the distant outpost of Riberalta. There, Fawcett watched a boat pulling along the bank. A worker yelled, "Here come the cattle!"—and Fawcett saw guards with whips driving a chain of about thirty Indian men and women onshore, where buyers began to inspect them. Fawcett asked a customs officer who these people were. Slaves, the officer replied.

Fawcett was shocked to learn that, because so many workers died in the jungle, rubber barons, in order to replenish their labor supply, dispatched armed posses into the forest to kidnap and enslave tribes. In one instance along the Putumayo River in Peru, the horrors inflicted on the Indians became so notorious that the British government launched an investigation after it was revealed that the perpetrators had sold shares in their company on the London Stock Exchange. Evidence showed that the Peruvian Amazon Company had committed virtual genocide in attempting to pacify and enslave the native population: it castrated and beheaded Indians, poured gasoline on them and lit them afire, crucified them upside down, beat them, mutilated them, starved them, drowned them, and fed them to dogs. The company's henchmen also raped women and girls and smashed children's heads open. "In some sections such an odour of putre-fying flesh arises from the numerous bodies of the victims that the places must be temporarily abandoned," said an engineer who visited the area, which was dubbed the "devil's paradise." Sir Roger Casement, the British consul general who led the investigation, estimated that some thirty thou-sand Indians had died at the hands of this one rubber company alone. A British diplomat concluded, "It is no exaggeration to say that this informa-tion as to the methods employed in the collection of rubber by the agents of the company surpass in horror anything hitherto reported to the civi-lized world during the last century."

Long before the Casement report became public, in 1912, Fawcett denounced the atrocities in British newspaper editorials and in meetings with government officials. He once called the slave traders "savages" and "scum." Moreover, he knew that the rubber boom had made his own mis-sion exceedingly more difficult and dangerous. Even previously friendly tribes were now hostile to foreigners. Fawcett was told of one party of eighty men in which "so many of them were killed with poisoned arrows that the rest abandoned the trip and retired"; other travelers were found buried up to their waists and left to be eaten alive by fire ants, maggots, and bees. In the journal of the Royal Geographical Society, Fawcett wrote that "the wretched policy which created a slave trade, and openly encour-aged a reckless slaughter of the indigenous Indians, many of them races of great intelligence," had imbued the Indians with a "deadly vengeance against the stranger" and constituted one of "the great dangers of South American exploration."

On September 25, 1906, Fawcett left Riberalta with Chivers, ac-companied by twenty desperadoes and native guides he had recruited on the frontier. Among them was a Jamaican prospector named Willis, who, despite a penchant for liquor, was a first-rate cook and fisherman ("He could smell out food and drink as a hound smells out a rabbit," Fawcett quipped), and a Bolivian former military officer who spoke fluent English and could serve as an interpreter. Fawcett had made sure that the men understood what they were getting themselves into. Anyone who broke a limb or fell sick deep in the jungle would have little chance of survival. To carry the person out would jeopardize the welfare of the entire party; the logic of the jungle dictated that the person be abandoned—or, as Fawcett grimly put it, "He has his choice of opium pills, starvation, or torture if he is found by savages."

Using canoes that they built from trees, Fawcett and his men meandered westward on their planned route of nearly six hundred miles along the frontier between Brazil and Bolivia. The river was barricaded with fallen trees, and from the canoes Chivers and Fawcett tried to slash through them with machetes. Piranhas were abundant, and the explorers were careful not to let their fingers skim the river's surface. Theodore Roosevelt, after exploring an Amazon tributary in 1914, called the piranha "the most ferocious fish in the world." He added, "They will rend and devour alive any wounded man or beast; for blood in the water excites them to madness . . . The head, with its short muzzle, staring malignant eyes and gaping, cruelly armoured jaws, is the embodiment of evil ferocity."

When bathing, Fawcett nervously checked his body for boils and cuts. The first time he swam across a river, he said, "there was an unpleasant sinking feeling in the pit of my stomach." In addition to piranhas, he dreaded candirus and electric eels, or *puraques*. The latter—about six feet long, with eyes set so far forward on their flattened heads that they nearly rested on their upper lips—were living batteries: they sent up to six hundred and fifty volts of electricity coursing through the bodies of their victims. They could electrocute a frog or a fish in a tank of water without ever touching it. The German explorer-scientist Alexander von Humboldt, who traveled along the Orinoco River in the Amazon at the beginning of the nineteenth century, drove, with the help of Indians holding harpoons, thirty horses and mules into a bog of water filled with electric eels to see what would happen. The horses and mules—manes erect, eyes inflamed—reared in terror as the eels surrounded them. Some horses tried to jump out of the water, but the

Indians forced them back with the harpoons. Within seconds, two horses had drowned, while the rest eventually broke through the Indians' blockade and collapsed to the ground, exhausted and numb. "One shock is sufficient to paralyze and drown a man—but the way of the *puraque* is to repeat the shocks to make sure of its victim," Fawcett wrote. He concluded that a person must do things in these parts that "carry no hope of epitaph—done in cold blood, and too often with an aftermath of tragedy."

One day Fawcett spied something along the edge of the sluggish river. At first it looked like a fallen tree, but it began undulating toward the canoes. It was bigger than an electric eel, and when Fawcett's companions saw it they screamed. Fawcett lifted his rifle and fired at the object until smoke filled the air. When the creature ceased to move, the men pulled a canoe alongside it. It was an anaconda. In his reports to the Royal Geographical Society, Fawcett insisted that it was longer than sixty feet ("Great Snakes!" blared one headline in the British press), though much of the anaconda was submerged and it was surely smaller: the longest officially recorded one is twenty-seven feet nine inches. (At that length, a single anaconda can still weigh over half a ton and, because of its elastic jaw muscles, swallow a deer whole.) Staring at the motionless snake in front of him, Fawcett removed his knife. He tried to slice off a piece of its skin, to put it in a specimen jar, but as he cut into the anaconda it jolted toward Fawcett and his party—sending them fleeing in fear.

As the expedition pushed onward, its members gazed at the jungle. "It was one of the gloomiest journeys I had made, for the river was threatening in its quiet, and the easy current and deep water seemed to promise evils ahead," Fawcett wrote months after leaving Riberalta. "The demons of the Amazonian rivers were abroad, manifesting their presence in lowering skies, downpours of torrential rain and somber forest walls."

Fawcett enforced a strict regimen. According to Henry Costin, a former British corporal who went on several later expeditions with Fawcett, the party woke at first light with one person calling reveille. Then the men rushed down to the river, washed, brushed their teeth, and packed, while the person on breakfast duty started a fire. "We lived simply," Costin re-called. "Breakfast would usually be porridge, tinned milk, lots of sugar." Within minutes, the men were on their way. Collecting the extensive data for Fawcett's RGS reports—including surveys, sketches of the landscape, barometric and temperature readings, and catalogs of the flora and fauna—required painstaking work, and Fawcett toiled furiously. "Inactivity was what I couldn't stand," he once said. The jungle seemed to exaggerate his fundamental nature: his bravery and toughness, along with his irascibility and intolerance of others' weakness. He allowed his men only a brief pause for lunch—a snack of a few biscuits—and trekked up to twelve hours a day.

Just before sundown, he would finally signal to his men to set up camp. Willis, the cook, was in charge of preparing supper and supple-mented their powdered soup with whatever animals the group had hunted. Hunger turned anything into a delicacy: armadillos, stingrays, tur-tles, anacondas, rats. "Monkeys are looked on as good eating," Fawcett ob-served. "Their meat tastes rather pleasant; but at first the idea revolted me because when stretched over a fire to burn off the hair they looked so hor-ribly human."

While moving through the forest, Fawcett and his men were more susceptible to predators. Once, a pack of white-lipped wild pigs stampeded toward Chivers and the interpreter, who fired their guns in every direc-tion as Willis scampered up a tree to avoid being shot by his companions. Even frogs could be deadly to the touch: a *Phyllobates terribilis*, which is found in the Colombian Amazon, has enough toxins in it to kill a hundred people. One day Fawcett stumbled upon a coral snake, whose venom shuts down the central nervous system of its victim, causing the person to suffo-cate. In the Amazon, Fawcett marveled, the animal kingdom "is against man as it is nowhere else in the world."

But it wasn't the big predators that he and his companions fretted about most. It was the ceaseless pests. The sauba ants that could reduce the men's clothes and rucksacks to threads in a single night. The ticks that attached like leeches (another scourge) and the red hairy chiggers that consumed human tissue. The cyanide-squirting millipedes. The parasitic worms that caused blindness. The berne flies that drove their ovipositors through clothing and deposited larval eggs that hatched and burrowed under the skin. The almost invisible biting flies called piums that left the explorers' bodies covered in lesions. Then there were the "kissing bugs," which bite their victim on the lips, transferring a protozoan called *Trypanosoma cruzi*; twenty years later, the person, thinking he had escaped the jungle unharmed, would begin to die of heart or brain swelling. Nothing, though, was more hazardous than the mosquitoes. They transmitted everything from malaria to "bone-crusher" fever to elephantiasis to yellow fever. "[Mosquitoes] constitute the chief single reason why Amazonia is a frontier still to be won," Willard Price wrote in his 1952 book *The Amazing Amazon*.

Fawcett and his men wrapped themselves in netting, but even this was insufficient. "The piums settled on us in clouds," Fawcett wrote. "We were forced to close both ends of the [boat's] palm-leaf shelter with mosquito-nets, and to use head-veils as well, yet in spite of that our hands and faces were soon a mass of tiny, itching blood-blisters." Meanwhile, polvorina, which are so small they resemble powder, hid in the hair of Fawcett and his companions. Often, all that the men could think about was insects. They came to recognize the different pitch of each insect's wings rubbing together. ("The *Tabana* came singly, but advertised their presence by a probe like the thrust of a needle," Fawcett said.) The bugs tormented the explorers to the point of madness, as a diary of a naturalist who went on a later expedition with Fawcett showed:

10/20: Attacked in hammocks by tiny gnat not over $\frac{1}{10}$ inch in length; mosquito nets no protection; gnats bite all night allowing no sleep.

10/21: Another sleepless night account of blood-sucking gnats.

10/22: My body mass of bumps from insect bites, wrists and hands swollen from bites of tiny gnats. 2 nights with almost no sleep—simply terrible . . . Rain during noon, all afternoon and most of night. My shoes have been soaked since starting . . . Worst ticks so far.

10/23: Horrible night with worst biting gnats yet; even smoke of no avail.

10/24: More than half ill from insects. Wrists and hands swollen. Paint limbs with iodine.

10/25: Arose to find termites covering everything left on the ground . . . Blood-sucking gnats still with us.

10/30: Sweat bees, gnats and "polverinahs" (blood-sucking gnats) terrible.

11/2: My right eye is sadly blurred by gnats.

11/3: Bees and gnats worse than ever; truly "there's no rest for the weary."

11/5: My first experience with flesh and carrion-eating bees. Biting gnats in clouds—very worst we have encountered—rendering one's food unpalatable by filling it with their filthy bodies, their bellies red and disgustingly distended with one's own blood.

Six months into the expedition, most of the men, including Chivers, were sick with fever. They were overcome with insatiable thirst, skull-splitting headaches, and uncontrollable shivering. Their muscles throbbed so much that it was hard to walk. They had contracted, in most cases, either yellow fever or malaria. If it was yellow fever, what the men feared most was spitting up mouthfuls of blood—the so-called black vomit—which meant that death was near. When it was malaria—which, according to one estimate, more than 80 percent of the people then working in the Amazon contracted—the men sometimes experienced hallucinations, and could slip into a coma and die. At one point, Fawcett shared a boat with four passengers who fell ill and perished. Using paddles, he helped to dig their graves along the shore. Their only monument, Fawcett noted, was "a couple of crossed twigs tied with grass."

One morning Fawcett noticed a trail of indentations on a muddy bank. He bent down to inspect them. They were human footprints. Fawcett searched the woods in the vicinity and discovered broken branches and trampled leaves. Indians were tracking them.

Fawcett had been told that the Pacaguara Indians lived along the banks of the Abuná River and had a reputation for kidnapping trespassers and carrying them into the forest. Two other tribes—the Parintinin, farther to the north, and the Kanichana, in the southern Mojo plains—were said to be cannibalistic. According to a missionary in 1781, "When [the Kanichana] captured prisoners in their wars they either kept them forever as slaves or roasted them to devour them in their banquets. They used as drinking cups the skulls of those whom they had killed." Although Westerners were fixated on cannibalism (Richard Burton and some friends had started a soiree called the Cannibal Club) and often exaggerated its extent in order to justify their conquest of indigenous people, there is no question that some Amazonian tribes practiced it, either for ritualistic reasons or for vengeance. Human meat was typically prepared two ways: roasted or boiled. The Guayaki, who practiced ritualistic cannibalism when members of the tribe died, cut bodies into quarters with a bamboo knife, severing the head and the limbs from the trunk. "The head and the intestines are not treated according to the same 'recipe' as the muscular parts or the internal organs," explained the anthropologist Pierre Clastres, who spent time studying the tribe in the early 1960s. "The head is first carefully shaved . . . then boiled, as are the intestines, in ceramic cooking pots. Regarding the meat proper and the internal organs, they are placed on a large wooden grill under which a fire is lit . . . The meat is roasted slowly and the fat released by the heat is absorbed gradually with the koto [brush]. When the meat is considered 'done' it is divided among all those present. Whatever is not eaten on the spot is set aside in the women's baskets and used as nutriment the next day. As far as the bones are concerned, they are broken and their marrow, of which the women are particularly fond, is sucked." The Guayaki's preference for human skin is the reason that they call themselves Aché Kyravwa—"Guayaki Eaters of Human Fat."

Fawcett studied the forest around him, looking for Indian warriors. Amazon tribes were expert at stalking their enemies. While some liked to announce their presence before an attack, many used the forest to enhance their stealth. They painted their bodies and faces with black charcoal and with red ointments distilled from berries and fruits. Their weapons—blow darts and arrows—struck silently, before anyone had time to flee. Certain tribes exploited the very things that made the forest so hazardous to Fawcett and his men—dipping the points of their weapons in the lethal toxins from stingrays and dart frogs or using biting soldier ants to suture their wounds in battle. In contrast, Fawcett and his party had no experience in the jungle. They were, as Costin confessed during his first journey, "greenhorns." Most were sick and debilitated and hungry—the perfect prey.

That night, Fawcett and his men were all on edge. Before they set off, Fawcett had made each of them agree to a seemingly suicidal edict: they were not to fire their weapons on Indians under any circumstances. When the Royal Geographical Society learned of Fawcett's instructions, one member familiar with the region warned that such a method would "court assassination." Fawcett conceded that his nonviolent approach involved "mad risks." Yet he argued that it was not just the moral course; it was also the only way for a small and easily outnumbered party to demonstrate its friendly intentions to tribes.

As the men now lay in their hammocks, a small fire crackling, they listened to the tumult of the forest. They tried to distinguish each sound: the plopping of a nut in the river, the rubbing of branches, the whine of mosquitoes, the roar of a jaguar. Occasionally, the jungle would seem silent, then a screech would shatter the darkness. While the men couldn't see anyone, they knew they could be seen. "It was trying to the nerves, knowing all the time that our every movement was watched, yet seeing almost nothing of those who were watching," Fawcett wrote.

On the river one day the boats came to a series of rapids, and a pilot went inland to look for a place to circumvent them. A long time elapsed with no word from him, so Fawcett went with several men to find him. They hacked through the forest for half a mile and suddenly came upon the pilot's body, pierced with forty-two arrows.

The men were beginning to panic. At one point, drifting on the boat toward the rapids, Willis yelled, "Savages!"—and there they were standing on the banks. "Their bodies [were] painted all over," Fawcett wrote, and "their ears had pendulous lobes, and quills were thrust from side to side through their nostrils." He wanted to try to establish contact, but the other men on board were shouting and paddling frantically away. The Indians took aim with six-foot bows and fired their arrows. "One ripped through the side of the boat with a vicious smack—through wood an inch and a half in thickness," Fawcett said. The boat then slipped down a chute of rapids, leaving, for the moment, the tribe behind.

Even before this confrontation, Fawcett had noticed his men, especially Chivers, unraveling. "I had observed his gradual break-up," Fawcett wrote. He decided to relieve Chivers of his duties and sent him and several other members of the party back to the frontier. Still, two of the men died of their fevers. Fawcett himself longed for his family. What kind of a fool was he, Fawcett wondered, to exchange the comfort of his previous postings for such conditions? His second son, Brian, had been born in his absence. "I was tempted to resign and return home," Fawcett wrote. Yet, unlike his men, Fawcett was in good health. He was hungry and wretched, but his skin wasn't yellow and his temperature was normal and he wasn't vomiting blood. Later, John Keltie, the secretary of the Royal Geographical Society, wrote a letter to Fawcett's wife, saying, "Unless he had an exceptional constitution, I do not see how he could survive." Fawcett noted that in these parts "the healthy person was regarded as a freak, an exception, extraordinary."

Despite his yearnings for home, Fawcett continued with Willis and the interpreter to survey the border between Bolivia and Brazil, hacking for miles through the jungle. In May 1907, he completed his route and presented his findings to members of the South American boundary commission and the RGS. They were incredulous. He had redefined the borders of South America—and he had done it nearly a year ahead of schedule.

THE

SECRET PAPERS

When I was in England, I tried to track down Fawcett's descendants, who, perhaps, could tell me more about the explorer and his route to Z. Fawcett's wife and children had died long ago, but in Cardiff, Wales, I located one of his grandchildren, Rolette de Montet-Guerin, whose mother was Fawcett's only daughter, Joan. She lived in a single-story house, with stucco walls and wood frame windows—an unassuming place that seemed somehow at odds with all the fanfare that had once surrounded her family. She was a petite, energetic woman in her fifties, with short black hair and glasses, who referred affectionately to her grandfather by his initials, PHF. ("That's what my mum and everyone in the family always called him.") Fawcett's wife and children, after years of being hounded by reporters, had retreated from the public eye, but Rolette welcomed me into the kitchen. As I told her about my plans to trace Fawcett's route, she said, "You don't look much like an explorer."

"Not really."

"Well, you best be well fed for the jungle."

She started to open cupboards, taking out pots and pans, and turned on the gas stove. The kitchen table was soon laden with bowls of risotto, steamed vegetables, homemade bread, and hot apple crumb cake. "It's all vegetarian," she said. "PHF believed it gave you greater stamina. Plus, he never liked to kill animals unless he had to."

As we sat down to eat, Rolette's twenty-three-year-old daughter, Isabelle, appeared. She had shorter hair than her mother's and eyes that held some of her great-grandfather's intensity. She was a pilot for British Airways. "I envy my great-grandfather, really," Isabelle said. "In his day, you could still go marching off and discover some hidden part of the world. Now where can you go?"

Rolette placed an antique silver chalice in the center of the table. "I brought that out especially for you," she said. "It was PHF's christening cup."

I held it up to the light. On one side were engraved flowers and buds, on the other was inscribed the number 1867, the year Fawcett was born.

After we ate and chatted for a while, I asked her something I had long pondered—whether, in determining my route, I should rely, like so many other parties, on the coordinates for Dead Horse Camp cited in *Exploration Fawcett*.

"Well, you must be careful with those," Rolette said.

"What do you mean?"

"PHF wrote them to throw people off the trail. They were a blind."

The news both astounded and unsettled me: if true, it meant that many people had headed, possibly fatally, in the wrong direction. When I asked why Brian Fawcett, who had edited *Exploration Fawcett*, would have perpetrated the deception, she explained that he had wanted to honor the wishes of his father and brother. The more she spoke, the more I realized that what for many was a tantalizing mystery was for her family a tragedy. As we finished supper, Rolette said, "When someone disappears, it's not like an ordinary death. There is no closure." (Later she told me, "You know, when my mother was dying, I said to her, 'At least you'll finally know what happened to PHF and Jack.' ") Now Rolette paused for a long time, as if trying to make up her mind about something. Then she said, "You really want to find out what happened to my grandfather?"

"Yes. If it's possible."

"I want to show you something."

She led me into a back room and opened a large wooden trunk. Inside were several leather-bound books. Their covers were worn and tattered, their bindings breaking apart. Some were held together only by strings, tied in bows.

"What are they?" I asked.

"PHF's diaries and logbooks." She handed them to me. "You can look through them, but you must guard them carefully."

I opened one of them, marked 1909. The cover left a black stain on my fingertips—a mixture, I imagined, of Victorian dust and jungle mud. The pages almost fell out when I turned them, and I held them gingerly between my index finger and thumb. Recognizing Fawcett's microscopic handwriting, I felt a strange sensation. Here was something that Fawcett had also held, something that contained his most private thoughts and that few had ever seen. The writer Janet Malcolm once compared a biographer to a "professional burglar, breaking into a house, rifling through certain drawers that he has good reason to think contain the jewelry and money, and triumphantly bearing his loot away."

I sat down on the couch in the living room. There was a book for almost every year from 1906 (his first expedition) to 1921 (his penultimate trip); he had obviously carried a diary on each of his expeditions, jotting down observations. Many of them were replete with maps and surveying calculations. On the inside covers were the poems he had copied down in order to read in the jungle when he was alone and desperate. One seemed meant for Nina:

Oh love, my love! Have all your will—
I am yours to the end.

Fawcett had also scribbled down lines from Ella Wheeler Wilcox's "Solitude":

> But no man can help you die.
> There is room in the halls of pleasure
> For a long and lordly train,
> But one by one we must all file on
> Through the narrow aisles of pain.

Many of the diaries were filled with the mundane, from someone with no expectation of history: "9 July . . . Sleepless night . . . Much rain and wet through by midday . . . 11 July . . . Heavy rain from midnight. Reached [camp] on trail, caught fish . . . 17 July . . . swimming across for balsa." Then, suddenly, a casual remark revealed the harrowing nature of his existence: "Feel very bad . . . Took 1 [vial] of morphine last night to rest from foot pain. It produced a violent stomachache and had to put finger down throat to relieve."

A loud noise sounded in the other room and I looked up. It was Isabelle playing a video game on the computer. I picked up another of the books. It had a lock to protect the contents. "That's his 'Treasure Book,' " Rolette said. The lock was unfastened, and inside were stories Fawcett had collected of buried treasures, like Galla-pita-Galla, and maps of their suspected locations: "In that cave is a treasure, the existence of which is known to me and to me alone."

In later diaries, as he developed his case for Z, Fawcett made more archaeological notations. There were drawings of strange hieroglyphics. The Botocudo Indians, now virtually extinct, had told him a legend of a city "enormously rich in gold—so much so as to blaze like fire." Fawcett added, "It is just conceivable this may be Z." As he seemed to be nearing his goal, he became more secretive. In the 1921 log, he outlined a "code" he had apparently devised, with his wife, to send messages:

78804 Kratzbank = Discoveries much as described

78806 Kratzfuss = Rich, important and wonderful

78808 Kratzka = Cities located—future now secure

Poring through the log, I noticed a word on the margins of one page: "DEAD." I looked at it more closely and saw two other words alongside it. They spelled out "DEAD HORSE CAMP." Underneath them were coordinates, and I quickly flipped through my notebook where I had scribbled down the position of the camp from *Exploration Fawcett*. They were significantly different.

For hours, I went through the diaries, taking notes. I thought there was nothing left to glean, when Rolette appeared and said that she wanted to show me one more item. She vanished into the back room, and I could hear her rummaging through drawers and cabinets, muttering to herself. After several minutes, she emerged with a photograph from a book. "I don't know where I put it," she said. "But I can at least show you a picture of it."

It was a photograph of Fawcett's gold signet ring, which was engraved with the family motto, *"Nec Aspera Terrent"*—essentially, "Difficulties Be Damned." In 1979, an Englishman named Brian Ridout, who was making a wildlife film in Brazil, heard rumors that the ring had turned up at a store in Cuiabá, the capital of Mato Grosso. By the time Ridout tracked down the shop, the proprietor had died. His wife, however, searched through her possessions and found Colonel Fawcett's ring. "It's the last concrete item we have from the expedition," Rolette said.

She said that she had been desperate to learn more and had once shown the ring to a psychic.

"Did you learn anything?" I asked.

She looked down at the picture, then up at me. "It had been bathed in blood."

THE

GREEN HELL

A re you game?" Fawcett asked.

He was back in the jungle not long after his previous expedition, trying to persuade his new second-in-command, Frank Fisher, to explore the Rio Verde, along the Brazilian and Bolivian border.

Fisher, who was a forty-one-year-old English engineer and a member of the RGS, hesitated. The boundary commission had not contracted with the party to explore the Verde—it had asked the men to survey a region in southwest Brazil near Corumbá—but Fawcett insisted on also tracing the river, which was in such uncharted territory that nobody even knew where it began.

Finally, Fisher said, "Oh, I'll come," though he added, "Surely the contracts don't call for it."

It was only Fawcett's second South American expedition, but it would prove critical to his understanding of the Amazon and to his evolution as a scientist. With Fisher and seven other recruits, he set out from Corumbá, trekking northwest more than four hundred miles, before shoving off on two makeshift wooden rafts. The rapids, fueled by rains and by steep descents, were intense, and the rafts were propelled over precipices before tumbling down into the foam and rocks—the grinding roar—as the men hollered to hold on and Fawcett, eyes flashing, Stetson cocked, steered with a bamboo pole held to one side, so it wouldn't spear his chest. White-water rafting was not yet a sport, but Fawcett anticipated it: "When . . . the enterprising traveler has to construct and manage his own balsa [raft], he will realize an exhilaration and excitement that few sports provide." Still, it was one thing to ride the rapids of a familiar river, and another to descend unmarked chutes that might at any moment drop hundreds of feet. If a member of the party fell overboard, he could not grab onto a raft without capsizing it. The only honorable course was to drown.

The explorers paddled past the Ricardo Franco Hills, eerie sandstone plateaus that rose three thousand feet. "Time and the foot of man had not touched those summits," Fawcett wrote. "They stood like a lost world, forested to their tops, and the imagination could picture the last vestiges of an age long vanished." (Conan Doyle reportedly based the setting of *The Lost World* at least partly on these tablelands.)

As Fawcett and his team wound through the canyon, the rapids became impassable.

"What'll we do now?" one of the men asked.

"There's no help for it," Fawcett said. "We must leave all we can't carry on our back and follow the river's course by land."

Fawcett ordered the men to keep only their essential items: hammocks, rifles, mosquito nets, and surveying instruments.

What about our stores of food? Fisher asked.

Fawcett said they'd bring only enough rations for a few days. Then they'd have to live off the land, like the Indians whose fire they had seen burning in the distance.

Despite cutting, chopping, pulling, and pushing through jungle from morning till night, they usually advanced no more than half a mile per day. Their legs sank in mud. Their shoes disintegrated. Their eyes blurred from a tiny species of bee that is drawn to sweat, and that invaded their pupils. (Brazilians called the bees "eye lickers.") Still, Fawcett counted his paces and crawled up banks to better see the stars and to fix their position, as if reducing the wilderness to figures and diagrams might enable him to overcome it. His men didn't need such signposts. They knew where they were: the green hell.

The men were supposed to conserve their rations, but most broke down and consumed them quickly. By the ninth day of marching, the expedition had run out of food. It was now that Fawcett discovered what explorers since Orellana had learned and what would become the basis of the scientific theory of a counterfeit paradise: in the world's thickest jungle, it was hard to find a morsel to eat.

Of all the Amazon's tricks, this was perhaps the most diabolical. As Fawcett put it, "Starvation sounds almost unbelievable in forest country, and yet it is only too likely to happen." Scrounging for food, Fawcett and his men could make out only buttressed tree trunks and cascades of vines. Chemical-laced fungi and billions of termites and ants had stripped bare much of the jungle floor. Fawcett had been taught to scavenge for dead animals, but there were none to be found: every corpse was instantly recycled back into the living. Trees drained even more nutrients from a soil already leached by rain and floods. Meanwhile, vines and trees stampeded over each other as they strove to reach the canopy, to absorb a ray of light. One kind of liana called the matador, or killer, seemed to crystallize this competition: it wrapped itself around a tree, as if offering a tender embrace, then began to strangle it, stealing both its life and its place amid the forest.

Although this death struggle for the light above created a permanent midnight below, few mammals roamed the jungle floor, where other creatures could attack them. Even those animals that Fawcett and his party should have been able to see remained invisible to their untutored eyes. Bats hid in tents of leaves. Armadillos burrowed in the ground. Moths looked like bark. Caimans became logs. One kind of caterpillar had a more frightening deception: it transformed its body into the shape of a deadly pit viper, with an enlarged, swaying triangular head and big gleaming eyes. As the writer Candice Millard explained in *The River of Doubt*, "The rain forest was not a garden of easy abundance, but precisely the opposite. Its quiet, shaded halls of leafy opulence were not a sanctuary, but rather the greatest natural battlefield anywhere on the planet, hosting an unremitting and remorseless fight for survival that occupied every single one of its inhabitants, every minute of every day."

On this battlefield, Fawcett and his men found themselves outmatched. For days, Fawcett, a world-class hunter, scoured the land with his party, only to turn up a handful of nuts and palm leaves. The men tried fishing, which they were sure, given how many piranhas and eels and dolphins were in other Amazonian rivers, would provide sustenance, but to the explorers' amazement they could not catch a single fish. Fawcett speculated that something had polluted the waters, and indeed some trees and plants produce tannic acids that poison rivers in the Amazon, creating what the biologists Adrian Forsyth and Kenneth Miyata have called "the aquatic equivalents of desert."

And so Fawcett and his party were forced to wander hungry through the jungle. The men wanted to turn back, but Fawcett was determined to find the Verde's source. They stumbled forward, mouths open, trying to capture every drop of rain. At night, chills swept through their bodies. A *tocandira*—a poisonous ant that can cause vomiting and intense fever—had infected Fisher, and a tree had fallen on the leg of another member of the party, so that his load had to be dispersed among the others. Nearly a month after they started on foot, the men reached what appeared to be the source of the river, Fawcett insisting on taking measurements, even though he was so depleted that he had trouble moving his limbs. The party paused momentarily for a photograph: they looked like dead men, their cheeks whittled to the bones, their beards matted against their faces like growth from the forest, their eyes half-mad.

Fisher muttered that they were going to "leave our bones here." Others prayed for salvation.

Fawcett tried to find an easier route back, but each time he chose a path, the expedition ended up at a cliff and was forced to turn around. "How long could we carry on was the vital question," Fawcett wrote. "Unless food was obtained soon, we should be too feeble to make our way out by any route." They had gone for more than a month with almost no food, and were starving; their blood pressure plummeted, and their bodies consumed their own tissue. "The voices of the others and the sounds of the forest seemed to come from a vast distance, as though through a long tube," Fawcett wrote. Unable to think about the past or the future, about anything other than food, the men became irritable, apathetic, and paranoid. In their weakened state, they were more susceptible to disease and infection, and most of them had developed severe fevers. Fawcett feared mutiny. Had they begun to look at one another differently, not as companions but as meat? As Fawcett wrote about cannibalism, "Starvation blunts one's finer feelings," and he told Fisher to collect the other men's guns.

Fawcett soon noticed that one of the men had vanished. He eventually came upon him sitting collapsed against a tree. Fawcett ordered the man to get up, but he begged Fawcett to let him die there. He refused to move, and Fawcett took out his knife. The blade gleamed before the man's eyes; Fawcett ached with hunger. Waving the knife, Fawcett forced him to his feet. If we die, Fawcett said, we'll die walking.

As they staggered on, many of the men, inured to their fate, no longer tried to slap at the pestilent mosquitoes or keep watch against the Indians. "[An ambush], in spite of its moment of terror and agony, is quickly over, and if we regard these matters in a reasonable way it would be considered merciful" compared with starvation, Fawcett wrote.

Several days later, as the group was slipping in and out of consciousness, Fawcett caught sight of a deer, almost out of range. He had one shot, then it would be gone. "For God's sake don't miss, Fawcett!" one of the men whispered. Fawcett unslung his rifle; his arms had atrophied, and his muscles strained to hold the barrel steady. He inhaled and pulled the trigger. The report echoed through the forest. The deer seemed to vanish, as if it had been a figment of their delirium. Then, as they stumbled closer, they saw it on the ground, bleeding. They cooked it over a fire, eating every bit of flesh, sucking every bone. Five days later, they came across a settlement. Still, five of Fawcett's men—more than half his team—were too weak to recover and soon died. When Fawcett returned to La Paz, people pointed and stared at him—he was a virtual skeleton. He sent off a telegram to the Royal Geographical Society. It said, "Hell Verde Conquered."

Dead Horse
Camp

T here," I said to my wife, pointing at a satellite image of the Amazon on my computer screen. "That's where I'm going."

The image revealed the cracks in the earth where the massive river and its tributaries had ruthlessly carved the land. Later, I was able to show her the coordinates more clearly using Google Earth, which was unveiled in the summer of 2005 and allowed anyone, in seconds, to zoom within meters of virtually every place on the globe. First, I typed in our Brooklyn address. The view on the screen, which had shown a satellite image of the earth from outer space, zoomed, like a guided missile, toward a patchwork of buildings and streets, until I recognized the balcony of our apartment. The level of clarity was incredible. Then I typed in Fawcett's last published coordinates and watched the screen race over images of the Caribbean and the Atlantic Ocean, past a faint outline of Venezuela and Guyana, before zeroing in on a blur of green: the jungle. What was once blank space on the map was now visible in an instant.

My wife asked how I knew where to go, and I told her about Fawcett's diaries. I showed her on the map the location that everyone assumed was Dead Horse Camp and then the new coordinates, more than a hundred miles south, which I had found in Fawcett's logbook. Then I revealed a copy of a document with the word "CONFIDENTIAL" printed on it, which I had discovered at the Royal Geographical Society. Unlike other documents written by Fawcett, this one was neatly typed. Dated April 13, 1924, it was titled "Case for an Expedition in the Amazon Basin."

Desperate for funding, Fawcett had seemingly relented to the Society's demand that he be more forthcoming about his plans. After nearly two decades of exploring, he said, he had concluded that in the southern basin of the Amazon, between the Tapajós and the Xingu tributaries, were "the most remarkable relics of ancient civilization." Fawcett had sketched a map of the region and submitted it with a proposal. "This area represents the greatest area of unexplored country in the world," he wrote. "Portuguese exploration, and all subsequent geographical research by Brazilians or foreigners, has been invariably confined to waterways." Instead, he planned to blaze a path overland between the Tapajós and the Xingu and other tributaries, where "none has penetrated." (Conceding how much more dangerous this course was, he requested extra money to "get the survivors back to England," as "I may be killed.")

On one page of the proposal, Fawcett had included several coordinates. "What are they for?" my wife asked.

"I think they're the direction he headed in after Dead Horse Camp."

The next morning I stuffed my gear and maps in my backpack, and said goodbye to my wife and infant son. "Don't be stupid," my wife said. Then I headed to the airport and boarded a plane for Brazil.

IN THE HANDS

OF THE GODS

O h, the "glorious prospect of home," Fawcett wrote in his diary. Streets paved and neatly aligned, thatched cottages covered in ivy, pastures filled with sheep, church bells tolling in the rain, stores crammed with jellies and soups and lemonades and tarts and Neapolitan ices and wines, pedestrians jostling in the streets with buses and trams and taxis. Home was all Fawcett could think about on the boat ride back to England at the end of 1907. And now he was back in Devon with Nina and Jack, Jack as big as could be, running and talking, already four years old, and little Brian staring at the man in the doorway as if he were a stranger, which he was. "I wanted to forget atrocities, to put slavery, murder and horrible disease behind me, and to look again at respectable old ladies whose ideas of vice ended with the indiscretions of so-and-so's housemaid," Fawcett wrote in *Exploration Fawcett*. "I wanted to listen to the everyday chit-chat of the village parson, discuss the uncertainties of the weather with the yokels, pick up the daily paper on my breakfast-plate. I wanted, in short, to be just 'ordinary.' " He bathed in warm water with soap and trimmed his beard. He dug in the garden, tucked his children into bed, read by the fire, and shared Christmas with his family—"as though South America had never been."

But before long he found himself unable to sit still. "Deep down inside me a tiny voice was calling," Fawcett said. "At first scarcely audible, it persisted until I could no longer ignore it. It was the voice of the wild places, and I knew that it was now part of me for ever." He added, "Inexplicably—amazingly—I knew I loved that hell. Its fiendish grasp had captured me, and I wanted to see it again."

So, after only a few months, Fawcett packed up his things again and fled what he called the "prison gate slowly but surely shutting me in." Over the next decade and a half, he conducted one expedition after another in which he explored thousands of square miles of the Amazon and helped to redraw the map of South America. During that time, he was often as neglectful of his wife and children as his parents had been of him. Nina compared her life to that of a sailor's wife: "a very uncertain and lonely" existence "without private means, miserably poor, especially with children." In a letter to the Royal Geographical Society in 1911, Fawcett professed that he would not "subject my wife to the perpetual anxiety of these risky journeys." (He had once shown her the lines on the palm of his hand and said, "Note this well!"—someday, she might have to "identify my dead body.") Yet he continued to subject her to his dangerous compulsions. In some ways, it must have been easier for his family when he was gone, for the longer he remained at home, the more his mood soured. Brian later confessed in his diary, "I felt relieved when he was out of the way."

Nina, for her part, subsumed her ambitions in her husband's. Fawcett's annual salary of about six hundred pounds from the boundary commission provided little for her and the children, and she was forced to shuttle the family from one rental house to the next, living in genteel poverty. Still, she made sure that Fawcett had little to worry about, performing the kinds of chores—cooking and cleaning and washing—to which she was unaccustomed and raising the children in what Brian called a "riotous democracy." Nina also acted as her husband's chief advocate, doing everything in her power to burnish his reputation. When she learned that a member of Fawcett's 1910 expedition was trying to publish an unauthorized account, she quickly alerted her husband so that he could put a stop to it. And when Fawcett wrote to her about his exploits, she immediately tried to publicize them by funneling the information to the Royal Geographical Society and, in particular, to Keltie, the institution's longtime secretary, who was one of Fawcett's biggest boosters. (Keltie had agreed to be the godfather of Fawcett's daughter, Joan, who was born in 1910.) In a typical communiqué, Nina wrote of Fawcett and his men, "They have had some miraculous escapes from death—once they were shipwrecked—twice attacked by huge snakes." Fawcett dedicated *Exploration Fawcett* to his beloved "Cheeky"—"because," he said, "she as my partner in everything shared with me the burden of the work."

Yet at times Nina longed to be not the person at home but the one in the wild. "I, personally, am quite ready now for accompanying P.H.F. on a Brazilian journey," she once told a friend. She learned how to read the stars, like a geographer, and kept herself in "splendid health"; in 1910, while visiting Fawcett in South America, she wrote an unpublished dispatch for the RGS about her journey by train from Buenos Aires, Argentina, to Valparaiso, Chile, which she thought might be "interesting to those who are fond of travel." At one point, she could see "the snow-capped peaks of the Cordillera flushed with the rosy light of the rising sun"—a vista so "beautiful and grand as to stamp itself on the memory forever."

Fawcett never consented to take her with him into the jungle. But Nina confided to a friend that she believed staunchly in the "equality . . . between man and woman." She encouraged Joan to build her stamina and take physical risks, including swimming for miles in rough seas. Writing to Keltie about his goddaughter, Nina said, "Some day perhaps she may win the laurels of the Royal Geographical Society as a lady-geographer, and so fulfill the ambition that her mother has striven for in vain—so far!" (Fawcett also spurred Joan, like all his children, to take extreme risks. "Daddy gave us a tremendous amount of fun, because he didn't realize the danger," Joan later recalled. "But he should have realized. He was always encouraging us to climb across roofs and up trees . . . Once I fell on the cervical vertebrae of my neck and that cost me a fortnight in bed with high delirium and unconscious. Since I had that accident my neck has always been slightly stooped.")

It was Jack, however, who most yearned to be like his father. "By the look of it, my little son Jack is going to pass through the same phase as I did when he reaches early manhood," Fawcett once remarked proudly. "Already he is fascinated by the stories we tell him of Galla-pita-Galla." Fawcett wrote and illustrated stories for Jack, depicting him as a young adventurer, and when Fawcett was home the two did everything together—hiking, playing cricket, sailing. Jack was "the real apple of his eye," one relative recalled.

In 1910, when Jack was heading off to boarding school along with Raleigh Rimell, Fawcett sent him a poem from "far away in the wild." It was called "Jack Going to School" and read, in part:

Never forget us brave little man
Mother and father trust in you
Be brave as a lion, yet kind returning
Ready to fight and averse to wrong . . .
Never forget you're a gentleman
And never a fear you'll do.

Life is short and the world is wide
We're just a ripple on life's great pool
Enjoy your life to the best you can
All will help to enrich the span
But never forget you're a gentleman

And the time will come when we all with pride
Will think of your days at school.

In a separate letter to Nina, Fawcett spoke about his older son's character and future: "A leader of men, I think—possibly an orator—always an independent, loveable, erratic personality, which may go far . . . a bundle of nerves—inexhaustible nervous energy—a boy of boys—capable of extremes—sensitive and proud—the child we longed for, and, I think, born for some purpose as yet obscure."

WORD OF FAWCETT'S feats as an explorer, meanwhile, was beginning to spread. Although his deeds lacked that single crystalline achievement, like reaching the North Pole or the top of Mount Everest—Amazonia defied such triumphs: no single person could ever conquer it—Fawcett, progressing inch by inch through the jungle, tracing rivers and mountains, cataloging exotic species, and researching the native inhabitants, had explored as much of the region as anyone. As one reporter later put it, "He was probably the world's foremost expert on South America." William S. Barclay, a member of the RGS, said of Fawcett, "I have for years regarded him as one of the best of his class that ever lived."

His feats came at a time when Britain, with the death of Queen Victoria and the rise of Germany, had grown anxious about its empire. These doubts were exacerbated by an English general's claim that 60 percent of the country's young men were unfit to meet the requirements of military service, and by a rash of apocalyptic novels—including *Hartmann the Anarchist; or, The Doom of the Great City*, by Fawcett's older brother, Edward. Published in 1893, the cult science-fiction novel detailed how an underground cell of anarchists ("a *disease* bred by an effete form of civilization") invented an airplane prototype christened the *Attila* and, in a scene that presaged the Blitz of World War II, used it to bomb London. ("Of the

Houses of Parliament pinnacles were collapsing and walls were being riven asunder as the shells burst within them.") The public had grown so agitated over the state of Victorian manhood that the government created an investigative body called the Inter-Departmental Committee on Physical Deterioration.

The press seized upon Fawcett's accomplishments, portraying him like one of his childhood heroes and holding him up as the perfect counterpoint to the national crisis of confidence. One newspaper declared, " 'The lure of the wild' has not lost its power upon men of the fearless and resourceful type represented by Maj. Fawcett." Another journal urged children to emulate him: "There is a true Scout for you to follow! He gives up all thought of his own safety or comfort, so that he may carry out the duty that has been given to him."

In early 1911, at a lecture before the Royal Geographical Society, where he presented his findings, dozens of scientists and explorers from across Europe crowded into the hall to glimpse the "Livingstone of the Amazon." Beckoning him to the front of the hall, Charles Darwin's son Leonard, who was now the Society's president, described how Fawcett had mapped "regions which have never before been visited by Europeans" and had traveled up rivers that had "never before been ascended by one." Darwin added that Fawcett had demonstrated that there was still a place "where the explorer can go forth and exhibit perseverance, energy, courage, forethought, and all those qualities which go to make up the qualities of an explorer of the times now passing away."

Although Fawcett liked to protest that he was not "a great seeker for publicity," he clearly relished the attention. (One of his hobbies was to paste newspaper accounts about himself into a scrapbook.) Showing lantern slides of the jungle and sketches of his maps, he told the crowd:

> What I hope is that the publicity of these explorations may attract other adventurous spirits into this neglected part of the world. But it

should be remembered that the difficulties are great and the tale of disasters a long one, for the few remaining unknown corners of the world exact a price for their secrets. Without any desire whatever for self-glorification, I can vouch for it that it requires a great enthusiasm to successfully bridge, year after year, the wide gulf which lies between the comforts of civilization and the very real risks and penalties which dog every footstep in the unexplored forests of this still little-known continent.

A Bolivian emissary who was there said of the emerging map of South America, "I must tell you that it is owing to Major Fawcett's bravery that this has been accomplished . . . If we had a few more men like him, I am sure there would not be a single corner of the unexplored regions."

Fawcett's growing legend was predicated on the fact that not only had he made journeys that no one else had dared but he had done so at a pace that seemed inhuman. He accomplished in months what others took years to do—or, as Fawcett once put it matter-of-factly, "I am a rapid worker and have no idle days." Incredibly, he rarely, if ever, seemed to get sick. "He was fever-proof," said Thomas Charles Bridges, a popular adventure writer at the time who knew Fawcett. The trait caused rampant speculation about his physiology. Bridges attributed this resistance to his having "a pulse below the normal." One historian observed that Fawcett had "a virtual immunity from tropical disease. Perhaps this last quality was the most exceptional. There were other explorers, although not many, who equaled him in dedication, courage and strength, but in his resistance to disease he was unique." Even Fawcett began to marvel at what he called the "perfect constitution."

In addition, he was struck by his ability to elude predators. Once, after leaping over a pit viper, he wrote in his journal, "What amazed me more than anything was the warning of my subconscious mind, and the instant muscular response . . . I had not seen it till it flashed between my legs, but the 'inner man'—if I can call it that—not only saw it in time, but judged its striking height and distance exactly, and issued commands to the body accordingly!" His RGS colleague William Barclay, who worked in Bolivia and knew Fawcett's methods as an explorer as well as anyone, said that over the years the explorer had developed "the conviction that no danger could touch him" and that, like a mythic hero, "his actions and happenings were fore-ordained." Or, as Fawcett liked to say, "I am in the hands of the Gods."

Yet the very things that made Fawcett a great explorer—demonic fury, single-mindedness, and an almost divine sense of immortality—also made him terrifying to be with. Nothing was allowed to stand in the way of his object—or destiny. He was "prepared to travel lighter and fare harder than most people would consider either possible or proper," the journal of the Royal Geographical Society reported. In a letter to the Society, Nina said, "By the way, you will be amused to hear Major Fawcett contemplated cutting through 100 miles of forest . . . in a month! The others fairly gasped at the thought!!!"

To those who could keep up with him, he showed tremendous loyalty. To those who couldn't—well, Fawcett came to believe that their sickness, even their death, only confirmed their underlying cowardice. "Such journeys cannot be executed" faintly, Fawcett wrote Keltie, "or I should never have got anywhere. For those who can do [them] I have nothing but gratitude and praise—for those who can't I have little sympathy for they accept the job with their eyes open—but for the lazy or incompetent I have no use whatever." In his private papers, Fawcett denounced a former assistant as a "hopeless rotter! A typical waster!"—the words scribbled beneath the man's obituary. (He had drowned in a river in Peru.) Several men were expelled from his expeditions or, aggrieved and bitter, deserted him. "Why he would not stop to let us eat or sleep," a former member of his party complained to another South American explorer. "We were working twenty-four hours a day and driven like bullocks before the lash."

"The strain has always been too much for members of my own parties," Fawcett informed Keltie, adding, "I have no mercy for incompetence."

Keltie gently chided his friend: "I am very glad to think that you are keeping so very fit. You must have a wonderful constitution to stand all that you have stood and be none the worse. I am afraid this makes you perhaps a little intolerant of men who are not so very fit as you are."

Keltie no doubt had in mind one man in particular, an explorer whose collaboration with Fawcett, in 1911, ended in catastrophe.

IT SEEMED LIKE the perfect match: James Murray, the great polar scientist, and Fawcett, the great Amazon explorer. Together, they would break through hundreds of miles of unexplored jungle surrounding the Heath River along Bolivia's northwestern border with Peru, to map the region and study its inhabitants and wildlife. The Royal Geographical Society had encouraged the excursion, and why not?

Born in Glasgow in 1865, Murray was the brilliant, peripatetic son of a grocer who, as a young man, had become obsessed with the recent discovery of microscopic creatures and, armed with little more than a microscope and a collecting jar, transformed himself into a virtually self-taught, world-renowned expert in the field. In 1902, he helped survey the muddy depths of the Scottish lochs. Five years later, Ernest Shackleton enlisted Murray for his expedition to Antarctica, where he carried out groundbreaking recordings on marine biology, physics, optics, and meteorology. Afterward, he co-wrote a book called *Antarctic Days*, which described hauling a sled across the snow: "Pulling, you are uncomfortably hot, resting, you are uncomfortably cold. Always, you are hungry. Ahead is the barrier surface, stretching away to the horizon." Voraciously curious, vainglorious, rebellious, eccentric, daring, autodidactic: Murray seemed like Fawcett's doppelgänger. He was even an artist. And in September 1911, when Murray arrived at San Carlos, an outpost on the Bolivian-Peruvian border, Fawcett proclaimed in a letter to the Royal Geographical Society, "He is an admirable man for the job."

But had anyone peered closer at their characters he might have seen warning signs. Although only two years older than Fawcett, Murray, at forty-six, looked crumpled and wizened; his face, with its well-trimmed mustache and graying hair, was filled with crags, his body was ill shapen. During the Scottish expedition, he had suffered a physical breakdown. "I had had rheumatism, inflamed eyes, and God knows what not," he said. On the Shackleton expedition, he had been in charge of the base camp and had not endured the most brutal conditions.

Moreover, the qualifications for a great polar explorer and for an Amazon one are not necessarily the same. Indeed, the two forms of exploration are, in many ways, the antithesis of each other. A polar explorer has to endure temperatures of nearly a hundred degrees below zero, and the same terrors over and over: frostbite, crevices in the ice, and scurvy. He looks out and sees snow and ice, snow and ice—an unrelenting bleakness. The psychological horror is in knowing that this landscape will never change, and the challenge is to endure, like a prisoner in solitary confinement, sensory deprivation. In contrast, an Amazon explorer, immersed in a cauldron of heat, has his senses constantly assaulted. In place of ice there is rain, and everywhere an explorer steps some new danger lurks: a malarial mosquito, a spear, a snake, a spider, a piranha. The mind has to deal with the terror of constant siege.

Fawcett had long been convinced that the Amazon was more grueling and of greater scientific import—botanically, zoologically, geographically, and anthropologically—than what he dismissed as the exploration of "barren regions of eternal ice." And he resented the hold that polar explorers had on the public's imagination and the extraordinary funding they received. Murray, in turn, seemed certain that his journey with Shackleton— a journey more heralded than any that Fawcett had undertaken—had elevated him above the man in charge of his latest expedition.

While the two explorers were sizing each other up, they were joined by Henry Costin, the British corporal who in 1910, bored with military life, had answered a newspaper advertisement that Fawcett had posted seeking an adventurous companion. Short and stocky, with a bold Kiplingesque mustache and heavily hooded eyes, Costin had proven Fawcett's most durable and capable assistant. He was exceedingly fit, having been a gymnastics instructor in the Army, and was a world-class marksman. One of his sons later summed him up this way: "A tough bugger who hated bullshit."

Rounding out the party was Henry Manley, a twenty-six-year-old Englishman who listed his profession as "explorer," though he had not yet been to many places, and a handful of native porters.

On October 4, 1911, the expedition prepared to leave San Carlos to begin the trek northward along the banks of the Heath River. A Bolivian officer had warned Fawcett against traveling in this direction. "It's impossible," he said. "The Guarayos [Indians] are bad, and there are so many of them that they even dare to attack us armed soldiers right here! . . . To venture up into the midst of them is sheer madness."

Fawcett was undeterred. So, too, was Murray—after all, how difficult could the jungle be compared with the Antarctic? Early on, the men had the benefit of pack animals, which Murray used to carry his microscope and collecting jars. One night Murray was astonished to see vampire bats swarming from the sky and attacking the animals. "Several mules with ugly wounds, and streaming with blood," he wrote in his diary. The bats had front teeth as sharp as razor blades, which punctured the skin so swiftly and surgically that a sleeping victim often didn't awake. The bats would use their grooved tongues to lap up blood for up to forty minutes, secreting a substance to keep the wound from clotting. The bats could also transmit a lethal protozoan.

The men cleaned and dressed the mules' wounds quickly to ensure they didn't become infected, but that wasn't their only concern: vampire bats also fed on humans, as Costin and Fawcett had discovered from a previous trip. "We were all bitten by vampire bats," Costin later recalled in a letter. "The major had his wounds on the head, while my four bites were on each knuckle of my right hand . . . It is surprising the amount of blood lost from such small wounds."

"We awoke to find our hammocks saturated with blood," Fawcett said, "for any part of our persons touching the mosquito-nets or protruding beyond them were attacked by these loathsome animals."

In the jungle, a pack animal would falter every few steps, tripping over sludge-covered tree trunks or sinking into a mud hole, and the men had to poke and prod and beat the miserable creatures forward. "Surely an iron-bound rock-ribbed stomach is required to walk behind and drive" these animals, a companion of Fawcett's once wrote in his diary. "I am frequently besmirched with wet clots of rotting blood and other putrid matter that drops from their sore heads that are kept in a state of constant irritation by insects. Yesterday I probed out the maggots with a stick and filled the wounds with warm candle grease and sulphur mixed but it is doubtful whether this will prove effective." The animals generally survived no more than a month in such conditions. Another Amazon explorer wrote, "The animals themselves are pitiful sights; bleeding from great, sloughing wounds . . . foam dripping from their mouths, they lunge and strain through this veritable hell on earth. For men and beasts alike it is a miserable existence, though a merciful death usually terminates the careers of the latter." Fawcett finally announced that they would abandon the pack animals and proceed on foot with only a pair of dogs, which he considered the best sorts of companions: able to hunt, uncomplaining, and loyal to the bitter end.

Over the years, Fawcett had honed the number of items that his team carried on their backs, so that each pack weighed about sixty pounds. As the men loaded their gear, Fawcett asked Murray to carry one more thing: his pan for sifting gold. The weight of the pack startled Murray as he began to hump it through dense jungle and hip-deep mud. "My strength quite gave out, and I went slowly, resting now and again," he wrote in his diary. Fawcett was forced to send a porter to help him carry his pack. The next day, Murray seemed even more exhausted and fell behind the rest of the party while ascending a summit littered with fallen trees. "I climbed over them for an hour, killing work with the heavy pack, and had not made one hundred yards," Murray wrote. "All trace of the path was lost, I couldn't get forward, I couldn't get up the steep hill, I couldn't go back."

Scanning the forest for Fawcett and the others, Murray heard the sound of a river below and, hoping that it might lead to an easier path, took out his machete and tried to reach it, slashing at the grasping vines and enormous tree roots. "Without a machete," he realized, "it means death to be lost in such forest." His boots chafed his feet, and he threw his backpack in front of him, then picked it up and threw it once more. The roar of the river was growing louder and he hurried toward it, but he came at the rushing water too quickly and lost his balance, sending something tumbling out of his backpack . . . *A portrait of his wife and letters from her.* As he watched the water envelop them, he was overcome by "a superstitious depression of spirits."

He pushed on, desperate to find the others before night erased what little light seeped into the forest. He noticed footprints on the muddy bank. Could they be those of the Guarayos he had been told so much about, whose tribal name meant "warlike"? Then he spotted a tent in the distance and staggered toward it, only to get there and realize it was a boulder. His mind was deceiving him. He had been marching since sunrise, but he had progressed scarcely a few hundred yards. It was getting dark, and in a fit of panic he fired his rifle in the air. There was no response. His feet ached, and he sat down and removed his boots and socks; the skin had peeled off his ankles. He had no food other than a pound of caramels, which Nina Fawcett had prepared for the expedition. The box was intended to be shared among the team, but Murray devoured half the contents, washing them down with the river's milky water. Lying alone in the blackness, he smoked three Turkish cigarettes, trying to stifle his hunger. Then he passed out.

In the morning, the group found him, and Fawcett reprimanded Murray for slowing the group's progress. But each day Murray lagged farther and farther behind. He was unaccustomed to intense hunger—the ceaseless, oppressive gnawing that ate away at mind and body alike. Later, when Murray was given some cornmeal, he scooped it greedily into his mouth with a leaf and let it melt over his tongue. "I wish no more than to be assured such food for the rest of my time," he said. The entries in his diary became choppier, more frantic:

> Very hot work, quite exhausted; suggest short rest, Fawcett refuses it; stay behind alone, when able to struggle on, fearfully dense scrub, cannot get through it, cut way back to river bank, very rough going there . . . see another playa [beach] away at next bend of the river, try to wade to it, gets too deep, return to mud playa, now night; gather some dead branches and canes and lianas and make fire to dry clothes; no food, some saccharine pellets, smoke three cigarettes, suck some of the cold fruits, mosquitoes pretty bad, cannot sleep from bites, cold and tiredness, try opium sedative, no use; weird noises in river and forest, [anteater] comes down to drink on opposite side, making great row. Think hear voices come across the river, and imagine they may be Guarayos. All clothes full of grit, gets in mouth, miserable night.

He tried to do some scientific work but soon gave up. As another biologist who later traveled with Fawcett put it, "I thought that I would get many valuable natural history notes but my experience is that when undergoing severe physical labor the mind is not at all active. One thinks of the particular problem in hand or perhaps the mind just wanders not performing coherent thought. As to missing various phases of civilized life, one has no time to miss anything save food or sleep or rest. In short one becomes little more than a rational animal."

One night when Fawcett, Murray, and the others reached camp, they were so weak that most of them collapsed on the ground without pitching their hammocks. Later, Fawcett, apparently sensing the atmosphere of despair, and heeding what he had learned in exploring school, tried to encourage merriment. He pulled a recorder from his pack and played "The Calabar," a gallows-humor Irish folk song about a shipwreck. He sang:

> Next day we ran short of buttermilk—it was all the captain's
> fault—
> So the crew were laid up with scurvy, for the herrings were
> terrible salt.
> Our coloured cook said the meat was done, there wasn't a bap on
> the shelf;
> "Then we'll eat the soap," the captain cried, "let no man wash
> himself."

Murray hadn't heard the song in thirty years and joined in along with Costin, who took out his own recorder. Manley lay listening, as the sound of their voices and instruments drowned out the howl of monkeys and the whir of mosquitoes. For a moment, they seemed, if not happy, at least able to mock the prospect of their own death.

"YOU HAVE NO RIGHT TO BE TIRED!" Fawcett snapped at Murray.

They were on one of two rafts that they had built to go up the Heath River. Murray said that he wanted to wait for a boat that was trailing them, but Fawcett thought that he was making another excuse to rest. As Costin warned, internal discord was common in the miserable conditions, and was perhaps the biggest threat to a party's survival. During the first European expedition down the Amazon, in the early 1540s, members were accused of deserting their commander in the "greatest cruelty that faithless men have ever shown." In 1561, members of another South American expedition stabbed their leader to death while he slept, then, not long after, murdered

Percy Harrison Fawcett was considered "the last of the individualist explorers"—those who ventured into blank spots on the map with little more than a machete, a compass, and an almost divine sense of purpose. He is seen here in 1911, the year of his fourth major Amazon expedition.

Copyright © R. de Montet-Guerin

Fawcett mapping the frontier between Brazil and Bolivia in 1908.

Courtesy of the Royal Geographical Society

At the age of eighteen Fawcett graduated from Britain's Royal Military Academy, where he learned to be "a natural leader of men . . . fearless." *Sandhurst Collection, Royal Military Academy Sandhurst*

Nina, whom Fawcett met in Ceylon and married in 1901, once compared her situation to that of a sailor's wife: "very uncertain and lonely" and "miserably poor." *Copyright © R. de Montet-Guerin*

E. A. Reeves, the Royal Geographical Society's map curator, was charged with turning Fawcett into a gentleman explorer. *Courtesy of the Royal Geographical Society*

For centuries Europeans viewed the Amazon as a mythical landscape where Indians might have heads in the middle of their chests, as this sixteenth-century drawing illustrates. *Courtesy of The Hispanic Society of America, New York*

The legendary kingdom of El Dorado depicted in a sixteenth-century illustration printed in Germany. *Courtesy of The Hispanic Society of America, New York*

Dr. Alexander Hamilton Rice, Fawcett's main rival, was a multimillionaire "as much at home in the elegant swirl of Newport society as in the steaming jungles of Brazil." *Courtesy of the Royal Geographical Society*

"How long could we carry on" was the vital question: Fawcett (foreground right) and his men facing starvation during their search for the source of the Rio Verde in 1908. *Courtesy of the Library of Congress*

(Above) A member of Dr. Rice's 1919–20 expedition deploys a wireless telegraphy set—an early radio—allowing the party to receive news from the outside world. *Courtesy of the Royal Geographical Society*

(Right) Dr. Rice's 1924–25 expedition included a machine that would revolutionize exploration: the airplane. *Courtesy of the Royal Geographical Society*

(Above) Fawcett's younger son, Brian, pored over his father's diaries and drew illustrations depicting his adventures. The drawings, like this one, were published in *Exploration Fawcett* in 1953 and further fueled Percy Fawcett's legend. *Copyright © R. de Montet-Guerin*

Fawcett's longtime assistant Henry Costin posing, in 1914, with an Amazonian tribe that had never before seen a white man. *Courtesy of Michael Costin*

Acclaimed biologist James Murray was a member of Shackleton's British Antarctic Expedition and later joined Fawcett on a horrific journey in the Amazon. *Scott Polar Research Institute, University of Cambridge*

An Indian in the Xingu fishes with bow and arrow in 1937.
Many scientists believed the Amazon could not provide sufficient
food to sustain a large, complex civilization.
Courtesy of the Royal Geographical Society

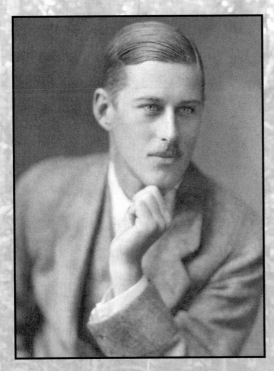

Fawcett's older son, Jack, who dreamed of being a movie star, accompanied his father on his deadly quest for Z. *Copyright © R. de Montet-Guerin*

"Strong as horses and keen as mustard": Jack Fawcett and his best friend, Raleigh Rimell, on the 1925 expedition. *Courtesy of the Royal Geographical Society*

Percy Fawcett with Raleigh Rimell and one of their guides shortly before the expedition vanished. *Courtesy of the Royal Geographical Society*

"I have never felt so well," Jack Fawcett wrote his mother during the fateful expedition. *Courtesy of the Royal Geographical Society*

In 1928 Commander George M. Dyott launched
the first major mission to rescue Fawcett.

Courtesy of the Royal Geographical Society

The Washington Post Magazine

WASHINGTON, D.C., SUNDAY, SEPTEMBER 30, 1934

Deep in the Fearful Amazon Jungle,

SAVAGES SEIZE MOVIE ACTOR

Seeking to Rescue Fawcett

By Robert Talley.

DOWN in the man-killing jungle of the Amazon where creeping death lurks behind every leafy bush and savage Indians guard the secrets of a vast region that has never been explored by white men, a new chapter in one of the greatest adventure stories of our time is being written today.

The hero is a 66-year-old Englishman, a man of evident wealth and

Hollywood knew this aristocratic and elderly Britisher for ten years, though there is some reason to doubt that it was his real one. About him there was an aura of wealth and social position suggestive of English estates and titles, but as to his past—which he never discussed—one could only guess.

Convinced Fawcett Was Still Alive.

race. Swallowed into oblivion with Col. Fawcett were his son, Jack Fawcett, 21, and Raleigh Rimmel, 23, a Los Angeles youth. Convinced that Col. Fawcett and his companions still lived and were perhaps held in slavery by some remote Indian tribe, DeWinton plunged into the jungle early in 1933 to find them. His mission was much the same as that of Henry M. Stanley, who penetrated Darkest Africa to res-

alive, DeWinton began his present expedition last January 10. He went to Cuyaba, quaint little capital of the Brazilian state of Matto Grosso that lies near the border of Bolivia, and from this outpost of civilization he entered the wilderness, accompanied only by a few Indian guides, along the route taken by Fawcett. Month elapsed—months during which Hollywood practically forgot the distinguished looking, but very

A news story about Albert de Winton, the Hollywood actor who, in 1933, had vowed to find Fawcett dead or alive. *From "Deep in the Fearful Amazon Jungle, Savages Seize Movie Actor Seeking to Rescue Fawcett," Washington Post, September 30, 1934*

(Below) Brian Fawcett, who had been left behind on the 1925 expedition, was eventually drawn into the jungle himself. *Bettmann/Corbis*

(Above) The Brazilian journalist Edmar Morel with Dulipé—the "White God of the Xingu"—who, in the 1940s, became a central figure in the Fawcett mystery. *From "The Strange Case of Colonel Fawcett," Life, April 30, 1951*

In 1951 Orlando Villas Boas, the revered Brazilian pioneer, thought that he had found proof of Fawcett's fate. *Photo by Edward A. Gourley, reproduced with permission from Douglas A. Gourley*

The Kalapalo Indians—including these, photographed by a missionary in 1937—were believed to know what really happened to Fawcett and his party. *Courtesy of the Royal Geographical Society*

(Below) James Lynch and his sixteen-year-old son, James, Jr., set out into the jungle in 1996, in the hopes of finally solving the Fawcett mystery. *Courtesy of James Lynch*

Paolo Pinage (left), who guided the author into the Amazon, rests in the house of a Bakairí Indian during our trip. *Courtesy of Paolo Pinage*

The author (front) treks with Bakairí Indians through the jungle along the same route that Fawcett followed eighty years earlier. *Courtesy of Paolo Pinage*

Two Kuikuro Indians dance in celebration of the
"whirlwind" spirit. *Courtesy of Michael Heckenberger*

Kuikuro Indians participate in one of their most sacred rituals, the Kuarup,
which honors the dead. *Courtesy of Michael Heckenberger*

The archaeologist Michael Heckenberger chats with Afukaká, the chief of the Kuikuro Indians. *Courtesy of Michael Heckenberger*

An aerial shot of the Kuikuro settlement with its circular plaza and domed houses along the perimeter. *Courtesy of Michael Heckenberger*

the man they had chosen to replace him. Fawcett had his own view of mutiny: as a friend once warned him, "Every party has a Judas."

With each day, tensions mounted between Fawcett and Murray. There was something about the man whom Costin reverently called "chief" that scared Murray. Fawcett expected "every man to do as much as he can" and was "contemptuous" of anyone who succumbed to fear. (Fawcett once described fear as "the motive power of all evil" which had "excluded humanity from the Garden of Eden.") Every year in the jungle seemed to make him harder and more fanatical, like a soldier who had experienced too much combat. He rarely cut a clean path through the forest; rather, he slashed his machete in every direction, as if he were being stung by bees. He painted his face with bright colors from berries, like an Indian warrior, and spoke openly of going native. "There is no disgrace in it," he said in *Exploration Fawcett*. "On the contrary, in my opinion it shows a creditable regard for the real things of life at the expense of the artificial." In his private papers, he jotted down thoughts under the heading "Renegades from Civilization": "Civilization has a relatively precarious hold upon us and there is an undoubted attraction in a life of absolute freedom once it has been tasted. The 'call o' the wild' is in the blood of many of us and finds its safety valve in adventure."

Fawcett, who seemed to approach each journey as if it were a Buddhist rite of purification, believed that the expedition would never get anywhere with Murray. Not only was the biologist ill suited for the Amazon; he drained morale by complaining incessantly. Because Murray had served under Shackleton, he seemed to think that he could question Fawcett's authority. Once, while walking a raft loaded with gear across a river, Murray was swept off his feet by the current. Ignoring Fawcett's instructions, he grabbed onto the raft's edge, threatening to topple it. Fawcett told him to let go and swim to safety, but he wouldn't, which confirmed him, in Fawcett's parlance, as "a pink-eyed weakling."

Fawcett soon came to suspect the scientist of something more serious than cowardice: stealing. In addition to the missing caramels, other communal provisions had been pilfered. Few crimes were graver. "On such an expedition the theft of food comes next to murder as a crime and should by rights be punished as such," Theodore Roosevelt said of his 1914 Amazon journey. When Fawcett confronted Murray about the thefts, the biologist was indignant. "Told them what I had eaten," he wrote bitterly, adding, "It seems my honorable course would have been to starve." Not long after, Costin caught Murray with maize that seemed to belong to reserves for later in the trip. Where did you get that? Costin demanded.

Murray said it was surplus from his own private store.

Fawcett ordered that because Murray had taken a handful, he wouldn't be permitted to eat the bread made from the maize. Murray pointed out that Manley had eaten corn from his own private store. Fawcett was unmoved. It was a matter of principle, he said.

"If it was," Murray said, "it was the principles of a fool."

The mood continued to deteriorate. As Murray put it one evening, "There is no singing in camp tonight."

MANLEY WAS the first stricken. His temperature rose to 104 degrees, and he shook uncontrollably—it was malaria. "This is too much for me," he muttered to Murray. "I can't manage it." Unable to stand, Manley lay on the muddy bank, trying to let the sun bake the fever out of him, though it did little good.

Next, Costin contracted espundia, an illness with even more frightening symptoms. Caused by a parasite transmitted by sand flies, it destroys the flesh around the mouth, nose, and limbs, as if the person were slowly dissolving. "It develops into . . . a mass of leprous corruption," Fawcett said. In rare instances, it leads to fatal secondary infections. In Costin's case, the disease eventually became so bad, as Nina Fawcett later informed the Royal Geographical Society, that he had "gone off his rocker."

Murray, meanwhile, seemed to be literally coming apart. One of his fingers grew inflamed after brushing against a poisonous plant. Then the nail slid off, as if someone had removed it with pliers. Then his right hand developed, as he put it, a "very sick, deep suppurating wound," which made it "agony" even to pitch his hammock. Then he was stricken with diarrhea. Then he woke up to find what looked like worms in his knee and arm. He peered closer. They were maggots growing inside him. He counted fifty around his elbow alone. "Very painful now and again when they move," Murray wrote.

Repulsed, he tried, despite Fawcett's warnings, to poison them. He put anything—nicotine, corrosive sublimate, permanganate of potash—inside the wounds and then attempted to pick the worms out with a needle or by squeezing the flesh around them. Some worms died from the poison and started to rot inside him. Others grew as long as an inch and occasionally poked out their heads from his body, like a periscope on a submarine. It was as if his body were being taken over by the kind of tiny creatures he had studied. His skin smelled putrid. His feet swelled. Was he getting elephantiasis, too? "The feet are too big for the boots," he wrote. "The skin is like pulp."

Only Fawcett seemed unmolested. He discovered one or two maggots beneath his skin—a species of botfly plants its eggs on a mosquito, which then deposits the hatched larvae on humans—but he did not poison them, and the wounds caused by their burrowing remained uninfected. Despite the party's weakened state, Fawcett and the men pressed on. At one point, a horrible cry rang out. According to Costin, a puma had pounced upon one of the dogs and was dragging it into the forest. "Being unarmed except for a machete, it was useless to follow," Costin wrote. Soon after, the other dog drowned.

Starving, wet, feverish, pocked with mosquito bites, the party began to eat itself from within, like the maggots corkscrewing through Murray's body. One night Murray and Manley fought bitterly over who would sleep on which side of the fire. By then, Fawcett had come to believe that Murray was a coward, a malingerer, a thief, and, worst of all, a cancer spreading throughout his expedition. It was no longer a question of whether Murray's slowness would cause the expedition to fail, Fawcett thought; it was whether he would keep the party from getting out at all.

Murray believed that Fawcett simply lacked empathy—"no mercy on a sick or tired man." Fawcett could slow down to "give a lame man a chance for his life," but he refused. As the party pushed ahead again, Murray began to fixate on Fawcett's gold-washing pan, until he couldn't bear it any longer. He opened his backpack and dumped the pan, along with most of his possessions, including his hammock and clothes. Fawcett warned him that he would need these things, but Murray insisted that he was trying to save his life, since Fawcett wouldn't wait for him.

The lighter pack improved Murray's speed, but without his hammock he was forced to sleep on the ground in the pouring rain with bugs crawling on him. "By this time the Biologist . . . was suffering badly from his sores and from lack of a change of clothes, for those he possessed were stinking," Fawcett wrote. "He was beginning to realize how foolish he had been to throw away all but immediate necessities in his pack, and became increasingly morose and frightened." Fawcett added, "As we had thunderstorms every day with deluges of rain, he grew worse instead of better. I was frankly anxious about him. If blood poisoning set in he would be a dead man, for there was nothing we could do about it."

"The prospect of getting out recedes; food is nearly done," Murray wrote in his diary.

Murray's body had become swollen with pus and worms and gangrene; flies swirled around him as if he were already a corpse. With their route not even half done, the moment had arrived that Fawcett had warned every expedition member of, were he too sick to carry on: abandonment.

Although Fawcett had prepared for such a contingency, he had never actually enforced it, and he consulted with Costin and Manley as Murray looked on grimly. "There was a curious discussion in camp tonight, on the question of my abandonment," Murray wrote. "When traveling in the uninhabited forest, without other recourses than you carry with you, every man realized that if he falls sick or can't keep up with the others he must take the consequences. The others can't wait and die with him." Still, Murray felt that they were close enough to a frontier outpost where he could be left behind. "This calm admission of the willingness to abandon me . . . was a queer thing to hear from an Englishman, though it did not surprise me, as I had gauged his character long before."

In the end, Fawcett, with his customary impetuousness, took a step that for him was almost as radical as leaving a man to die: he diverted his mission, at least long enough to try to get Murray out. Bitterly and reluctantly, he looked for the nearest settlement. Fawcett ordered Costin to remain beside Murray and ensure his evacuation. According to Costin, Murray showed signs of delirium. "I will not detail the physical force methods I had to adopt with him," Costin later recalled. "Suffice it to say I took away his revolver, so that he could not shoot me . . . But it was the only alternative to leaving him to die."

Eventually, the party came across a frontiersman with a mule, who promised to try to carry the biologist back to civilization. Fawcett offered Murray some money to pay for food, though the enmity between them still burned. Costin told Murray that he hoped that any harsh words they had exchanged in the jungle would be forgotten. He then glanced at Murray's infected knee. "You know that knee of yours is far worse than you think," he said.

Murray gathered from his manner that Costin and the others expected him to die—that they would never see him again. The men loaded him onto the mule. His limbs, like his knee, had begun to discharge foul matter. "It is surprising the quantity that comes from both arm and knee," Murray wrote. "The matter from the arm is very inflammatory and makes the whole forearm red flesh and very painful. The discharge from the knee is more copious; it runs down in streams from half-a-dozen holes and saturates my stockings." He could barely sit up on the mule. "Feel more ill than ever I did, knee very bad, heel very bad, kidneys upset, whether from food or poison and must pass water frequently." He prepared to die: "Lie awake all night wondering how the end will be, and whether it is justifiable to make it easier, with drugs or otherwise"—an apparent allusion to suicide. He continued, "Cannot say afraid of the end itself, but wonder if it will be very difficult."

Fawcett, Manley, and Costin, meanwhile, trudged on, trying to complete at least part of the mission. A month later, when they left the jungle in Cojata, Peru, there was no word of Murray. He had vanished. Later, in La Paz, Fawcett sent off a letter to the Royal Geographical Society:

> Murray is, I regret to say, missing . . . The Govt. of Peru is instituting searching enquiries, but I fear he must have received some accident on the dangerous Cordillera trails, or have died en route of gangrene. The British Minister has his case in hand and his family will not be communicated with unless there is definite news of some kind or all hopes of his existence are abandoned.

Pointing out that Manley had almost died as well, Fawcett concluded, "I am well and fit myself but want a rest."

Then, miraculously, Murray emerged from the forest. It turned out that, after more than a week, he had made it on the mule with the settler to Tambopata, a frontier outpost on the border of Bolivia and Peru that consisted of a single house; there a man named Sardon and his family had nursed him for weeks. They slowly squeezed out "a good many dead maggots, big fat fellows," drained the pus from his sores, and fed him. When he was strong enough, they put him on a mule and sent him to La Paz. Along the way, he "read enquires about Senor Murray, supposed dead in this region." He reached La Paz in the beginning of 1912. His arrival shocked authorities, who discovered that he was not only alive but furious.

Murray accused Fawcett of all but trying to murder him, and was incensed that Fawcett had insinuated that he was a coward. Keltie informed Fawcett, "I understand that there is a possibility that the matter may be put into the hands of a well known solicitor. James Murray has got powerful and wealthy friends behind him." Fawcett insisted, "Everything that could humanely speaking be done for him was done . . . Strictly speaking, he owed his condition to unsanitary habits, insatiability for food, and excessive partiality for strong liquor—all of which are suicidal in such places." Fawcett added, "I have little sympathy with him. He knew to a detail what he would have to put up with and that on such journeys of a pioneering character illness and accidents cannot be allowed to jeopardize the safety of the party. Everyone who goes with me understands that much clearly before hand. It was only that he and Mr. Manley both were sick which compelled me to abandon the journey projected. That he was rushed rather mercilessly . . . was a matter of food supply and the necessity of saving his life, of which he himself was inclined to be pessimistic." Costin was willing to testify on Fawcett's behalf, as was Manley. The Royal Geographical Society, examining the initial evidence, suspected that Fawcett "did not neglect Murray, but did his best for him under the circumstances." Nevertheless, the Society pleaded with Fawcett to quietly put the matter to rest before it became a national scandal. "I am sure you don't want to do Murray any injury and now you are both in a temperate climate I think you might take steps to come to an understanding," Keltie said.

Whether Fawcett extended an apology to Murray or vice versa is not clear, but the full details of the feud were never made public, including how close Fawcett had come to deserting his countryman in the jungle. Costin, meanwhile, was now the one on the verge of death. His espundia was rapidly growing worse, and was compounded by other possible infections. "So far they have been unable to cure him," Fawcett informed Keltie. "But he is undergoing a fresh and peculiarly painful course of treatment at the School of Tropical Medicine [in London]. I sincerely hope he will recover." After an official from the RGS visited Costin, he told Fawcett in a letter, "What a dreadful sight he is poor man." Gradually, Costin recovered his health, and when Fawcett announced that he planned to return to the Amazon he decided to accompany him. As he put it, "It's hell all right, but one kind of likes it." Manley, too, despite his brush with death, pledged to go with Fawcett. "He and Costin were the only assistants I could ever call completely reliable and fully adaptable, and never have I wished for better company," Fawcett said.

Murray, for his part, had had enough of the tropics. He longed for the familiar bleakness of ice and snow, and in June 1913 joined a Canadian scientific expedition to the Arctic. Six weeks later, the ship he was on, the *Karluk*, became embedded in the ice and eventually had to be abandoned. This time Murray helped to lead a mutiny against the captain, and with a breakaway faction he escaped with sleds across the barren snow. The captain was able to rescue his party. Murray and his party, however, were never seen again.

13

—◦—

RANSOM

When I landed in São Paulo, Brazil, I went to see the person who I was sure could assist me on my expedition: James Lynch. He was the Brazilian explorer who, in 1996, had led the last major expedition to uncover evidence of Fawcett's missing party and who, along with his sixteen-year-old son and ten other explorers, had been abducted by Indians. I had heard that, after Lynch had managed to escape from captivity and returned to São Paulo, he had left his job at Chase Bank and started a financial consulting firm. (Part of its name was, aptly, Phoenix.) When I phoned him, he agreed to meet me at his office, which was situated in a skyscraper downtown. He seemed older and gentler than the figure I had conjured in my imagination. He wore an elegant suit, and his blond hair was neatly combed. He led me into his office, on the ninth floor, and peered out the window. "São Paulo makes New York City seem almost small, doesn't it?" he said, noting that the metropolitan area had eighteen million people. He shook his head with wonder and sat down at his desk. "So how can I help you?"

I told him about my plans to trace Fawcett's route.

"You got the Fawcett bug, huh?" he said.

By then, I had it more than I cared to admit, and I said simply, "It seems like an interesting story."

"Oh, that it is. That it is."

When I asked how he had escaped from captivity, he stiffened slightly in his chair. He explained that, after he and his group were transported up-river, the Indians had forced them out of the boats and up a massive clay embankment. At the top, the Indians posted guards and set up a makeshift camp. Lynch said that he had tried to make a note of everything and everyone—to find a weak spot—but darkness soon enveloped them, and he could distinguish his captors only by their voices. Strange noises emanated from the forest. "Have you ever heard the sound of a jungle?" Lynch asked. I shook my head. "It's not what you imagine," he went on. "It's not really loud or anything like that. But it's always talking."

He recalled how he had told his son, James, Jr., to try to sleep, and how he, too, eventually collapsed from exhaustion. He wasn't sure how long he had nodded off, he said, when he opened his eyes and saw, in the morning sunlight, the tip of a spear flickering in the forest.

He turned around and saw another gleaming point, as more and more Indian men, all armed, emerged from the forest. There were over a hundred of them. James, Jr., who had also been woken up by the noise, whispered, "They're everywhere."

"I told him everything was going to be okay, though I knew it wasn't," Lynch recalled.

As the tribesmen formed a circle around Lynch and his son, five older Indians, who appeared to be chiefs, sat down on wooden stumps in front of the group. "That's when I knew our fate was about to be determined," Lynch said.

The young Indian who had led the original assault stepped forward and argued angrily before what appeared to be a council; occasionally, after he made a point, several Indians pounded their wooden clubs in assent.

Others addressed the chiefs, and every so often an Indian, who spoke some broken Portuguese, translated for the benefit of Lynch and his group, explaining that they were being accused of trespassing. The negotiations went on for two days. "There would be these endless hours of debate, and we didn't know what was going on," Lynch recalled, "and then this translator would sum up everything in a single sentence. It was, like, *bam,* 'They will tie you over the river and let the piranhas eat you.' Or, *bam,* 'They shall cover you in honey and let the bees sting you to death.' "

Just then the door to Lynch's office opened and a young man walked in. He had a round, handsome face. "This is my son, James, Jr.," Lynch said.

He was now twenty-five and engaged to be married. When James, Jr., learned that we were discussing the Fawcett expedition, he said, "You know, I had a lot of romantic notions about the jungle and this kind of finished that."

Lynch said that the tribe began to target his son, touching and taunting him, and Lynch thought about telling him to bolt into the forest, though death there was no less certain. Then Lynch noticed that four of the chiefs seemed to defer to a fifth one, who appeared to be the least swayed by the violent exhortations. As several Indians indicated that they intended to tie up his son and kill him, Lynch rose anxiously and approached the fifth chief. Relying on the Indian translator, Lynch said that he was sorry if his men had offended his people in any way. Assuming the role of a chief, Lynch said, he began to negotiate directly with him and agreed to hand over his group's boats and equipment in exchange for the party's release. The elderly chief turned and spoke to the council for several minutes, and, as he did, the Indians became more riled. Then the council fell quiet, and the commanding chief said something to Lynch in an unflinching voice. Lynch waited for the translator, who seemed to struggle to find the words. Finally, he said, "We accept your gifts."

Before the council could change its mind, Lynch obtained his radio, which had been confiscated by the tribe, to send an SOS with his coordinates, and a bush plane was dispatched to rescue them. The value of the ransom came to thirty thousand dollars.

Lynch said that he was the last member of the party to be released and that it wasn't until he boarded the plane and was safely in the air that he thought about Colonel Fawcett again. He wondered if Fawcett and his son had also been taken hostage, and if they had tried and failed to proffer a ransom. Looking out the airplane window, Lynch recalled, he could see the embankment where he and his team had been held for three days. The Indians were gathering their things, and Lynch watched as they faded into the forest.

"I don't think anyone will ever solve the mystery of Fawcett's disappearance," Lynch said. "It's impossible."

On a computer on Lynch's desk, I noticed a satellite image of jagged mountains. To my surprise, it was for Lynch's next expedition. "I leave in two days. We're going to the top of the Andes."

"Not me," James, Jr., said. "I have a wedding to plan."

James, Jr., said goodbye to me and left the room, and Lynch talked about his upcoming adventure. "We're looking for this plane that crashed in the Andes in 1937," he said. "No one's ever been able to find the thing." He sounded excited, when, in the midst of his explanation, he stopped and said, "Don't tell my son, but I wouldn't mind tagging along with you. If you find anything about Z, you must tell me. Please."

I said I would. Before I left, Lynch offered some advice. "First, you need a top-notch guide, someone who has ties to the tribes in the area," he said. "Second, you need to go in as quietly as possible. Fawcett was right: too big a party only calls attention to itself." He warned me to be careful. "Remember: My son and I were lucky. Most of these Fawcett expeditions never come back."

THE CASE
FOR Z

There was no epiphany, no bolt of lightning. Rather, the theory developed over time, with a clue here and a clue there, in fits and starts and with unexpected turns, the trail of evidence reaching as far back as his days in Ceylon. At Fort Frederick, Fawcett had first learned that it was possible for a great kingdom to seclude itself in the jungle and, after time had taken its inexorable toll, for its palaces and thoroughfares to vanish under creeping vines and roots. But the notion of Z—of a lost civilization concealed in the Amazon—began truly to take hold when Fawcett encountered the hostile Indians he had been warned to avoid at all costs.

In 1910, he was riding in canoes with Costin and several other companions, exploring an unknown part of the Heath River in Bolivia, when seven-foot-long poisonous arrows started to rain down, boring into the side of the canoe. A Spanish friar once described watching a companion who had been hit by such a weapon: "The moment that it struck him he felt a great pain . . . for the foot in which he had been wounded turned very black, and the poison gradually made its way up through the leg, like a living thing, without its being possible to head it off, although they applied many cauteries to it with fire . . . and when it had mounted to his heart, he died, being in great pain until the third day, when he gave his soul to God, who had created it."

A member of Fawcett's team dived into the water, shouting, "Retire! Retire!" But Fawcett insisted on pulling the boats to the opposite bank, as arrows continued to cascade from the sky. "One of these came within a foot of my head, and I actually saw the face of the savage who fired it," Costin later recalled. Fawcett ordered his men to drop their rifles, but the barrage of arrows persisted. And so Fawcett instructed one of the men, as further demonstration of their peaceful intentions, to pull out his accordion and play it. The rest of the party, commanded to stand and face their deaths without protest, sang along as Costin, first in a trembling voice, then more fervently, called out the words to "The Soldiers of the Queen": "In the fight for England's glory, lads / Of its world wide glory let us sing."

Fawcett then did something that shocked Costin so much that he would recall it vividly even as an old man: the major untied the handkerchief around his neck and, waving it above his head, waded into the river, heading directly into the fusillade of arrows. Over the years, Fawcett had picked up scraps of Indian dialects, scribbling the words in his logbooks and studying them at night, and he called out the few fragments of vocabulary he knew, repeating *friend*, *friend*, *friend*, not sure if the word that he was shouting was even right, as the water from the river rose to his armpits. Then the arrows ceased. For a moment, no one moved as Fawcett stood in the river, hands above his head, like a penitent being baptized. According to Costin, an Indian appeared from behind a tree and came down to the edge of the river. Paddling out toward Fawcett in a raft, he took the handkerchief from Fawcett's hand. "The Major made signs for him to be taken across," Costin later recounted in a letter to his daughter, and the Indian "poled back to his side with Fawcett kneeling on his flimsy craft."

"On climbing the opposite bank," Fawcett said, "I had an unpleasant anticipation of receiving a shot in the face or an arrow in the stomach."

The Indians led him away. "[Fawcett] disappeared into the forest, and we were left wondering!" Costin said. The party feared that its leader had been slaughtered until, nearly an hour later, he emerged from the jungle with an Indian cheerfully wearing his Stetson.

In such fashion, Fawcett made friends with a group of Guarayos. "[They] helped us to make camp, remaining in it all night and giving us yucca, bananas, fish, necklaces, parrots, and in fact of all they had," Fawcett wrote in one of his dispatches.

Fawcett did not carry a craniometer and relied instead on his eyes to record observations of the Indians. He had been accustomed to meeting tribes that had been conquered by whites and acculturated by force, their members weakened by disease and brutality. By contrast, these hundred and fifty or so forest Indians seemed robust. "The men are finely developed, and of a warm brown, black haired, good looking and well clothed in dyed cotton shirts, plenty of which were in course of manufacture in their huts," Fawcett wrote. He was struck by the fact that, unlike the emaciated explorers, they had substantial resources of food. One Guarayo crushed a plant with a stone and let its juice spill into a stream, where it formed a milky cloud. "After a few minutes a fish came to the surface, swimming in a circle, mouth gaping, then turned on its back apparently dead," Costin recalled. "Soon there were a dozen fish floating belly up." They had been poisoned. A Guarayo boy waded into the water and picked out the fattest ones for eating. The quantity of poison only stunned them and posed no risk to humans when the fish were cooked; equally remarkable, the fish that the boy had left in the water soon returned to life and swam away unharmed. The same poison was often used for toothaches. The Indians, Fawcett was discovering, were masters of pharmacology, adept at manipulating their environment to suit their needs, and he concluded that the Guarayos were "a most intelligent race of people."

After his 1910 expedition, Fawcett, suspecting that the Indians of the Amazon held secrets long overlooked by historians and ethnologists, started to seek out various tribes, no matter how fierce their reputation. "There are problems to solve out here . . . which shout for someone to undertake them," he informed the RGS. "But experience is essential. It is a folly to enter the unexplored parts without it—and in these days suicide." In 1911, he resigned from the boundary commission to pursue inquiries into the burgeoning new field of anthropology. Once, not far from the Heath River, Fawcett was sitting with Costin and the rest of his team eating when a band of Indians encircled them with drawn bows. "Without any hesitation," Costin wrote, "Fawcett dropped his belt and machete, to show he was unarmed, and advanced toward them, hands above his head. There was a slight pause in doubt and then one of 'los barbaros' [the savages] put down his arrows and walked to meet him. We had made friends with the Echojas!"

Over time, this became Fawcett's signature approach. "Whenever he came upon the savages," Costin said, "he would walk slowly towards them . . . with hands stretched in the air." As with his method of traveling in radically small parties, without protection from armed soldiers, his means of establishing relations with tribes, some of which had never before seen a white man, struck many as both heroic and suicidal. "I know, from persons who have informed me, how he crossed the river in front of a whole tribe of hostile savages, and simply by his bravery induced them to cease firing, and accompanied them to their village," a Bolivian official reported to the Royal Geographical Society of Fawcett's meeting with the Guarayos. "I must say they are indeed very hostile, because I have been among them myself, and in 1893 General Pando not only lost some of his men, but also lost his nephew, and the engineer, Mr. Muller, who, tired of the journey, decided to cross from one of the rivers up to the Modeidi, and up to this day we have not heard anything about them."

Fawcett's ability to succeed where so many others failed contributed to a growing myth of his invincibility, which he himself began to believe. How could one explain, he wondered, "standing deliberately in front of savages with whom it was vital to make friends, arrows fixing past one's head, between one's legs, even between arm and body, for several minutes, and yet being untouched"? Nina also thought that he was indestructible.

Once, after he had approached a hostile Indian tribe with his modus operandi, she informed the RGS, "His encounter with the savages and the way he handled them is one of the bravest episodes I have ever heard of—and I am glad he behaved as he did—personally, I have no fears whatever regarding his safety, for I am so certain that on occasions like that he will do the right thing."

Costin wrote that on their five expeditions Fawcett invariably made friends with the tribes they met. There was, however, one exception. In 1914, Fawcett sought out a group of Maricoxis in Bolivia, of whom the other Indians in the area had told him to be wary. When he made his usual overtures, the Indians reacted violently. As they came in for the kill, Fawcett's men pleaded for permission to use their guns. We *must* fire, Costin yelled.

Fawcett hesitated. "He did not wish to do so, for we had never fired before," Costin recalled. But at last Fawcett relented. Later, Fawcett said that he had ordered his men to fire only at the ground or in the air. But, according to Costin, "we could see that one [Indian] at least had been hit in the stomach."

If Costin's account is correct, and there is little reason to doubt it, then it was the one time Fawcett violated his own edict, and he was apparently so mortified that he doctored his official reports to the RGS and concealed the truth his entire life.

ONE DAY, WHILE staying with a tribe of Echojas in the Bolivian region of the Amazon, Fawcett stumbled across further evidence that seemed to contradict the prevailing notion that the jungle was a death trap in which small bands of hunter-gatherers led a miserable existence, abandoning and killing their own to survive. Fawcett had reinforced this image with accounts of his own harrowing journeys, and he was stunned to find that, like the Guarayos, the Echojas had stockpiled mass quantities of food. They often used the Amazonian floodplains, which were more fertile than terra firma, to grow crops, and they had developed elaborate ways of hunting and fishing. "Food problems never bothered them," Fawcett said. "When hungry, one of them would go off into the forest and call for game; and I joined him on one occasion to see how he did it. I could see no signs of an animal in the bush, but the Indian plainly knew better. He set up ear-piercing cries and signed to me to keep still. In a few minutes a small deer came timidly through the bush . . . and the Indian shot it with bow and arrow. I have seen them draw monkeys and birds out of the trees above by means of these peculiar cries." Costin, an award-winning marksman, was equally amazed to watch the Indians succeed where he, with his rifle, failed again and again.

And it wasn't just the Indians' ability to generate an abundant food supply—a precursor to any densely populated, sophisticated civilization—that intrigued Fawcett. Though the Echojas seemed to have no defenses against imported European diseases like measles, which is one reason Fawcett suspected their population was still small, they had developed an array of medicinal herbs and unorthodox treatments to protect themselves against the daily assault of the jungle. They were even adept at removing the maggots that had tortured Murray. "[The Echojas] would make a curious whistling noise with their tongues, and at once the grub's head would issue from the blowhole," Fawcett wrote. "Then the Indian would give the sore a quick squeeze, and the invader was ejected." He added, "I sucked, whistled, protested, and even played the flute to mine, with absolutely no effect." A Western doctor who was traveling with Fawcett considered such methods witchcraft, but Fawcett regarded them, along with an assortment of herbal cures, as a marvel. "With illness and disease so prevalent it is no wonder that herbal remedies are used," Fawcett said. "It seems as though every disorder has its appropriate nature-cure." He added, "Of course, the medical profession does not encourage people to make use of them. Yet the cures they effect are often remarkable, and I speak as one who has tried several with complete success." Adopting herbal medicines and native methods of hunting, Fawcett was better able to survive off the land. "In 99 cases out of a 100 there is no need to starve," he concluded.

But even if the Amazon could, as he supposed, sustain a large civilization, had the Indians ever actually constructed one? There was still no archaeological evidence. There was not even evidence of dense populations in the Amazon. And the notion of a complex civilization contradicted the two main ethnological paradigms that had prevailed for centuries and that originated with the first encounter between Europeans and Native Americans, more than four hundred years earlier. Though some of the first conquistadores were in awe of the civilizations that Native Americans had developed, many theologians debated whether these dark-skinned, scantily clad peoples were, in fact, human; for how could the descendants of Adam and Eve have wandered so far, and how could the biblical prophets have been ignorant of them? In the mid-sixteenth century, Juan Ginés de Sepúlveda, one of the Holy Roman Emperor's chaplains, argued that the Indians were "half men" who should be treated as natural slaves. "The Spanish have a perfect right to rule these barbarians of the New World," Sepúlveda declared, adding, "For there exists between the two as great a difference as between . . . apes and men."

At the time, the most forceful critic of this genocidal paradigm was Bartolomé de Las Casas, a Dominican friar who had traveled throughout the Americas. In a famous debate with Sepúlveda and in a series of treatises, Las Casas tried to prove, once and for all, that Indians were equal humans ("Are these not men? Do they not have rational souls?"), and to condemn those "pretending to be Christians" who "wiped them from the face of the earth." In the process, however, he contributed to a conception of the Indians that became an equal staple of European ethnology: the "noble savage." According to Las Casas, the Indians were "the simplest people in the world," "without malice or guile," "never quarrelsome or belligerent or boisterous," who "are neither ambitious nor greedy, and are totally uninterested in worldly power."

Although in Fawcett's era both conceptions remained prevalent in scholarly and popular literature, they were now filtered through a radical new scientific theory: evolution. Darwin's theory, laid out in *On the Origin of Species* in 1859, suggested that people and apes shared a common ancestor, and, coupled with recent discoveries of fossils revealing that humans had been on earth far longer than the Bible stated, helped irrevocably to sever anthropology from theology. Victorians now attempted to make sense of human diversity not in theological terms but in biological ones. The manual *Notes and Queries on Anthropology*, which was recommended reading in Fawcett's exploring school, included chapters titled "Anatomy and Physiology," "Hair," "Colour," "Odour," "Motions," "Physiognomy," "Pathology," "Abnormalities," "Reproduction," "Physical Powers," "Senses," and "Heredity." Among the questions that Fawcett and other explorers were told to answer were:

> Is there any notable peculiarity of odour attached to the persons of the tribe or people described? What is the habitual posture in sleep? Is the body well balanced in walking? Is the body erect and the leg straightened? Or do they stand and move with the knee slightly bent? Do they swing the arm in walking? Do they climb trees well? Is astonishment expressed by the eyes and mouth being opened wide, and by the eyebrows being raised? Does shame excite a blush?

The Victorians wanted to know, in effect, why some apes had evolved into English gentlemen and why some hadn't.

Whereas Sepúlveda had argued that Indians were inferior on religious grounds, many Victorians now claimed that they were inferior on biological ones—that they were possibly even a "missing link" in the evolutionary chain between apes and men. In 1863, the Anthropological Society of London was created to investigate such theories. Richard Burton, one of the Society's founders, postulated that Indians, like blacks, with their "quasi-gorillahood," belonged to a "sub-species." (Darwin himself, who never subscribed to the extreme racialism that emerged in his name, described the Fuegians he saw in South America—"these poor wretches . . . stunted in their growth, their hideous faces bedaubed with white paint, their skins filthy and greasy, their hair entangled, their voices discordant, and their gestures violent and without dignity"—as if it were hard to "believe they are fellow-creatures, and inhabitants of the same world.") Many anthropologists, including Burton, practiced phrenology—the study of the protuberances on human skulls, which were thought to indicate intelligence and character traits. One phrenologist comparing two Indian craniums with those of Europeans said that the former were marked by "firmness" and "secretiveness" and that their shape explained "the magnanimity displayed by the Indians in their endurance of torture." Francis Galton, in his theory of eugenics, which once counted among its followers John Maynard Keynes and Winston Churchill, argued that human intelligence was inherited and immutable and that native peoples of the New World were intrinsically "children in mind." Even many Victorians who believed in a "psychic unity to mankind" assumed that Indian societies were in a different stage of evolutionary development. By the early twentieth century, the then-popular diffusionist school of anthropologists maintained that if a sophisticated ancient civilization ever did exist in South America, its origins were either Western or Near Eastern—in the lost tribes of Israel, for example, or in seafaring Phoenicians. "There are all sorts of theories among anthropologists regarding the distribution of the human race," Keltie, of the Royal Geographical Society, noted, adding that diffusionist anthropologists "maintain that the Phoenicians navigated the whole of the Pacific Ocean, and that many of them penetrated South America."

Fawcett was deeply influenced by such ideas—his writings are rife with images of Indians as "jolly children" and "ape-like" savages. When he first saw an Indian cry, he expressed befuddlement, sure that physiologically Indians had to be stoic. He struggled to reconcile what he observed with everything he had been taught, and his conclusions were filled with convolutions and contradictions. He believed, for instance, that the jungle contained "savages of the most barbarous kind, ape-men who live in holes in the ground and come out only at night"; yet he nearly always described the Indians whom he met as being "civilized," and often far more so than Europeans. ("My experience is that few of these savages are naturally 'bad,' unless contact with 'savages' from the outside world has made them so.") He vigorously opposed the destruction of indigenous cultures through colonization. In the jungle, the absolutist became a relativist. After he witnessed a tribe cannibalize one of its dead as part of a religious ceremony—the body "roasted over a big fire" and "cut up and divided amongst the various families"—Fawcett beseeched Europeans not to deplore the "elaborate ritual." He hated to classify unacculturated Indians as "savages"—then the common terminology—and he noted that the kind, decent Echojas were "plain proof of how unjustified is the general condemnation of all the wild forest people." Along with adopting Indian mores, he learned to speak myriad indigenous languages. "He knew the Indians as few white men have ever known them, and he had the gift of tongues," observed the adventure writer and Fawcett associate Thomas Charles Bridges. "Few men have ever possessed that gift to such a marked degree." Costin, summing up Fawcett's relationship with the natives of the Amazon, said simply, "He understood them better than anyone."

Yet Fawcett could never find his way out of what the historian Dane Kennedy has called the "mental maze of race." When Fawcett detected a highly sophisticated tribe, he frequently tried to find racial markers—more "whiteness" or "redness"—that might reconcile the notion of an advanced Indian society with his Victorian beliefs and attitudes. "There are three kinds of Indians," he once wrote. "The first are docile and miserable people . . . [T]he second, dangerous, repulsive cannibals very rarely seen; the third, a robust and fair people, who must have a civilized origin."

The notion that the Americas contained a tribe of "fair" people, or "white Indians," had endured since Columbus claimed that he had seen several natives who were as "white as we are." Later, conquistadores said that they had found an Aztec room filled with "men, women and children, white at birth in the face, body, hair and eyelashes." The legend of "white Indians" had taken hold perhaps most fervently in the Amazon, where the first Spanish explorers to descend the river described female warriors as "very white and tall." Many of these legends undoubtedly had their origins in the existence of tribes with markedly lighter skin. One group of uncommonly tall, pale Indians in eastern Bolivia were called the Yurucares, which literally means "white men." The Yanomami of the Amazon were also known as "white Indians" owing to their lightness, as were the Wai-Wai of Guyana.

In Fawcett's day, the "white Indian question," as it was called, gave credence to the diffusionists' theory that Phoenicians or some other Westerners, such as the Atlanteans or the Israelites, had migrated into the jungle thousands of years earlier. Fawcett was initially skeptical of the existence of "white Indians," calling the evidence "weak," but over time they seemed to give him a way out of his personal mental maze of race: if the Indians had descended from Western civilization, there could be no doubt that they could build a complex society. Fawcett could never take the final leap of a modern anthropologist and accept that complex civilizations were capable of springing up independently of each other. As a result, while some anthropologists and historians today consider Fawcett enlightened for his era, others, like John Hemming, depict him as a "Nietzschean explorer" who spouted "eugenic gibberish." In truth, he was both. As much as Fawcett rebelled against Victorian mores—becoming a Buddhist who lived like an Indian warrior—he could never transcend them. He escaped virtually every kind of pathology in the jungle, but he could not rid himself of the pernicious disease of race.

What is consistent in his writings is the growing belief that the Amazon and its people were not what everyone assumed them to be. Something was amiss. He had seen during his *autopses* too many tribes that did not resemble the general European ethnology.

. . .

IN 1914, FAWCETT was traveling with Costin and Manley in a remote corner of the Brazilian Amazon, far from any major rivers, when the
jungle suddenly opened into a huge clearing. In the burst of light, Fawcett
could see a series of beautiful dome-shaped houses made of thatch; some
were seventy feet high and a hundred feet in diameter. Nearby were plant-
ings of maize, yucca, bananas, and sweet potato. There didn't seem to be
anyone in the vicinity, and Fawcett signaled to Costin to look into one
of the houses. When Costin reached the entrance, he saw a solitary old
woman leaning over a fire, cooking a meal. The scent of yucca and pota-
toes wafted toward him, and, overcome with hunger, he found himself being pulled inside, despite the danger. Fawcett and Manley smelled the
aroma as well, and followed him. The men motioned to their stomachs,
and the startled woman handed them bowls of food. "Probably none of us
had ever tasted anything so good," Fawcett later recalled. As the explorers
were eating, paint-streaked warriors began to appear all around them.
"They slipped in by various entrances not previously noticed, and through
the doorway beside us we could see the shadows of more men outside,"
Fawcett wrote. Their nostrils and mouths were pierced with wooden
pegs; they carried drawn bows and blowpipes.

Fawcett whispered to Costin and Manley, "Don't move!"

According to Costin, Fawcett slowly untied the handkerchief around
his neck and placed it on the ground, as a gift, before a man who appeared
to be the chief. The man picked it up and examined it in stern silence.
Fawcett told Costin, *You must give them something.*

"I myself made a blunder," Costin later recalled. "I not only produced a match, but struck it."

There was a flutter of panic, and Fawcett quickly delved in his
pocket for another gift—a glittering necklace. A member of the tribe, in
turn, handed to its visitors gourds full of nuts. "Our friendship was now
accepted," Fawcett wrote, "and the chief himself sat down on a curved

stool and shared the peanuts with us." They had befriended a previously unknown group of Indians that Fawcett classified as the Maxubis. And, while staying there, Fawcett discovered something he had never seen before: a large population numbering in the several thousands. Moreover, the village was surrounded by indigenous settlements with thousands more people. (Fawcett's discovery of so many previously unknown Indians prompted a president of the American Geographical Society to proclaim, "We do not know of anything so amazing in the history of recent exploration.") It dawned on Fawcett that in regions far from the major rivers, where most European travelers and slave raiders went, tribes were healthier and more populous. Physically, they were less decimated by diseases and alcoholism; culturally, they remained vibrant. "Perhaps this is why the ethnology of the continent has been built on a misconception," Fawcett said.

The Maxubis, in particular, showed evidence of a sophisticated culture, he thought. They made exquisite pottery and had names for the planets. "The tribe is also exceedingly musical," Fawcett noted. Describing their songs, he added, "In the utter silence of the forest, when the first light of day had stilled the nightlong uproar of insect life, these hymns impressed us greatly with their beauty." It was true, he wrote, that he had encountered some tribes in the jungle that were "intractable, hopelessly brutal," but others, like the Maxubis, were "brave and intelligent," "utterly refuting the conclusions arrived at by ethnologists, who have only explored the rivers and know nothing of the less accessible places." What's more, many of these tribes told legends about their ancestors who lived in settlements that were even grander and more beautiful.

THERE WERE OTHER clues. On rocks throughout the jungle, Fawcett had observed what appeared to be ancient paintings and carvings of human and animal figures. Once, while climbing a desolate mound of earth above the floodplains of the Bolivian Amazon, he noticed something sticking out of the ground. He scooped it into his hand: it was a shard of pottery. He started to scour the soil. Virtually everywhere he scratched, he later informed the RGS, he turned up bits of ancient, brittle pottery. He thought the craftsmanship was as refined as anything from ancient Greece or Rome or China. Yet there were no inhabitants for hundreds of miles. Where had the pottery come from? To whom had it once belonged?

Even as the mystery seemed to deepen, some patterns were emerging. "Wherever there are 'alturas,' that is high ground above the plains" in the Amazon basin, Fawcett told Keltie, "there are artifacts." And that wasn't all: extending between these *alturas* were some sort of geometrically aligned paths. They looked, he could almost swear, like "roads" and "causeways."

As FAWCETT WAS developing his theory of an ancient Amazonian civilization, he was conscious of growing competition from other explorers, who were racing into the interior of South America to survey one of the last uncharted realms. They were an eclectic, fractious, monomaniacal bunch, each with his own pet theory and obsession. There was, for instance, Henry Savage Landor, who had attracted worldwide renown for his travelogues in which he told of nearly being executed in Tibet, of climbing the Himalayas without ropes and clamps, and of crossing the deserts of Persia and Baluchistan by camel, and who was now wandering through parts of the Amazon dressed as if he were heading off to a luncheon in Piccadilly Circus ("I did not masquerade about in fancy costumes such as are imagined to be worn by explorers") while his men mutinied and nearly shot him. There was the Brazilian colonel and part-Indian orphan Cândido Mariano da Silva Rondon, who had helped to lay telegraph lines across the jungle, lost a toe to piranhas, and started the Indian Protection Service. (Its motto, like his, was "Die if you must, but never kill.") There was Theodore Roosevelt, who, after being defeated in the 1912 presidential election, sought refuge in the Amazon and surveyed with

Rondon the River of Doubt. (By the end of the journey, the former president, who had advocated "the strenuous life," was reduced to near death from hunger and fever, and kept repeating the opening lines to Samuel Taylor Coleridge's poem "Kubla Khan": "In Xanadu did Kubla Khan / A stately pleasure dome decree.")

But perhaps the rival Fawcett most feared was Alexander Hamilton Rice, a tall, debonair American doctor who, like Fawcett, had trained under Edward Ayearst Reeves at the Royal Geographical Society. In his late thirties, with a barrel chest and bushy mustache, Rice had graduated from Harvard Medical School in 1904. An interest in tropical diseases led him to the Amazon, where he investigated lethal parasites by dissecting monkeys and jaguars and where he soon became obsessed with the region's geography and ethnology. In 1907, while Fawcett was conducting his first surveying expedition, Dr. Rice was trekking over the Andes with a then-unknown amateur archaeologist named Hiram Bingham. Later, Dr. Rice descended into the northern basin of the Amazon, searching for the sources of several rivers and studying the native inhabitants. In a letter to a friend, Dr. Rice wrote, "I am going very slowly, studying everything carefully, and coming only to conclusions after long meditation. If I am in doubt about anything, I return to work over it again."

After that expedition, Dr. Rice, realizing that he lacked sufficient technical training, enrolled at the School of Astronomy and Surveying at the Royal Geographical Society. Upon graduating in 1910 ("We look upon him, in a very special degree, as a child of our Society," an RGS president later noted), he returned to South America to explore the Amazon basin. Whereas Fawcett was impetuous and daring, Dr. Rice approached his mission with the calm precision of a surgeon. He did not so much want to transcend the brutal conditions as transform them. He assembled teams of as many as a hundred men, and was fixated on gadgetry—new boats, new boots, new generators—and on bringing the latest methods of modern science into the wild. During one expedition, he paused to perform emergency surgery on a native suffering from anthrax and on an Indian with an abscess near her liver. The RGS noted that the latter procedure was "probably the first surgical operation under chloroform carried out in this primeval wilderness." Although Dr. Rice did not push his men the way Fawcett did, on at least one occasion they mutinied, deserting him in the jungle. During that same expedition, Dr. Rice's leg became so infected that he took his surgical blade and plunged it into his flesh to remove part of the tissue, operating on himself while he was still conscious. As Keltie told Fawcett, "He is a medical man and very clever in all his work."

Fawcett may have been confident that no one could surpass his abilities as an explorer, but he knew that his chief rival had an advantage that he could never match: money. Dr. Rice, who was the wealthy grandson of a former mayor of Boston and governor of Massachusetts, had married Eleanor Widener, the widow of a Philadelphia tycoon who had been one of the richest men in America. (Her first husband and her son were on the *Titanic* when it sank.) With a fortune worth millions of dollars, Dr. Rice and his wife—who donated the Widener Library at Harvard University in memory of her late son—helped to finance a new lecture hall at the Royal Geographical Society. In the United States, Dr. Rice often showed up at appointments in his chauffeured blue Rolls-Royce, dressed in a full-length fur coat. He was, one newspaper wrote, "as much at home in the elegant swirl of Newport society as in the steaming jungles of Brazil." With unlimited money to bankroll his expeditions, he could afford the most advanced equipment and the best-trained men. Fawcett, meanwhile, was constantly begging foundations and capitalists for financial support. "Explorers are not often those happy and irresponsible rovers which fancy paints," he once complained in a letter to the RGS, "but are born without the proverbial silver spoon."

Despite the vastness of the Amazon, it seemed unable to accommodate all of these explorers' egos and ambitions. The men tended to eye one another hawkishly, jealously guarding their routes for fear of being beaten to a discovery. They even conducted reconnaissance on each other's activities. "Keep your ears open as to any information about the movements of Landor," the RGS advised Fawcett in a communiqué in 1911. Fawcett needed no prodding: he maintained the paranoia of a spy.

At the same time, the explorers were quick to cast doubt upon, and even denigrate, a rival's accomplishments. After Roosevelt and Rondon announced that they had explored for the first time a nearly thousand-mile-long river—renamed Rio Roosevelt in the president's honor—Landor told reporters it was impossible that such a tributary existed. Branding Roosevelt a "charlatan," he accused the former president of plagiarizing events from the narrative of Landor's own journey: "I see he even has had the same sickness as I experienced and, what is more extraordinary, in the very same leg I had trouble with. These things happen very often to big explorers who carefully read the books of some of the humble travelers who preceded them." Roosevelt snapped back that Landor was "a pure fake, to whom no attention should be paid." (It was not the first time Landor had been called a fake: after he ascended a peak in the Himalayas, Douglas Freshfield, one of the most distinguished climbers of his day and a future president of the RGS, said that "no mountaineer can accept the marvelous feats of speed and endurance Mr. Landor believes himself to have accomplished" and that his "very sensational tale" affects "the credit, both at home and on the Continent, of English travellers, critics and scientific societies.") Dr. Rice, for his part, initially found Roosevelt's account "unintelligible"; but after Roosevelt furnished him with more details he apologized. Though Fawcett never doubted Roosevelt's discovery, he dismissed it tartly as a good journey "for an elderly man."

"I do not wish to deprecate other exploration work in South America," Fawcett told the RGS, "only to point out the vast difference between river journeys with their freedom from the great food problem, and forest journeys on foot—when one has perforce to put up with circumstances and deliberately penetrate Indian sanctuaries." Nor was Fawcett impressed by Landor, whom he considered "a humbug from the first." Fawcett told

Keltie that he had no desire to be "counted in with the Savage Landors and Roosevelts of the so-called exploring fraternity."

Fawcett had often expressed admiration for Rondon, but eventually he grew suspicious of him, too. Fawcett argued that Rondon sacrificed too many lives by traveling in large parties. (In 1900, Rondon embarked on an expedition with eighty-one men and returned with only thirty—the rest had either died or been hospitalized, or had deserted.) Rondon, a proud, deeply patriotic man, did not understand why Fawcett—who told the RGS he preferred in his parties English "gentlemen, owing to greater powers of endurance and enthusiasm for adventure"—always resisted taking Brazilian soldiers on expeditions. A colleague of Rondon's said that the colonel disliked "the idea of a foreigner's coming here to do what he said Brazilians could do for themselves."

Despite Fawcett's imperviousness to the most brutal conditions in the jungle, he was hypersensitive to the smallest personal criticism. An official from the RGS advised Fawcett, "I think you worry yourself a great deal too much as to what people say about you. I should not trouble myself about it if I were you. Nothing succeeds like success."

Still, as Fawcett pieced together his evidence of a lost civilization in the Amazon, he worried that someone like Dr. Rice might be on the same trail. When Fawcett hinted to the RGS the new direction of his anthropological inquiries, Keltie wrote back saying that Dr. Rice was "sure to go out again" and might be "disposed to take up the task which you indicate."

In 1911, the cohort of South American explorers, along with the rest of the world, was astounded by the announcement that Hiram Bingham, Dr. Rice's old traveling companion, had, with the aid of a Peruvian guide, uncovered the Incan ruins of Machu Picchu, nearly eight thousand feet above sea level, in the Andes. Although Bingham had not discovered an unknown civilization—the Incan empire and its monumental architectural works were well documented—he had helped to illuminate this ancient world in remarkable fashion. *National Geographic*, which devoted an entire issue to Bingham's find, noted that Machu Picchu's stone temples and

palaces and fountains—most likely a fifteenth-century retreat for Incan no-
bility—may "prove to be the most important group of ruins discovered in
South America." The explorer Hugh Thomson subsequently called it "the
pin-up of twentieth-century archeology." Bingham was catapulted into the
stratosphere of fame; he was even elected to the U.S. Senate.

The discovery fired Fawcett's imagination. It undoubtedly stung,
too. But Fawcett believed that the evidence he had gathered suggested
something potentially more momentous: remnants of a yet unknown civilization in the heart of the Amazon, where for centuries the conquistadores
had searched for an ancient kingdom—a place they called El Dorado.

El Dorado

The chronicles were buried in the dusty basements of old churches and libraries, and scattered around the world. Fawcett, exchanging his explorer's uniform for more formal clothing, searched everywhere for these scrolls, which recounted the early conquistadores' journeys into the Amazon. The papers were often neglected and forgotten; some, Fawcett feared, had been lost altogether, and when he discovered one he would copy critical passages from it into his notebooks. The process was time-consuming, but slowly he pieced together the legend of El Dorado.

"THE GREAT LORD . . . goes about continually covered in gold dust as fine as ground salt. He feels that it would be less beautiful to wear any other ornament. It would be crude and common to put on armour plates of hammered or stamped gold, for other rich lords wear those when they wish. But to powder oneself with gold is something exotic, unusual, novel and more costly—for he washes away at night what he puts on each morning, so that it is discarded and lost, and he does this every day of the year."

So, according to the sixteenth-century chronicler Gonzalo Fernández de Oviedo, began the story of El Dorado. The name means "the gilded man." Indians told the Spaniards about this ruler and his glorious land, and the kingdom became synonymous with the man. Another chronicler reported that the king slathered himself in gold and floated on a lake, "gleaming like a ray of the sun," while his subjects made "offerings of gold jewelry, fine emeralds and other pieces of their ornaments." If these reports were not enough to excite the conquistadores' acquisitive hearts, it was believed that the kingdom contained vast swaths of cinnamon trees—a spice that was then nearly as precious as gold.

As fanciful as these stories seemed, there was precedent for finding magnificent cities in the New World. In 1519, Hernán Cortés marched across a causeway and into the Aztec capital of Tenochtitlán, which floated amid a lake and shimmered with pyramids, palaces, and ornaments. "Some of our soldiers even asked whether the things we saw were not a dream?" the chronicler Bernal Díaz del Castillo wrote. Fourteen years later, Francisco Pizarro conquered Cuzco, the capital of the Incas, whose empire once encompassed nearly two million square kilometers and included more than ten million people. Echoing Díaz, Gaspar de Espinosa, the governor of Panama, said that the Incan civilization's riches were "like something from a dream."

In February of 1541, the first expedition in search of El Dorado was launched by Gonzalo Pizarro, Francisco's younger half brother and the governor of Quito. He wrote to the king of Spain, saying, "Because of many reports which I received in Quito and outside that city, from prominent and very aged chiefs as well as from Spaniards, whose accounts agreed with one another, that the province of La Canela [Cinnamon] and Lake El Dorado were a very populous and very rich land, I decided to go and conquer and explore it." Daring and handsome, greedy and sadistic—a prototypical conquistador—Gonzalo Pizarro was so confident that he would succeed that he sank virtually his entire fortune into assembling a force, which surpassed even the one that had captured the Incan emperor.

Marching in the procession were more than two hundred soldiers mounted on horses and outfitted like knights, with iron hats, swords, and shields; and four thousand enslaved Indians, clad in animal skins, whom Pizarro had kept shackled until the day of departure. In their wake came wooden carts pulled by llamas and loaded with some two thousand squealing pigs, followed by nearly two thousand hunting dogs. To the natives, the scene must have been as amazing as any vision of El Dorado. The expedition headed eastward from Quito over the Andes, where a hundred Indians died from the cold, and into the Amazon basin. Hacking through the jungle with swords, sweating in their armor, thirsty, hungry, wet, and miserable, Pizarro and his men came across several cinnamon trees. Oh, the stories were true: "Cinnamon of the most perfect kind." But the trees were scattered over territories so vast that it would be fruitless to try to cultivate them. They were another of the Amazon's pitiless cons.

Shortly after, Pizarro encountered several Indians in the jungle and demanded to know where the kingdom of El Dorado was. When the Indians looked at him blankly, Pizarro had them strung up and tortured. "The butcher Gonzalo Pizarro, not content with burning Indians who had committed no fault, further ordered that other Indians should be thrown to the dogs, who tore them to pieces with their teeth and devoured them," the sixteenth-century historian Pedro de Cieza de León wrote.

Meanwhile, the expedition, less than a year after it had set out, was in tatters. The llamas perished from the heat, and before long the pigs, horses, and even most of the dogs were eaten by the famished explorers. Moreover, almost all of the four thousand Indians whom Pizarro had forced into the jungle died of disease or hunger.

By a vast meandering river, Pizarro decided to split the surviving members of the party into two groups. While the majority continued to scour the shore with him, his second-in-command, Francisco de Orellana, took fifty-seven Spaniards and two slaves downriver on a boat they had built, in hopes of finding food. The Dominican friar Gaspar de Carvajal, who was with Orellana, wrote in his diary that some in the party were so weak that they crawled on all fours into the jungle. Many, Carvajal said, were "like mad men and did not possess sense." Rather than return to find Pizarro and the rest of the expedition, Orellana and his men decided to continue down the massive river until, as Carvajal put it, they would "either die or see what there was along it." Carvajal reported passing villages and coming under attack by thousands of Indians, including female Amazon warriors. During one assault, an arrow struck Carvajal in the eye and "went in as far as the hollow region." On August 26, 1542, the men's boat was finally expelled into the Atlantic Ocean, and they became the first Europeans to travel the length of the Amazon.

It was both an incredible feat of exploration and a fiasco. When Pizarro discovered that Orellana had abandoned him, an act he considered mutiny, he was forced to turn back and try to retreat with his starving troops over the Andes. By the time he entered Quito in June 1542, only eighty men from his once-gallant army survived, and they were stripped almost naked. One person reportedly tried to offer Pizarro clothing, but the conquistador refused to look at him or anyone else, and simply went into his house and secluded himself.

Although Orellana went back to Spain, El Dorado still glimmered in his mind, and in 1545 it was his turn to pour all of his money into an expedition. Spanish authorities maintained that his fleet, with a crew of a few hundred people—including his wife—was unseaworthy and denied him permission to sail, but Orellana sneaked out of the harbor anyway. A plague soon swept through the crew, killing nearly a hundred people. Then a ship was lost at sea, with seventy-seven additional souls. Upon reaching the mouth of the Amazon and sailing barely a hundred leagues, fifty-seven more members of his crew perished from disease and hunger. Indians then attacked his ship, killing seventeen others. At last, Orellana collapsed on deck in a fever and muttered an order to retreat. His heart stopped, as if he could no longer bear the disappointment. His wife wrapped him in a Spanish flag and buried him on the banks of the Amazon, watching, in the words of one writer, "as the brown waters that had so long possessed his mind, now possessed his body."

Still, the allure of this terrestrial paradise was too great to resist. In 1617, the Elizabethan poet and explorer Walter Raleigh, convinced that there was not only one gilded man but thousands of them, set out on a ship named the *Destiny* with his twenty-three-year-old son to locate what he called "more rich and bewtifull cities, more temples adorned with golden Images, more sepulchers filled with treasure, then either Cortéz found in Mexico or Pazzaro in Peru." His son—"more desirous of honour than of safety," as Raleigh put it—was promptly killed during a clash with the Spanish along the Orinoco River. In a letter to his wife, Raleigh wrote, "God knows, I never knew what sorrow meant till now . . . [M]y brains are broken." Raleigh returned to England with no evidence of his kingdom, and was beheaded by King James in 1618. His skull was embalmed by his wife and occasionally displayed to visitors—a stark reminder that El Dorado was, if nothing else, lethal.

Other expeditions that searched for the kingdom descended into cannibalism. A survivor of a party in which two hundred and forty men died confessed, "Some, contrary to nature, ate human meat: one Christian was found cooking a quarter of a child together with some greens." On hearing of three explorers who had roasted an Indian woman, Oviedo exclaimed, "Oh, diabolical plan! But they paid for their sin, for those three men never reappeared: God willed that there should be Indians who later ate them."

Financial ruin, destitution, starvation, cannibalism, murder, death: these seemed to be the only real manifestations of El Dorado. As a chronicler said of several seekers, "They marched like madmen from place to place, until overcome by exhaustion and lack of strength they could no longer move from one side to the other, and they remained there, wherever this sad siren voice had summoned them, self-important, and dead."

. . .

WHAT COULD FAWCETT learn from such madness?

By the early twentieth century, most historians and anthropologists had dismissed not just the existence of El Dorado but even most of what the conquistadores claimed to have witnessed during their journeys. Scholars believed these chronicles were products of fervid imaginations, and had been embellished to excuse to monarchs the disastrous nature of the expeditions—hence the mythological woman warriors.

Fawcett agreed that El Dorado, with its plethora of gold, was an "exaggerated romance," but he was not ready to dismiss the chronicles altogether, or the possibility of an ancient Amazonian civilization. Carvajal, for instance, was a respected priest, and others in the expedition had affirmed his account. Even the Amazon warriors had some basis in reality, Fawcett thought, for he had encountered women chiefs along the Tapajós River. And if some details in the accounts were embellished, it did not mean that all of them were. Indeed, Fawcett viewed the chronicles as a generally accurate portrait of the Amazon before the European onslaught. And what the conquistadores described, in his opinion, was a revelation.

During Fawcett's era, the banks of the Amazon River and its major tributaries contained little more than small, scattered tribes. The conquistadores, however, uniformly reported vast and dense indigenous populations. Carvajal had noted that some places were so "thickly populated" that it was dangerous to sleep on land. ("All that night we continued to pass by numerous and very large villages, until the day came, when we had journeyed more than twenty leagues, for in order to get away from the inhabited country our companions did nothing but row, and the farther we went, the more thickly populated and the better did we find the land.") When Orellana and his men went ashore, they saw "many roads" and "fine highways" leading into the interior, some of which were "like royal highways and wider."

The accounts seemed to describe what Fawcett had seen, only on a grander scale. When the Spaniards invaded one village, Carvajal said, they discovered a "great quantity of maize (and there was also found great quantity of oats), from which the Indians make bread, and very good wine resembling beer, and this is to be had in great aplenty. There was found in this village a dispensing place for this wine, [a thing so unusual] that our companions were not a little delighted, and there was found a very good quality of cotton goods." Villages overflowed with maniocs, yams, beans, and fish, and there were thousands of turtles cultivated in pens for food. The Amazon seemed to sustain large civilizations, and highly complex ones. The conquistadores observed "cities that glistened in white," with temples, public squares, palisade walls, and exquisite artifacts. In one settlement, Carvajal wrote, "there was a villa in which there was a great deal of . . . plates and bowls and candelabra of this porcelain of the best that has ever been seen in the world." He added that these objects were "all glazed and embellished with all colors, and so bright that they astonish, and, more than this, the drawings and paintings which they make on them are so accurately worked out that [one wonders how] with [only] natural skill they manufacture and decorate all these things [making them look just] like Roman [articles]."

The failure of Victorian explorers and ethnographers to find any similar settlements reinforced the belief that the conquistadores' accounts were "full of lies," as one historian had earlier described Carvajal's report. Yet why had so many of the chroniclers provided such similar testimony? Recounting a German-led expedition, for instance, a sixteenth-century historian wrote:

> Both the General and all the rest saw a town of disproportionate size, quite close . . . It was compact and well-ordered and in the middle was a house that greatly surpassed the rest in size and height. They asked the chief they had as a guide: "Whose house was that, so remarkable and eminent among the others?" He answered that it

was the house of the chief, called Qvarica. He had some golden ef-
figies or idols the size of boys, and a woman all made of gold who
was their goddess. He and his subjects possessed other riches. But a
short distance beyond, there were other chiefs who exceeded that
one in the number of subjects and quantity of riches.

A soldier on another expedition later recalled that "they had seen very
large towns, of such an extent that they were astounded."

Fawcett wondered where all these people had gone. He speculated
that the "introduction of small-pox and European disease wiped out the
indigenes by millions." Still, the Amazon's populations seemed to collapse
so swiftly and so completely that he contemplated whether something
more dramatic had occurred, even a natural disaster. The Amazon, he'd
begun to believe, contained "the greatest secrets of the past yet preserved
in our world of today."

THE

LOCKED BOX

I am afraid there is no way for you to see the document. It's locked in a vault."

I had arrived in Rio de Janeiro and was speaking on the phone to a university student who had been helping me track down one more manuscript, what Fawcett considered the final piece of evidence supporting his theory of a lost civilization in the Amazon. The manuscript was in Brazil's National Library in Rio, and was so old and in such poor condition that it was kept in a safe. I had filed formal requests and made appeals by e-mail. Nothing worked. Finally, as a last effort, I had flown to Rio to make my case in person.

Situated downtown in a beautiful neoclassical building with Corinthian columns and pilasters, the library contains more than nine million documents—the largest archive in Latin America. I was escorted upstairs into the manuscript division, a chamber lined with books that climbed several stories toward a stained-glass ceiling, where a faint light seeped through, revealing, amid the room's grandeur, a hint of disrepair—dilapidated wooden desks and dusty lightbulbs. The area was quiet, and I could hear the soles of my shoes clapping against the floor.

I had arranged an appointment with the head of the manuscript division, Vera Faillace, an erudite woman with shoulder-length dark hair and glasses. She greeted me at the security gate, and when I inquired about the document she said, "It is, without question, the most famous and sought-after item we have in the manuscript division."

"How many manuscripts do you have?" I asked, surprised.

"Around eight hundred thousand."

She said that scientists and treasure hunters from all over the world have wanted to study this particular document. After it became known that Fawcett had drawn on the manuscript for his theory, she said, his devotees have treated it almost like a religious icon. Apparently, it was the Holy Grail for the Fawcett freaks.

I had rehearsed everything I planned to say to persuade her to let me see the original document, including how important it was for me to assess its authenticity and how I promised not to touch it—a speech that began soberly enough but grew, in my desperation, more abstract and grandiose. Yet before I could start Faillace waved me through the security gate. "This must be very important to you to come all this way without knowing you'd be able to see the document," she said. "I've put it on the table for you."

And there, only a few feet away, opened like a Torah, was the roughly sixteen-inch-by-sixteen-inch manuscript. Its pages had turned almost a golden brown; its edges had crumbled. "This paper is not parchment," Faillace explained. "It was from before wood pulp was added to paper. It's a kind of fabric."

Scrawled across the pages, in black ink, was beautiful calligraphy, but many sections had been washed out or eaten through by worms and insects.

I looked at the title on the top of the first page. It said in Portuguese,

"Historical account of a large, hidden, and very ancient city . . . discovered in the year 1753."

"Can you make out the next sentence?" I asked Faillace.

She shook her head, but farther down more words became legible, and a librarian who spoke fluent English helped me to slowly translate them. They had been written by a Portuguese *bandeirante*, or "soldier of fortune." (His name was no longer decipherable.) He described how he and his men, "incited by the insatiable greed of gold," had set out into the interior of Brazil in search of treasure: "After a long and troublesome peregrination . . . and almost lost for many years . . . we discovered a chain of mountains so high that they seemed to reach the ethereal regions, and they served as throne for the Wind or for the Stars themselves." Eventually, the *bandeirante* said, he and his party found a path between the mountains that appeared to have been "cut asunder by art rather than by nature." When they reached the top of the path, they looked out and saw a spell-binding vista: below them were the ruins of an ancient city. At dawn, the men loaded their weapons and crept down. Amid swarms of bats, they discovered stone archways, a statue, roads, and a temple. "The ruins well showed the size and grandeur which must have been there, and how populous and opulent it had been in the age when it flourished," the *bandeirante* wrote.

After the expedition returned to civilization, the *bandeirante* had sent the document with this "intelligence" to the viceroy, "in remembrance of the much that I owe to you." He urged his "Excellency" to dispatch an expedition to find and "utilize these riches."

It is not known what the viceroy did with the report, or if the *bandeirante* ever tried to reach the city again. Fawcett had uncovered the manuscript when he was scouring for documents in the National Library of Brazil. For more than a century after the manuscript was written, Fawcett said, it had been "pigeonholed" in bureaucratic archives. "It was difficult for an administration steeped in the narrow bigotry of an all-powerful Church to give much credence to such a thing as an old civilization," Fawcett wrote.

The librarian pointed to the bottom of the manuscript. "Look at that," she said.

There were several strange diagrams that resembled hieroglyphics. The *bandeirante* said that he had observed the images carved into some of the ruins. They seemed familiar, and I realized that they were identical to drawings I had noticed in one of Fawcett's diaries—he must have copied them after seeing the document.

The library was closing, and Faillace came to retrieve the ancient scroll. As I watched her carefully transport it back into the vault, I understood why Brian Fawcett, seeing the document years after his father and brother vanished, had proclaimed, "It feels genuine! It *must* be genuine!"

THE WHOLE
WORLD IS MAD

awcett had narrowed down the location. He was sure that he had found proof of archaeological remains, including causeways and pottery, scattered throughout the Amazon. He even believed that there was more than a single ancient city—the one that the *bandeirante* described was most likely, given the terrain, near the eastern Brazilian state of Bahia. But Fawcett, consulting archival records and interviewing tribesmen, had calculated that a monumental city, along with possibly even remnants of its population, was in the jungle surrounding the Xingu River in the Brazilian Mato Grosso. In keeping with his secretive nature, he gave the city a cryptic and alluring name, one that, in all his writings and interviews, he never explained. He called it simply Z.

In September of 1914, after a yearlong reconnaissance trip with Manley and Costin, Fawcett was ready to launch an expedition in search of the lost city. Yet when he emerged from the jungle he was greeted with the news that, more than two months earlier, the Austrian archduke Franz Ferdinand—who was the unlikely catalyst for Fawcett and Nina's first meeting in Ceylon—had been assassinated. World War I had begun.

Fawcett and his two British companions immediately set sail for England. "Of course experienced men like you are very much wanted: there is a great deficiency of trained officers," Keltie told Fawcett in a letter that December. "We have had tremendous losses, as you see, at the front, far more in proportion, I should think, than has ever been among officers before." Though Fawcett was forty-seven years old and a "renegade" from European life, he felt compelled to volunteer. He informed Keltie that he had his "finger on important discoveries" in the Amazon, but was obliged by "the patriotic desire of all able-bodied men to squash the Teuton."

Most of Europe was gripped by a similar zeal. Conan Doyle, who churned out propaganda that portrayed the war as a clash of chivalrous knights, wrote, "Fear not, for our sword will not be broken, nor shall it ever drop from our hands."

After a brief visit with his family, Fawcett made his way to the western front, where, as he told Keltie, he would soon be "in the thick of it."

As a major in the Royal Field Artillery, Fawcett was placed in charge of a battery of more than a hundred men. Cecil Eric Lewis Lyne, a twenty-two-year-old second lieutenant, recalled when the Amazon explorer arrived in his dark khaki uniform, carrying his revolver. He was, Lyne wrote in a diary, "one of the most colorful personalities I ever encountered"—a man of "magnificent physique and great technical ability."

As always, Fawcett was an electric and polarizing figure, and his men fell into two camps: the Costins and the Murrays. The Costins gravitated toward him, relishing his daring and élan, while the Murrays despised his ferocity and unforgivingness. An officer among the Murrays said that Fawcett "was probably the nastiest man I have ever met in this world and his dislike of me was only exceeded by my dislike of him." Yet Lyne was a Costin. "Fawcett and I, despite the disparity of our ages, became great friends."

Along with their men, Fawcett and Lyne dug trenches—sometimes only a few hundred yards from the Germans—in the area around Ploegsteert, a hamlet in western Belgium, near the border of France. One day

Fawcett spotted a suspicious-looking figure in the village wearing a long fur coat, a French steel helmet three sizes too small for his head, and a shepherd's smock—"queer garments," as Fawcett put it. Fawcett overheard the man saying, in a guttural voice, that this area would be ideal for an observation post, even though it struck Fawcett as "a bloody awful place." German spies were rumored to be infiltrating British lines dressed as Belgian civilians, and Fawcett, who knew what it meant to be a secret agent, rushed back to headquarters and reported, "We've got a spy in our sector!"

Before an arrest party was dispatched, further inquiries revealed that the man was none other than Winston Churchill, who had volunteered to command a battalion on the western front after being forced to resign as First Lord of the Admiralty in the wake of the disastrous invasion of Gallipoli. While visiting the trenches south of Fawcett's position, Churchill wrote, "Filth & rubbish everywhere, graves built into the defences & scattered about promiscuously, feet & clothing breaking through the soil, water & muck on all sides; & about this scene in the dazzling moonlight troops of enormous bats creep & glide, to the unceasing accompaniment of rifles & machine guns & the venomous whining & whirring of the bullets which pass overhead."

Fawcett, who was accustomed to inhuman conditions, was superb at holding his position, and in January 1916 he was promoted to lieutenant colonel and put in command of a brigade of more than seven hundred men. Nina kept Keltie and the Royal Geographical Society apprised of his activities. In a letter dated March 2, 1916, she wrote, "He is very well in spite of 3 months constantly under shell fire." Several weeks later, she said that he was overseeing nine batteries, far more than constituted a typical brigade. "So you can imagine how hard worked he is," she said, adding, "Of course I am glad he has an opportunity to use his powers of organization and leadership for it all helps in the struggle for victory." Nina was not the only one who touted his abilities. He was repeatedly cited in dispatches for his "gallant" and "distinguished" services under fire.

Even in the trenches, Fawcett tried to keep informed of events in the Amazon. He learned of expeditions being led by anthropologists and explorers from America, which was not yet engaged in the war, and these reports only intensified his fear that someone would discover Z before he did. In a letter to his old teaching mentor Reeves, he confided, "If you only knew what these expeditions cost in physical strain, you would, I feel sure, appreciate what a lot it means to me that I shall have the completion of the work."

He had reason to fret, in particular, about Dr. Rice. To Fawcett's shock, the RGS had, in 1914, presented Dr. Rice with a gold medal for his "meritorious work on the head waters of the Orinoco and the Northern tributaries of the Amazon." Fawcett was incensed that his own efforts had not received equal recognition. Then, in early 1916, he discovered that the doctor was preparing to launch another expedition. A bulletin in the *Geographical Journal* announced that "our medallist" Dr. Rice would ascend the Amazon and the Rio Negro, with "a view to still further extending our knowledge of the region previously explored by him." Why was the doctor returning to the same area? The bulletin said little more than that Dr. Rice was building a forty-foot motor-powered vessel that could navigate through swamps and carry seven hundred gallons of petrol. It must have cost a fortune, though what did that matter to a millionaire?

That spring, amid intense fighting, Fawcett received a letter from the Royal Geographical Society. It said that, in tribute to his historic mapping of South America, he, too, had been awarded a gold medal. (The Society gave out two gold medals, both equal in prestige: Fawcett's was the Founder's Medal and Dr. Rice's the Patron's.) The award was the same honor that had been bestowed upon the likes of Livingstone and Burton—"the dream of his life," as Nina put it. Not even the prospect of Dr. Rice's expedition or the continuation of the war could diminish Fawcett's delight. Nina, who told Keltie that such an occasion comes "only once in a life time," quickly set about planning for the award presentation on May 22. Fawcett obtained leave to attend. "I possess the medal and am content," he remarked.

After the ceremony, he hurried back to the front: he had received orders that the British command was launching an unprecedented assault, with the aim of ending the war. In early July 1916, Fawcett and his men took up their positions along a placid river in northern France, providing cover as tens of thousands of British soldiers clambered up ladders propped against the muddy trench walls and marched onto the battlefield, bayonets gleaming and arms swinging, like in a parade. From his perch, Fawcett would have seen the German gunners, who were supposed to have been destroyed by weeks of bombardment. They were emerging from cavernous holes, unleashing machine-gun fire. The British soldiers fell, one by one. Fawcett tried to offer cover, but there was no way to protect men walking into a hail of bullets and eighteen-pound shells and liquidy bursts from flamethrowers. No force of nature in the jungle had prepared him for this man-made onslaught. Bits of letters and photographs that men had carried into battle fluttered over their corpses like snow. The wounded crawled into shell holes, shrieking. Fawcett called it "Armageddon."

It was the Battle of the Somme—or what the Germans, who suffered massive casualties as well, referred to in letters home as "the bath of blood." On the first day of the offensive, nearly twenty thousand British soldiers died and almost forty thousand were wounded. It was the greatest loss of life in the history of the British military, and many in the West began to portray the "savage" as European rather than as some native in the jungle. Fawcett, quoting a companion, wrote that cannibalism "at least provides a reasonable motive for killing a man, which is more than you can say for civilized warfare."

When Ernest Shackleton, who had been trekking through Antarctica for nearly a year and a half, emerged in 1916 on the island of South Georgia, he immediately asked someone, "Tell me, when was the war over?" The person replied, "The war is not over . . . Europe is mad. The whole world is mad."

As the conflict dragged on, Fawcett often remained at the front lines, living among corpses. The air smelled of blood and fumes. Trenches became bogs of urine and excrement and bones and lice and maggots and rats. The walls caved in from rain, and occasionally men drowned in the slime. One soldier sank slowly for days in a mud hole, without anyone being able to reach him. Fawcett, who had always found refuge in the natural world, no longer recognized the wilderness of bombed-out villages, denuded trees, craters, and sunbaked skeletons. As Lyne wrote in his diary, "Dante would never have condemned lost souls to wander in so terrible a purgatory."

Periodically, Fawcett would hear a gong-like sound, which meant the gases were coming. Shells unleashed phosgene, chlorine, or mustard gas. A nurse described patients "burnt up and blistered all over with great mustard-coloured suppurating blisters, with blind eyes . . . all sticky and stuck together, and always fighting for breath, with voices a mere whisper, saying that their throats are closing and they know they will choke." In March 1917, Nina sent a letter to the RGS saying her husband had been "gassed" after Christmas. For once, Fawcett had been injured. "He was troubled for some time by the effects of the poison," Nina told Keltie. Certain days were worse than others: "He feels better but not quite right."

All around Fawcett, people he knew or had been associated with were dying. The war had claimed the lives of more than a hundred and thirty RGS members. Conan Doyle's oldest son, Kingsley, died of wounds and influenza. A surveyor with whom Fawcett had worked on the South American boundary commission was killed. ("He was a good fellow—we all thought so," Fawcett informed Keltie. "I am sorry.") A friend in his brigade was blown up when he rushed to help someone—an act, Fawcett wrote in his official report, "of purely unselfish self-sacrifice."

Toward the end of the war, Fawcett described some of the carnage that he had witnessed in a missive published in an English newspaper under the headline "British Colonel in Letter Here Tells of Enormous Slaughter." "If you can imagine 60 miles of front, to a depth of 1 to 30 miles, literally carpeted with dead, often in little hills," Fawcett wrote. "It is a measure of the price paid. Masses of men moved to the slaughter in endless waves, bridged the wires and filled the trenches with dead and dying. It was the irresistible force of an army of ants, where the pressure of the succeeding waves forced the legions in front, willingly or unwillingly, into the shambles. No thin line could withstand the human tidal wave, or go on killing forever. It is, I think, the most terrible testimony to the relentless effect of an unbridled militarism." He concluded, " 'Civilization!' Ye gods! To see what one has seen the word is an absurdity. It has been an insane explosion of the lowest human emotions."

Amid this onslaught, Fawcett continued to be heralded in dispatches for his bravery, and, as the *London Gazette* announced on January 4, 1917, he was awarded the Distinguished Service Order medal. But if his body remained intact, his mind appeared, at times, to be wavering. When he visited home on leave, he often sat for hours without speaking, holding his head in his hands. He sought solace in spiritualism and occult rituals that offered a way to communicate with missing loved ones—a refuge that many Europeans turned to in their grief. Conan Doyle described attending a séance where he heard a voice:

> I said, "Is that you, boy?"
>
> He said in a very intense whisper and a tone all his own, "Father!" and then after a pause, "Forgive me!"
>
> I said, "There was never anything to forgive. You were the best son a man ever had." A strong hand descended on my head which was slowly pressed forward, and I felt a kiss just above my brow.
>
> "Are you happy?" I cried.
>
> There was a pause and then very gently, "I am so happy."

Fawcett wrote to Conan Doyle about his own experiences with mediums. He recounted how his dreaded mother had spoken to him during a séance. The medium, who channeled her spirit, said, "She loved you so as a little boy and she has remorse for treating you badly." And, "She would like to send her love but fears it might not be accepted."

In the past, Fawcett's interest in the occult had been largely an expression of his youthful rebellion and scientific curiosity, and had contributed to his willingness to defy the prevailing orthodoxies of his own society and to respect tribal legends and religions. Now, though, his approach was untethered from his rigorous RGS training and acute powers of observation. He imbibed Madame Blavatsky's most outlandish teachings about Hyperboreans and astral bodies and Lords of the Dark Face and keys to unlocking the universe—the Other World seemingly more tantalizing than the present one. (In *The Land of Mist*, Conan Doyle's 1926 sequel to *The Lost World*, John Roxton, the character said to be partly based on Fawcett, embraces spiritualism and investigates the existence of ghosts.) There was a rumor among some officers that Fawcett used a Ouija board, a popular tool of mediums, to help make tactical decisions on the battlefield. "He and his intelligence officer . . . would retire to a darkened room and put their four hands, but not their elbows, on the board," Henry Harold Hemming, who was then a captain in Fawcett's corps, wrote in an unpublished memoir. "Fawcett would then ask the Ouija Board in a loud voice if this was a confirmed location [of the enemy's position], and if the miserable board skidded over in the right direction; not merely would he include it in his list of confirmed locations, but often order 20 rounds of 9.2 howitzer to be fired at the place."

More than anything, though, Fawcett was consumed with visions of Z, which, amid the war's horror, gathered only more luster—a glittering place seemingly immune to the rottenness of Western civilization. Or, as he told Conan Doyle, something of "The Lost World" really did exist. By all accounts, Fawcett thought about Z when he was firing howitzers, when he was being shot at in the trenches, when he was burying the dead. In an article published in the *Washington Post* in 1934, a soldier in Fawcett's unit recalled how "many times in France when the commander was 'marking time' between raids and attacks, he would tell of his explorations and adventures in South American jungles—of the heavy rains and the thick tangle of grass and bushes meeting overhanging vines and branches—

and the deep unbroken quiet of the interior." An officer from his brigade wrote in a letter that Fawcett was already "full of the hidden cities and treasures . . . he intended to search for."

Fawcett deluged Costin and Manley, who were also fighting on the western front, with letters, trying to secure their services in the future. And he petitioned the RGS for funding.

"It is a little awkward as you can understand, for us at the present moment, to make any definite promise as to what could be done after the war," Keltie responded to one of his appeals. "If you can only afford to wait."

"I am getting older and am, I daresay, impatient of lost years and months," Fawcett complained to Keltie in early 1918. Later that year, he told *Travel* magazine, "Knowing what these journeys in the real fastnesses of the forest mean to men a good deal younger than I am, I do not want to delay action."

On June 28, 1919, nearly five years after Fawcett returned from the Amazon and shortly before his fifty-second birthday, Germany finally signed a peace treaty in surrender. Some twenty million people had been killed and at least twenty million wounded. Fawcett described "the whole business" as "suicide" for Western civilization, and thought, "Many thousands must have come through those four years of mud and blood with a similar disillusionment."

Returning to his home in England, he saw his wife and children on a regular basis for the first time in years. He was astonished by how much Jack had grown, how much bigger he was through his shoulders and around his arms. Jack had recently celebrated his sixteenth birthday and was "now quite an inch, if not more, taller than his father!" Nina wrote in a letter to Harold Large, a family friend who lived in New Zealand. Jack had developed into a powerful athlete and was already honing his body for the day when he was old enough to venture with his father into the wilderness. "We all went to the sports on Saturday and saw him win the 2nd Prize for the High Jump and Putting the Weight," Nina said.

Fawcett and Jack played their usual sports together, only now the son often surpassed the father in ability. Jack wrote to Large, boasting, "I had a ripping cricket season, as I was vice-captain of the [school] team, and won the average ball, and was second in the batting averages. Also I never dropped a catch throughout the whole season." He wrote with a mixture of youthful cockiness and innocence. He noted that he had taken up photography and made "some ripping photos." Occasionally in his letters he'd include a pen-and-ink caricature of his brother or sister.

Despite his brashness and athletic grace, Jack remained, in many ways, an awkward teenager who, unsure how to interact with girls and desperate to uphold his father's monkish edicts, seemed mostly at ease in the company of his childhood friend Raleigh Rimell. Brian Fawcett said that Raleigh was Jack's "able and willing lieutenant." During the war, the two friends would shoot starlings off the roofs of surrounding houses, causing a furor among the neighbors and the local police. Once, Raleigh shattered a letter box and was summoned by the police and ordered to pay ten shillings to replace it. Whenever Raleigh passed the new letter box, he would polish it with a handkerchief and proclaim, "This is mine, you know!"

On the rare occasions when Raleigh wasn't present, it was Brian Fawcett who followed Jack around. Brian was different from his older brother—indeed, different from most Fawcett men. He lacked athletic prowess and was often, as he admitted, bullied by other kids "into a stupor." Suffering in the shadow of his brother, Brian recalled, "At school it was always Jack who distinguished himself in games, in fights, and by standing up to the severe canings of the headmaster."

Although Nina thought her children had no "hidden feeling of fear or distrust" toward their parents, Brian seemed roiled by his father's actions. Fawcett always seemed to want to play with Jack and touted him as a future explorer; he even gave Jack his Ceylon treasure map. Brian once noted in a letter to his mother that at least when his father was away there were "no favourites" in the house.

One day Brian followed Jack into the room where their father kept his collection of artifacts. It included a sword, stone axes, a spear tipped with bone, bows and arrows, and shell necklaces. The boys had previously devoured a bag of nuts that the chief of the Maxubis had given Fawcett as a present; now Jack removed a beautifully handcrafted musket called a jezail, which Fawcett had obtained in Morocco. Wondering if it would fire, Jack carried the jezail outside and loaded it with powder. Given its rust and age, the gun was likely to backfire, lethally, and Jack said that he and Brian should flip a coin to see who would pull the trigger. Brian lost. "My elder brother stood well clear, and goaded me on to fulfil my honourable obligation to risk suicide," Brian recalled. "I pulled the trigger, the pan flashed and sizzled—and nothing further seemed to happen. But things *were* happening. An appreciable time after pulling the trigger there was a loud, asthmatic sort of cough, and a huge cloud of red dust vomited out of the muzzle!" The gun didn't fire, but Brian had demonstrated, at least for an instant, that he was as daring as his older brother.

FAWCETT, MEANWHILE, was frantically trying to organize what he called his "path to Z." His two most trusted companions were no longer available: Manley had died of heart disease shortly after the war, and Costin had married and decided to settle down. The loss of these men was a blow that perhaps only Costin fully appreciated. He told his family that Fawcett's only Achilles' heel as an explorer was that he hated to slow down, and he needed someone whom he trusted enough to defer to when the person said, *"Enough!"* Without him or Manley, Costin feared, there would be no one to stop Fawcett.

Fawcett then suffered a more severe setback: the RGS and a number of other institutions turned down his requests for funding. The war had made money for scientific exploration harder to come by, but that wasn't the only reason. University-trained anthropologists and archaeologists were displacing "Hints to Travellers" amateurs; sub-specialization had rendered obsolete the man or woman who dared to try to provide an *autopsis* of the entire earth. Another South American explorer and contemporary of Fawcett's complained bitterly that "the general practitioner in this everyday world of ours is being squeezed out." And, although Fawcett remained a legend, most of the new specialists disputed his theory of Z. "I cannot induce scientific men to accept even the supposition that there are traces of an old civilization" in the Amazon, Fawcett wrote in his journals.

Colleagues had once doubted his theory of Z largely for biological reasons: the Indians were physically incapable of constructing a complex civilization. Now many of the new breed of scientists doubted him for environmental reasons: the physical landscape of the Amazon was too inhospitable for primitive tribes to construct any sort of sophisticated society. Biological determinism had increasingly given way to environmental determinism. And the Amazon—the great "counterfeit paradise"—was the most vivid proof of the Malthusian limits that the environment placed on civilizations.

The chronicles of the early El Dorado hunters that Fawcett cited only confirmed to many in the scientific establishment that he was an "amateur." An article in *Geographical Review* concluded that the Amazon basin was so bereft of humankind that it was like "one of the world's great deserts . . . comparable with the Sahara." The distinguished Swedish anthropologist Erland Nordenskiöld, who had met Fawcett in Bolivia, acknowledged that the English explorer was "an extremely original man, absolutely fearless," but that he suffered from "boundless imagination." An official at the RGS said of Fawcett, "He is a visionary kind of man who sometimes talks rather nonsense," and added, "I do not expect that his going in for spiritualism has improved his judgment."

Fawcett protested to Keltie, "Remember that I am a sane enthusiast and not an eccentric hunter of the Snark"—a reference to the make-believe creature in the Lewis Carroll poem. (According to the poem, Snark hunters often "suddenly vanish away, / And never be met with again.")

Within the RGS, Fawcett maintained a loyal faction of supporters, including Reeves and Keltie, who in 1921 became the Society's vice president. "Never mind what people say about you and about your so-called 'tall stories,' " Keltie told Fawcett. "That does not matter. There are plenty of people who believe in you."

Fawcett might have persuaded his detractors with delicacy and tact, but after so many years in the jungle he had become a creature of it. He did not dress fashionably, and in his house preferred to sleep in a hammock. His eyes were sunk deep in their sockets, like a doomsday prophet's, and even among the eccentrics at the RGS there was something vaguely frightening about what one official called his "rather queer" manner. After reports circulated within the Society that he was too intemperate, too uncontrollable, Fawcett grumbled to members of its council, "I don't lose my temper. I am not naturally tempestuous"—though his protestations suggested that he was being thrown into yet another pique.

In 1920, following the New Year, Fawcett used what little savings he had to move his family to Jamaica, saying that he wanted his children to have "an opportunity to grow up in the virile ambiente of the New World." Although sixteen-year-old Jack had to leave school, he was delighted, because Raleigh Rimell had also settled there with his family, after the death of his father. While Jack worked as a cowhand on a ranch, Raleigh toiled on a United Fruit Company plantation. At night, the two boys would often get together and plot their incandescent futures: how they would dig up the Galla-pita-Galla treasure in Ceylon and crawl through the Amazon in search of Z.

THAT FEBRUARY, Fawcett left again for South America, in the hope of securing funding from the Brazilian government. Dr. Rice, whose 1916 journey had ended prematurely owing to the entry of the United States into the war, was already back in the jungle, near the Orinoco—a region north of the one Fawcett had targeted, which for centuries had been speculated to be a possible location of El Dorado. As usual, Dr. Rice went with a large, well-armed party, which rarely veered far from the major rivers. Ever obsessed with gadgetry, he had designed a forty-five-foot boat to overcome, as he put it, "the difficulty of bad rapids, strong currents, submerged rocks, and shallow waters." The boat was shipped in pieces to Manaus, just as the city's opera house had been, and was assembled by laborers working around the clock. Dr. Rice christened the boat *Eleanor II*, for his wife, who accompanied him on a less risky leg of the journey. He had also brought along a mysterious forty-pound black box, with dials and with wires jutting from it. Vowing that it would transform exploration, he had loaded the contraption into his boat and taken it with him into the jungle.

One evening at camp, he carefully removed the box and placed it on a makeshift table. Slipping on a pair of earphones and twirling the dials as ants crawled over his fingertips, he could hear vague crackling sounds, as if someone were whispering from behind the trees—only the signals were coming from as far as the United States. Dr. Rice had picked them up using a wireless telegraphy set—an early radio—specially outfitted for the expedition. The device cost around six thousand dollars, the equivalent today of about sixty-seven thousand dollars.

Each night, as the rain dripped off the leaves and monkeys swung over his head, Dr. Rice would set up the machine and listen to the news: how President Woodrow Wilson had suffered a stroke and how the Yankees had purchased Babe Ruth from the Red Sox for $125,000. Although the machine could not send messages, it retrieved signals indicating the time of day at different meridians around the globe, so that Dr. Rice could more accurately fix longitude. "The results . . . far exceeded expectations," remarked John W. Swanson, a member of the expedition who helped operate the radio. "Time signals were received at every locality where they were desired and a daily newspaper, published from news reports received from radio-stations in the United States, Panama, and Europe, kept the members of the expedition fully informed of current events."

The expedition followed the Casiquiare, a two-hundred-mile natural canal that connected the Orinoco and the Amazon river systems. At one point, Dr. Rice and his men abandoned the boats and went on foot to explore a portion of jungle that was rumored to contain Indian artifacts. After cutting through the forest for about half a mile, they came upon several towering rocks with curious markings. The men quickly scraped away the moss and vines. The rock faces were painted with figures resembling animals and human bodies. Without more modern technology (radiocarbon dating wasn't available until 1949), it was impossible to determine their age, but they were similar to the ancient-looking rock paintings that Fawcett had seen and made diagrams of in his logbooks.

The expedition, excited, returned to the boat and continued to ascend the river. On January 22, 1920, two members of Dr. Rice's team were foraging along the shore when they thought they saw someone watching them. They bolted back to camp, sounding the alarm. In an instant, Indians fanned out on the opposite bank of the river. "A large, stout, dark, hideous individual gesticulated violently and kept shouting in an angry manner," Dr. Rice later wrote in his report to the RGS. "A thick, short growth of hair adorned his upper lip, and a great tooth was suspended from the lower. He was the leader of a band of which some sixty were visible at first, but more seemed to spring up each minute, until the bank was lined with them as far up and down as we could see."

They carried long bows, arrows, clubs, and blow darts. What was most striking, however, was their skin. It was "almost white in color," Dr. Rice said. The tribesmen were Yanomami, one of the groups of so-called white Indians.

During his previous expeditions, Dr. Rice had taken a cautious, paternalistic approach when contacting tribes. Whereas Fawcett believed that the Indians should, for the most part, remain "uncontaminated" by Westerners, Dr. Rice thought that they should be "civilized," and he and his wife had established a school in São Gabriel, along the Rio Negro, and several medical clinics staffed with Christian missionaries. After one visit to the school, Dr. Rice told the RGS that the change in the children's "dress, manners, and general appearance" and the "atmosphere of order and industry" were in "striking contrast to the squalid village of naked little savages" that had once prevailed.

Now, as the Yanomami approached, Dr. Rice's men stood watch, armed with an assortment of weapons, including a rifle, a shotgun, a revolver, and a muzzle-loader. Dr. Rice placed offerings of knives and mirrors on the ground, where the light could glint off them. The Indians, perhaps seeing the guns aimed at them, refused to take the gifts; instead, some Yanomami edged closer to the explorers, pointing their drawn bows. Dr. Rice ordered his men to fire a warning shot over their heads, but the gesture only provoked the Indians, who began to unleash their arrows, one landing by the doctor's foot. Dr. Rice then gave the command to open fire—shooting to kill. It is not known how many Indians died during the onslaught. In a missive to the RGS, Dr. Rice wrote, "There was no alternative, they being the aggressors, resenting all attempts at parley or truce, and compelling a defensive that resulted disastrously for them and was a keen disappointment to me."

As the Indians retreated under the fusillade, Dr. Rice and his men returned to their boats and fled. "We could hear their blood-curdling screams as they kept at our heels," Dr. Rice said. When the expedition eventually emerged from the jungle, the explorers were hailed for their bravery. Fawcett, however, was appalled, and told the RGS that to shoot indiscriminately at the Indians was reprehensible. He also could not resist pointing out that Dr. Rice had "skedaddled" the moment he encountered danger and was "rather too soft for the real game."

Yet reports that the doctor had uncovered ancient Indian paintings and intended to head back into the jungle with even more gadgetry put Fawcett in a frenzy as he tried to raise funding in Brazil. In Rio, he stayed with the British ambassador, Sir Ralph Paget, a close friend, who lobbied the Brazilian government on his behalf. Although the RGS had refused to devote its depleted resources to the expedition, it recommended its famous disciple to the Brazilian government, writing in a cable that "it is quite true that he has a reputation of being difficult to get on with . . . but all the same he has an extraordinary power of getting through difficulties that would deter anybody else." On February 26, a meeting was arranged with the Brazilian president, Epitácio Pessoa, and the renowned explorer and head of the Indian Protection Service, Cândido Rondon. Fawcett presented himself as a colonel, even though he had retired after the war as a lieutenant colonel. He had recently petitioned the British War Office to approve the change in rank, since he was returning to South America to raise money and "it is a matter of some importance." In a later plea, he was more explicit: "The higher rank has a certain importance in dealing with local officials, 'Lt Colonel' not only being locally equivalent to 'Commandante,' a grade below colonel, but as a rank having lost much of its local prestige owing to the large number of Temporary Officers who have retained it." The War Office refused his request on both occasions, but he inflated his rank anyway—a subterfuge he maintained so steadfastly that nearly everyone, including his family and friends, eventually knew him only as "Colonel Fawcett."

In the presidential palace, Fawcett and Rondon greeted each other cordially. Rondon, who had been promoted to general, was in uniform and wore a gold-braided cap. His graying hair gave him a distinguished look, and he stood ramrod straight. As another English traveler once noted, he commanded "instant attention—an atmosphere of conscious dignity and power that immediately singled him out." Aside from the president, there was no one else in the room.

According to Rondon, Fawcett gradually made his case for Z, emphasizing the importance of his archaeological research for Brazil. The president seemed sympathetic, and asked Rondon what he thought of "this valuable project." Rondon suspected that his rival, who remained secretive about his route, might have some ulterior motive—perhaps to exploit the jungle's mineral wealth for England. There were also rumors, later fanned by the Russians on Radio Moscow, that Fawcett was still a spy, though there was no evidence for this. Rondon insisted that it was not necessary for "foreigners to conduct expeditions in Brazil, as we have civilians and military men who are very capable of doing such work."

The president noted that he had promised the British ambassador that he would help. Rondon said that it was imperative, then, that the search for Z involve a joint Brazilian-British expedition.

Fawcett was convinced that Rondon was trying to sabotage him, and his temper grew. "I intend to go alone," he snapped.

The two explorers faced each other down. The president initially sided with his countryman and said that the expedition should include Rondon's men. But economic difficulties prompted the Brazilian government to withdraw from the expedition, though it gave Fawcett enough money to launch a bare-bones operation. Before Fawcett left their final meeting, Rondon told him, "I pray for the Colonel's good fortune."

Fawcett had enlisted for the expedition a British army officer and RGS member whom Reeves had recommended, but at the last minute the officer backed out. Undeterred, Fawcett posted an advertisement in newspapers and recruited a six-foot-five-inch Australian boxer named Lewis Brown and a thirty-one-year-old American ornithologist, Ernest Holt. Brown was the wild sort drawn to the frontier, and before leaving on the expedition he indulged his sexual appetites. "I'm flesh and blood like the rest!" he told Fawcett. Holt, in contrast, was a sensitive young man who, growing up in Alabama, had collected lizards and snakes and had long aspired to be a naturalist-explorer in the mold of Darwin. Like Fawcett, he wrote down poems in his diary to recite in the jungle, including Kipling's words "The Dreamer whose dream came true!" Holt also printed on his diary's cover, in bold letters, a relative's address, "IN CASE OF FATAL ACCIDENT."

The three gathered in Cuiabá, the capital of Mato Grosso. During the six years Fawcett had been away from the Amazon, the rubber boom had collapsed, and a central role in its demise was played by a former president of the Royal Geographical Society, Sir Clements Markham. In the 1870s, Markham had engineered the smuggling of Amazonian rubber-tree seeds to Europe, which were then distributed to plantations throughout British colonies in Asia. Compared with the brutal, inefficient, and costly extraction of wild rubber in the jungle, growing rubber on Asian plantations was easy and cheap, and the produce abundant. "The electric lights went out in Manaus," the historian Robin Furneaux wrote. "The opera house was silent and the jewels which had filled it were gone . . . Vampire bats circled the chandeliers of the broken palaces and spiders scurried across their floors."

Fawcett described Cuiabá as "impoverished and backward," a place that had degenerated into "little better than a ghost town." The streets were covered in mud and grass; only the main road was illuminated by electric lightbulbs. As Fawcett gathered provisions for his expedition, he feared that he was being spied on. In fact, General Rondon had vowed not to let the Englishman out of his sight until he discovered his true intentions. In his correspondence, Fawcett began to use a cipher to conceal his route. As Nina explained in a letter to a trusted friend, "Lat $x+4$ to $x + 5$, and Long $y + 2$, where 'x' is twice the number of letters in the name of the town where he stayed with us, and 'y' is the number of the building in London where I used to visit him." She added, "Keep the key to this cipher entirely to yourself."

Fawcett received a farewell note from his son Jack, who wrote that he had had a "dream" in which he entered an ancient temple in a city like Z. May "protection" be "with you at all stages of your journey," Jack told his father, and wished him Godspeed. Fawcett asked a local intermediary that if his family or friends "get alarmed at no news please soothe them with the confident assertion we shall come to no untoward end and shall be heard of in due course." And in a letter to Keltie he vowed, "I am going to reach this place and return from it." Trailed by his two companions, plus two horses, two oxen, and a pair of dogs, he then marched northward toward the Xingu River, holding his machete like a knight clutching his sword.

Soon after, everything began to unravel. Rains flooded their path and destroyed their equipment. Brown, despite his ferocious appearance, suffered a mental breakdown, and Fawcett, fearing another Murray-like disaster, dispatched him back to Cuiabá. Holt, too, grew feeble; he said that it was impossible to do fieldwork because of the horrific conditions, and he maniacally cataloged the bugs that were attacking him, until his diary contained details of almost nothing else. "More than half ill from insects," he scribbled, adding, "Days of toil, nights of torture—an explorer's life! Where is the romance now?"

Fawcett was irate. How could he get anywhere with "this cripple"? he wrote in his journals. Yet Fawcett, too, was, at the age of fifty-three, no longer immune to the forces of nature. His leg had become swollen and infected, "giving me so much pain at night that sleep was difficult," he confessed in his diary. One night he took opium pills and became violently ill. "It was rather unusual for me to be laid low in this way, and I was heartily ashamed of myself," he wrote.

A month into their journey, the animals started to collapse. "It is awful on one's nerves to watch one's pack animals slowly dying," Holt wrote. An ox that had been invaded by maggots lay down and never got up. One of the dogs was starving, and Holt shot it. A horse drowned. Then the other horse dropped in its tracks, and Fawcett put it out of its misery with a bullet—this was the site that became known as Dead Horse Camp. Finally, Holt prostrated himself and said, "Never mind me, Colonel. You go on—just leave me here."

Fawcett knew the expedition might be his last opportunity to prove the theory of Z, and he cursed the gods for conspiring against him— decried them for the weather, his companions, and the war that had held him back. Fawcett realized that if he left Holt behind he would die. "There was nothing for it," Fawcett later wrote, "but to take him back and give up the present trip as a failure—a sickening, heartrending failure!"

What he would not admit was that his own infected leg made proceeding almost impossible. As the expedition party struggled back to the nearest frontier outpost, enduring thirty-six hours without water, Fawcett told Holt, "The exit from Hell is always difficult."

When they emerged in Cuiabá in January 1921, Ambassador Paget sent a telegram to Nina saying only, "Your husband returned." Nina asked Harold Large, "What does it mean, think you?—Not failure I should say! Possibly, he may not have found the 'lost cities' but I should think he's found something important or surely he wouldn't have returned." Yet he had returned with nothing. General Rondon released a gloating statement to the press that said, "Col. Fawcett's expedition was abandoned . . . in spite of all his pride as an explorer . . . He came back thin, naturally disappointed for having been forced to retreat before entering the hardest part of the Xingu." Devastated, Fawcett made plans to return to the jungle with Holt, who was still under contract and whose services were all he could afford. The wife of the American vice-consul in Rio, who was a friend of the ornithologist's, sent Holt a letter beseeching him not to go:

> You are a strong, able-bodied young man, so *why* do you . . . deliberately throw your life away as you will if you go back to Mato Grosso? . . . We all realize that you are deeply interested in and love science, but how much good is it going to do you or the world to have you go aimlessly into the depths of nowhere? . . . What about your Mother and sister? Don't they count for anything? . . . Someday one or both of them may need you and where will you be. You have no right to sacrifice your life just because a man you do not know wants you to. Many lives are lost for the betterment of mankind, it is true, but how is this wild goose chase to help or give anything to the world?

Still, Holt was determined to see the expedition through, and went to Rio to collect supplies. Fawcett, meanwhile, was turning over in his mind every aspect of Holt's performance: each complaint, each misstep, each error. He even began to suspect, though he had no evidence, that Holt was a Judas, sending information back to Dr. Rice or another rival. Fawcett dispatched a message to Holt that said, "Unfortunately we live and think in different worlds and can no more mix than oil and water . . . And as the objects of this journey with me come first and personal considerations last, I prefer to finish it alone than to risk results unnecessarily."

Holt, dumbfounded, wrote in his diary, "After close association with Col. Fawcett for a period covering one year, I . . . find that the lesson most clearly impressed upon my mind is: Never again under any circumstances form any connections with any Englishman whatsoever." He lamented that, instead of earning fame, he remained a "vagabond ornithologist—or perhaps 'tramp birdskinner' would be nearer a true title." He concluded, "As far as my biased observation goes [Fawcett] possesses only 3 qualities that I admire: Nerve, kindness to animals, and quick forgetfulness of a row."

Fawcett told a friend that he had fired another expedition companion, who was "convinced I am sure that I am a lunatic."

Now, for the first time, the thought began to take hold: *If only my son could come.* Jack was strong and devoted. He would not complain like a pink-eyed weakling. He would not demand a large salary, or mutiny. And, most important, he believed in Z. "I longed for the day when my son would be old enough to work with me," Fawcett wrote.

For the moment, though, Jack, still only eighteen, was not ready, and Fawcett had no one. The logical choice was to postpone the journey, but instead he sold half his military pension to pay for provisions—gambling what little private savings he had—and came up with a new plan. This time he would try to reach Z from the opposite direction, heading from east to west. Starting in Bahia and passing where he thought the *bandeirante* had discovered the city in 1753, he would walk hundreds of miles inland toward the jungle in Mato Grosso. The plan seemed mad. Even Fawcett conceded to Keltie that if he went alone "the prospects of returning are diminished." Nevertheless, in August of 1921, he set out, unaccompanied. "Loneliness is not intolerable when enthusiasm for a quest fills the mind," he wrote. Thirsty and hungry, delirious and deranged, he marched on and on. At one point, he looked out at cliffs in the distant horizon and thought he saw the shapes of a city . . . or was his mind unraveling? His supplies were exhausted, his legs spent. After three months in the wilderness and facing death, he had no choice but to retreat.

"I must return," he vowed. "I *shall* return!"

A

SCIENTIFIC

OBSESSION

I t's up to you, Jack," Fawcett said.

The two were talking after Fawcett had come back from his 1921 expedition. While Fawcett had been away, Nina had moved the family from Jamaica to Los Angeles, where the Rimells had also gone and where Jack and Raleigh had been swept up in the romance of Hollywood, greasing their hair, growing Clark Gable mustaches, and hanging around Hollywood sets, in the hopes of landing roles. (Jack had met Mary Pickford and loaned her his cricket bat to use in the production of *Little Lord Fauntleroy*.)

Fawcett had a proposition for his son. Colonel T. E. Lawrence—the celebrated desert spy and explorer better known as Lawrence of Arabia—had volunteered to go with Fawcett on his next journey in search of Z, but Fawcett was wary of choosing a companion with a powerful ego who was unaccustomed to the Amazon. As Fawcett wrote to a friend, "[Lawrence] may be keen upon S. American exploration but in the first place he probably requires a salary I cannot pay him and in the second place excellent work in the Near East does not infer the ability or willingness to hump a 60 lbs pack, live for a year upon the forest, suffer from legions of insects and accept the conditions which I would impose." Fawcett told Jack that, instead of Lawrence, he could take part in the expedition. It would be one of the most difficult and dangerous expeditions in the history of exploration—the ultimate test, in Fawcett's words, "of faith, courage, and determination."

Jack didn't hesitate. "I want to go with you," he said.

Nina, who was present during these discussions, raised no objections. Partly, she was confident that Fawcett's seemingly superhuman powers would protect their son, and, partly, she believed that Jack, as his father's natural heir, would possess similar abilities. Yet her motivation seems to have gone deeper than that: to doubt her husband after so many years of sacrifice was to doubt her own life's work. Indeed, she needed Z just as much as he did. And even though Jack had no exploring experience and the expedition entailed extraordinary danger, she never considered, as she later told a reporter, trying to "hold" her son back.

Of course, Raleigh had to come, too. Jack said that he could not do the most important thing in his life without him.

Raleigh's mother, Elsie, was reluctant to permit her youngest son— her "boy," as she called him—to join such a dangerous venture. But Raleigh was insistent. His movie aspirations had foundered, and he was toiling in menial jobs in the lumber industry. As he told his older brother, Roger, he felt "unsatisfied and unsettled." This was his opportunity not only to earn a "pile of dough" but also to make good with his life.

Fawcett informed the RGS and others that he now had two ideal companions ("both strong as horses and keen as mustard") and tried once more to secure funding. "I can only say I am a Founder's Medallist . . . and therefore deserving of confidence," he maintained. Yet the failure of his previous expedition—even though it was only the first in an illustrious career—had given his critics further ammunition. And with no backers, and after exhausting what little savings he had on his previous expedition, he soon found himself bankrupt, like his father. In September 1921, unable to sustain the cost of living in California, he was forced to uproot his family again and return to Stoke Canon, England, where he rented an old, ramshackle house without running water or electricity. "All water has to be pumped and huge logs have to be sawn into blocks—all additional labour," Nina wrote to Large. The work was grueling. "I broke down utterly about 5 weeks ago and was very seriously ill," Nina said. Part of her wanted to run away and escape all the sacrifices and burdens—but, she said, "the family needed me."

"The situation is difficult," Fawcett admitted to Large. "One learns little from a smooth life, but I do not like roping others into the difficulties which have dogged me so persistently . . . It is not that I want luxuries. I care little about such things—but I hate inactivity."

He couldn't afford to send Jack to university, and Brian and Joan stopped attending school, in order to help with chores and do odd jobs to make money. They hawked photographs and paintings, while Fawcett sold off family possessions and heirlooms. "My man actually suggested a few days ago that he thought it would be a wise thing to sell those old Spanish chairs, if . . . they would fetch a good price," Nina wrote Large. By 1923, Fawcett had become so poor that he could not pay his annual three-pound membership dues to the RGS. "I wish you would give me the benefit of your advice as to whether I could resign . . . without something in the nature of a scandal for a Founder's Medallist," Fawcett wrote Keltie. "The fact is that the forced inertia and family . . . going to California have left me on the rocks. I had hoped to weather them, but such hopes seem to wilt away, and I do not think I can hang on." He added, "It is rather a fall from dreams."

Although he scraped up enough money to pay another year of dues, Nina was concerned about her husband. "P.H.F. was in the lowest depths of despair," she confided to Large.

"My father's impatience to start off on his last trip was tearing at him with ever increasing force," Brian later recalled. "From reticent he became almost surly."

Fawcett began to lash out at the scientific establishment, which he felt had turned its back on him. He told a friend, "Archeological and ethnological science is founded upon the sands of speculation, and we know what may happen to houses so constructed." He denounced his enemies at the RGS and detected "treachery" everywhere. He complained about "the money wasted on these useless Antarctic expeditions," about the "men of science" who had "in their day pooh-poohed the existence of the Americas—and, later, the idea of Herculaneum, Pompeii, and Troy," about how "all the skepticism in Christendom won't budge me an inch" from believing in Z, about how he was "going to see it through somehow or other even if I have to wait another decade."

He increasingly surrounded himself with spiritualists who not only confirmed but embroidered on his own vision of Z. One seer told him: "The valley and city are full of jewels, spiritual jewels, but also immense wealth of real jewels." Fawcett published essays in journals, such as the *Occult Review*, in which he spoke of his spiritual quest and "the treasures of the invisible World."

Another South American explorer and RGS fellow said that many people thought that Fawcett had become "a trifle unbalanced." Some called him a "scientific maniac."

In the spiritualist magazine *Light*, Fawcett contributed an essay titled "Obsession." Without mentioning his own idée fixe, he described how "mental storms" could consume a person with "fearful torture." "Undoubtedly obsession is the diagnosis of many cases of madness," he concluded.

Brooding day and night, Fawcett hatched various half-baked schemes— to mine nitrate in Brazil, to prospect for oil in California—in order to raise money for his expedition. "The Mining Syndicate fell through" because it was "a nest of crooks," Fawcett wrote Large in October 1923.

Jack told another family friend, "It seemed as if some evil genius was trying to put every possible obstacle in our way."

Still, Jack continued to train in case the money suddenly came through. Without Raleigh's lighthearted influence, he adopted his father's asceticism, shunning meat and liquor. "A short time ago I had the idea that I must set myself a certain immensely difficult trial requiring a tremendous spiritual effort," he wrote Esther Windust, a family friend who was a Theosophist. "By great effort I have been successful and have already felt the benefit." He added, "I enjoy immensely the life and teachings of Buddha [which] came somewhat as a surprise to me in their absolute adherence to my own ideas. You notice his dislike of creeds and dogma." A visitor to the house was struck by Jack's presence: "The capacity for love—and the slight ascetic restraint—makes one think of the knights of the Grail."

Fawcett, meanwhile, tried to hold out faith that sooner or later "the Gods will accept me for service." At one point, his friend Rider Haggard told Fawcett that he had something important he wanted to give the explorer. It was a stone idol, about ten inches tall with almond-shaped eyes and hieroglyphics carved on its chest. Haggard, who had kept it by his desk while writing the 1919 book *When the World Shook*, said that he had received the statue from someone in Brazil who believed it came from the Indians in the interior. Fawcett took the idol with him and had it examined by several museum experts. Most suspected it was fake, but Fawcett, in his desperation, even showed it to a psychic, and concluded that it might be a relic of Z.

In the spring of 1924, Fawcett learned that Dr. Rice, drawing on his bottomless bank account, was mounting one of the more extraordinary expeditions ever assembled. He had compiled a team that reflected the new demand for specialization. It included experts in botany, zoology, topography, astronomy, geography, and medicine, as well as one of the world's most distinguished anthropologists, Dr. Theodor Koch-Grünberg, and Silvino Santos, considered the first cinematographer of the Amazon. More breathtaking was the expedition's arsenal of equipment. There was the *Eleanor II*, along with another elegant vessel; and a new wireless radio system, this one able not only to receive signals but also to send them. These objects, however, were not what had created the greatest stir. As the *New York Times* reported, the doctor had with him a 160-horsepower, six-cylinder, three-person oak-propeller hydroplane with a complete outfit of aerial cameras.

Fawcett believed that Dr. Rice's equipment had limitations in the Amazon: existing radios were so bulky that they would confine the expedition to boats, and aerial observation and photography would not necessarily be able to penetrate the canopy. There was also the risk of landing a plane in hostile areas. The *Times* reported that the doctor's hydroplane was loaded with "a supply of bombs" to be used in "scaring the cannibal Indians"—a tactic that horrified Fawcett.

Nevertheless, Fawcett knew that an airplane could carry even the most inept explorer to extreme places. Dr. Rice proclaimed that "the whole method of exploration and geographical mapping will be revolutionized." The expedition—or at least the film that Santos planned to shoot—was called *No rastro do Eldorado*, or *On the Trail of El Dorado*. Although Fawcett believed that his rival was still searching too far north for Z, he was petrified.

That September, while Rice and his team were making their way into the Amazon, Fawcett met a swashbuckling British war correspondent and onetime member of the RGS named George Lynch. Well connected in both the United States and Europe, he frequented the Savage Club in London, where writers and artists would gather over drinks and cigars. Fawcett found Lynch, who was fifty-six, to be a "highly respectable man of unimpeachable character and excellent repute." What's more, Lynch was enthralled by the idea of finding Z.

In exchange for a percentage of the profits that would arise from the expedition, Lynch, who was a far more capable salesman than Fawcett, offered to help raise money. Fawcett had focused most of his fund-raising efforts on the financially strapped RGS. Now, with Lynch's assistance, he would look for support from the United States, that bustling new empire which was constantly expanding into new frontiers and was awash in capital. On October 28, Jack wrote Windust to say that Lynch had left for America "to get into touch with millionaires." Realizing the power of Fawcett's legend and the commercial value of his story—"the finest exploration story that I think has ever been written in our time," as Fawcett put it—Lynch initially mined his contacts in the media. Within days, he had secured thousands of dollars by selling the story rights for Fawcett's expedition to the North American Newspaper Alliance, or NANA—a consortium of publications that had a presence in almost every major city in the United States and Canada. The consortium, which included the *New York World*, the *Los Angeles Times*, the *Houston Chronicle*, the *Times-Picayune*, and the *Toronto Star*, was known for giving press credentials to nonprofessional reporters who could provide gripping dispatches from the most exotic and dangerous locales. (The consortium later enlisted Ernest Hemingway as a foreign correspondent during the Spanish civil war and funded expeditions like Thor Heyerdahl's 1947 crossing of the Pacific by raft.) While explorers had typically written about their adventures after the fact, Fawcett would send Indian runners out with dispatches *during* his journey—even, if possible, from "the forbidden city itself," as one newspaper reported.

Lynch also sold the rights to Fawcett's expedition to newspapers throughout the world, so that tens of millions of people on virtually every continent would read about his journey. Though Fawcett was wary of trivializing his scientific endeavors with "journalese," as he called it, he was grateful for any funding, not to mention the assured burst of glory. What made him most happy, though, was a cable from Lynch informing him that his proposal was generating equal enthusiasm among prestigious American scientific institutions. Not only did these foundations have more money than many of their European counterparts, but they were also more open to Fawcett's theory. The director of the American Geographical Society, Dr. Isaiah Bowman, had been a member of Hiram Bingham's expedition that discovered Machu Picchu, which scientists at the time had never expected to be found. Dr. Bowman told a reporter, "We have known of Colonel Fawcett for many years as a man of soundest character and the highest integrity. We have the highest confidence, both in his capacity and his competence and reliability as a scientist." The American

Geographical Society offered the expedition a thousand-dollar grant; the Museum of the American Indian followed with another thousand dollars.

On November 4, 1924, Fawcett wrote Keltie, saying, "I judge from Lynch's cable and letters that the whole affair . . . is catching the fancy of Americans. It is I suppose the romantic streak that has made and no doubt will make empires." Warning that it was bound to come out that "a modern Columbus was turned down in England," he offered the Society one last chance to support the mission. "The R.G.S. bred me as an explorer, and I don't want them to be out of" an expedition that was sure to make history, he said. Finally, with Keltie and other supporters lobbying on his behalf, and with scientists around the world gravitating toward the possibility of Z, the Society voted to support the expedition and help furnish it with equipment.

The total raised amounted to roughly five thousand dollars—less than the cost of one of Dr. Rice's radios. This was not enough money for Fawcett, Jack, or Raleigh to draw a salary, and much of the financing from newspapers would be paid only upon completion of their journey. "If they don't return there will be nothing" for the family to live on, Nina later wrote to Large.

"Not a sum which would inspire most explorers," Fawcett told Keltie. But he added in another letter, "In some ways I am rather glad that not one of the three of us makes a red cent unless the journey is successful, for nobody can say we were after money in undertaking this rather perilous quest. It is an honest scientific research animated by its own exceptional interest and value."

Fawcett and Jack paid a visit to the RGS, where all the ill feelings, all the frustrations, seemed to have evaporated. Everyone wished them luck. Reeves, the Society's map curator, later recalled what "a fine young fellow" Jack was: "well built, tall and strong, very like his father." Fawcett expressed his gratitude to Reeves and Keltie, who had never wavered in their support. "I shall rejoice in telling you the whole story in three years' time," he said.

Back at Stoke Canon, Fawcett, Jack, and the rest of the family were thrown into a whirl of packing and planning. It was decided that Nina and Joan, who was fourteen, would move to the Portuguese island of Madeira, where it was cheaper to live. Brian, who was devastated that his father had not chosen him for the expedition, had turned his attention to railroad engineering. With Fawcett's help, he found work with a railroad company in Peru and was the first to depart for South America. The family accompanied Brian, who was only seventeen at the time, to the train station.

Fawcett told Brian that he would be responsible for Nina and his sister's care during the expedition, and that any financial assistance he could give them would help them survive. The family made plans for the return of Fawcett and Jack as heroes. "In two years' time they would be back, and, when my first home leave fell due, we would all meet again in England," Brian later recalled. "After that we might make a family home in Brazil, where the work of the future years would undoubtedly lie." Brian said farewell to his family and stepped onto the train. As the carriage pulled away, he stared out the window, watching as his father and brother slowly disappeared from view.

On December 3, 1924, Fawcett and Jack said goodbye to Joan and Nina and boarded the *Aquitania* for New York, where they were to meet Raleigh. The path to Z finally seemed secure. When they landed in New York a week later, however, Fawcett discovered that Lynch, his business partner of "unimpeachable character," had sequestered himself, drunk and surrounded by prostitutes, in the Waldorf-Astoria Hotel. "[He] succumbed to the lure of the ubiquitous bottle in this Prohibition City," Fawcett wrote the RGS. He said that Lynch "must have suffered from alcoholic aberration. It may be more, for he was sexually disturbed." The aberration had cost more than a thousand dollars of the expedition's funds, and Fawcett feared that the mission was in danger of unraveling before it began. Yet the venture had already become an international sensation, prompting John D. Rockefeller Jr., the scion of the billionaire founder of Standard Oil and an ally of Dr. Bowman, to step forward with a check for forty-five hundred dollars, so that "the plan can be initiated at once."

With his path to Z again clear, Fawcett could no longer even work up his notorious wrath toward Lynch, who had returned to London in disgrace. "He did precipitate this exploration, which is something to his credit, and The Gods select curious agents for their purposes sometimes," Fawcett wrote the RGS. Plus, he said, "I am a great believer in the Law of Compensation." He was sure that he had sacrificed all he had to give to reach Z. Now he hoped to receive what he called "the honour of immortality."

An Unexpected

Clue

Yeah, I've heard of Fawcett," a Brazilian guide who offered tours of the Amazon told me. "Isn't he the one who disappeared looking for El Dorado or something?"

When I mentioned that I was seeking a guide to help me trace Fawcett's route and look for Z, he replied that he was *"muito ocupado,"* which seemed to be a polite way of saying, "You're out of your mind."

It was difficult to find someone not only willing to make the journey into the jungle but also with ties to the indigenous communities in Brazil, which function almost as autonomous countries, with their own laws and governing councils. The history of the interaction between *brancos* and *indios*—whites and Indians—in the Amazon often reads like an extended epitaph: tribes were wiped out by disease and massacres; languages and songs were obliterated. One tribe buried its children alive to spare them the shame of subjugation. But some tribes, including the dozens that remain uncontacted, have managed to insulate themselves in the jungle. In recent decades, as many indigenous people have organized themselves politically, the Brazilian government has stopped trying to "modernize" them and has worked more effectively to protect them. As a result, some Amazon tribes, particularly those in the Mato Grosso region, where Fawcett disappeared, have flourished. Their populations, after being decimated, are growing again; their languages and customs have endured.

The person I eventually persuaded to accompany me was Paolo Pinage, a fifty-two-year-old former professional samba dancer and theater director. Though Paolo was not of Indian descent, he had previously worked for FUNAI, the agency that succeeded Rondon's Indian Protection Service. Paolo shared its "Die if you must, but never kill" edict. During our initial phone conversation, I had asked him if we could penetrate the same region that Fawcett had, including part of what is now Xingu National Park, Brazil's first Indian reservation, which was created in 1961. (The park, along with an adjoining reservation, is the size of Belgium and is one of the largest swaths of jungle under Indian control in the world.) Paolo said, "I can take you there, but it's not easy."

Entering Indian territories, he explained, required elaborate negotiations with tribal leaders. He asked me to send him medical records attesting that I carried no contagious diseases. Then he began approaching various chiefs on my behalf. Many of the tribes in the jungle now had shortwave radios, a more modern version of what Dr. Rice had used, and for weeks our messages were relayed back and forth as Paolo assured them that I was a reporter and not a *garimpero*, or "prospector." In 2004, twenty-nine diamond miners trespassed onto a reservation in western Brazil, and members of the Cinta Larga tribe shot them or beat them to death with wooden clubs.

Paolo told me to meet him at the airport in Cuiabá. Although none of the tribes had agreed to my visit, he seemed optimistic when he greeted me. He was carrying several large plastic containers, instead of a suitcase or a backpack, and had a cigarette dangling from his lip. He wore a camouflage vest with myriad pockets, stuffed with supplies: a Swiss Army knife, a Japanese anti-itch medicine, a flashlight, a bag of peanuts, and more ciga-

rettes. He resembled someone returning from an expedition, not embarking on one. His vest was ragged, his face was bone thin and covered with a
gray-tinged beard, and his bald head had been seared by the sun. His English pronunciation was shaky, yet he spoke as fast as he smoked. "Come,
come, we go now," he said. "Paolo take care of everything."

We took a taxi to the center of Cuiabá, which was no longer the
"ghost town" Fawcett had described but had an air of modernity, with
paved roads and a few modest skyscrapers. Brazilian settlers had once been
lured into the interior by rubber and gold. Now the primary temptation
was the high price of commodities from ranching and farming, and the
city served as a staging ground for these latest pioneers.

We checked into a hotel named El Dorado ("A funny coincidence,
isn't it?" Paolo said) and began making preparations. Our first challenge
was to ensure that we correctly divined Fawcett's route. I filled Paolo in
about my trip to England and about everything Fawcett had done—
including planting false leads and using ciphers—to conceal his course.

"This colonel goes to many lengths to hide something that no one
has ever found," Paolo said.

I spread the relevant documents that I had obtained in British
archives on a wooden table. Among them were copies of several of Fawcett's original maps. They were meticulous, recalling pointillist paintings.
Paolo picked one up and examined it for several minutes under the light.
Fawcett had printed "UNEXPLORED" in bold letters atop one image,
which depicted the forests between the Xingu River and two other major
tributaries of the Amazon. On another map, he added several notations:
"small tribes . . . believed to be friendly"; "very bad Indian tribes—names
unknown"; "Indians probably dangerous."

One of the maps seemed somewhat crudely drawn, and Paolo asked
if Fawcett had made it. I explained that a notation on the map—which I
had found among several old documents from the North American Newspaper Alliance—indicated that it had belonged to Raleigh Rimell. He had

sketched on the map the expedition's route and given it to his mother. Although he made her promise to destroy it after he left, she had held on to it.

Paolo and I agreed that the documents confirmed that Fawcett and his team, after leaving Cuiabá, had proceeded north, to the territory of the Bakairí Indians. From there they had gone to Dead Horse Camp, and then, presumably, deep into what is today Xingu National Park. In the route that Fawcett had supplied in confidence to the Royal Geographical Society, he wrote that his party would turn due east around the eleventh parallel south of the equator and continue past the River of Death and the Araguaia River, until they reached the Atlantic Ocean. Fawcett noted in his proposal that it was preferable to maintain an eastward trajectory, toward Brazil's coastal regions, since it "would preserve a higher level of enthusiasm than one proceeding farther and farther into the wilds."

Yet one segment of the route Raleigh had drawn seemed to contradict this. At the Araguaia River, Raleigh indicated, the expedition would turn sharply northward, instead of continuing eastward, and would pass from Mato Grosso into the Brazilian state of Pará, before exiting near the mouth of the Amazon River.

"Maybe Raleigh made a mistake," Paolo said.

"That's what I thought, too," I said. "But then I read this."

I showed him the last letter that Jack had sent to his mother. Paolo read the line I had highlighted: "Next time I write will probably be from Para."

"I think Fawcett kept this last piece of his route secret even from the RGS," I said.

Paolo seemed increasingly intrigued by Fawcett, and with a black pen he began to trace Fawcett's route on a clean map, excitedly ticking off each of our intended destinations. Finally, he took his cigarette out of his mouth and said, "On to Z, no?"

HAVE NO FEAR

The train creaked toward the frontier. On February 11, 1925, Fawcett, Jack, and Raleigh had left Rio de Janeiro on their more than one-thousand-mile journey into the interior of Brazil. In Rio, they had stayed in the Hotel Internacional, where they tested their equipment in the garden and where virtually everything they did was chronicled in newspapers around the world. "At least forty million people [are] already aware of our objective," Fawcett wrote his son Brian, reveling in the "tremendous" publicity.

There were photographs of the explorers with headlines like "Three Men Face Cannibals in Relic Quest." One article said, "No Olympic games contender was ever trained down to a finer edge than these three reserved, matter-of-fact Englishmen, whose pathway to a forgotten world is beset by arrows, pestilence and wild beasts."

"Aren't the reports of the expedition in the English and American papers amusing?" Jack wrote his brother.

Brazilian authorities, fearing the demise of such an illustrious party on their territory, demanded that Fawcett sign a statement absolving them of responsibility, which he did without hesitation. "They do not want to be pressed . . . if we do not turn up," Fawcett told Keltie. "But we shall all turn up all right—even if it is just about as much as my fifty-eight years can put up with." Despite such concerns, the government and its citizens warmly received the explorers: the party would be given free transport to the frontier in railroad cars reserved for dignitaries—luxurious carriages with private baths and saloons. "We have met with unbounded sympathy and goodwill," Fawcett informed the RGS.

Raleigh seemed somewhat dispirited, though. On the voyage from New York, he had fallen in love, apparently with the daughter of a British duke. "I became acquainted with a certain girl on board, and as time went on our friendship increased till I admit it was threatening to get serious," he confessed in a letter to Brian Fawcett. He wanted to tell Jack about his turbulent emotions, but his best friend, who had become even more priestly while training for the expedition, complained that he was making "a fool of himself." Whereas before Raleigh had been intently focused on his adventure with Jack, now all he could think about was this . . . *woman.*

"[The colonel] and Jack were getting quite anxious, afraid I should elope or something!" Raleigh wrote. Indeed, Raleigh contemplated getting married in Rio, but Fawcett and Jack dissuaded him. "I came to my senses and realized I was supposed to be the member of an expedition, and not allowed to take a wife along," Raleigh said. "I had to drop her gently and attend to business."

"[Raleigh] is much better now," Jack wrote. Still, he worriedly asked Raleigh, "I suppose after we get back you'll be married within a year?"

Raleigh replied that he wouldn't make any promises, but, as he later put it, "I don't intend to be a bachelor all my life, even if Jack does!"

The three explorers stopped for a few days in São Paulo and went to visit the Instituto Butantan, one of the largest snake farms in the world. The staff carried out a series of demonstrations for the explorers, showing how various predators strike. At one point, an attendant reached into a cage with a long hook and removed a lethal bushmaster, while Jack and Raleigh stared at its fangs. "A whole lot of venom squirted out," Jack later wrote his brother. Fawcett was familiar with Amazonian snakes, but he still found the demonstrations enlightening, and he shared his notes in one of his dispatches for the North American Newspaper Alliance. ("A snake-bite which bleeds is nonpoisonous. Two punctures, plus a bluish and bloodless patch, is a sign of poison.")

Before leaving, Fawcett was handed what he most wanted: five years' worth of anti-snakebite serums, stored in vials marked "rattlesnakes," "pit vipers," and "unknown" species. He also received a hypodermic needle to inject them.

After local officials in São Paulo gave the explorers what Jack described as "a fine send-off," the three Englishmen again boarded a train, heading west toward the Paraguay River, along the border of Brazil and Bolivia. Fawcett had made the same trip in 1920, with Holt and Brown, and the familiar vista only intensified his chronic impatience. As sparks flew up from the rails, Jack and Raleigh looked out the window, watching the swamps and scrub forest pass, imagining what they would soon encounter. "I saw some quite interesting things," Jack wrote. "In the cattle country were numerous parrots, and we saw two flocks . . . of young rheas [ostrichlike birds] about four to five feet high. There was a glimpse of a spider's web in a tree, with a spider about the size of a sparrow sitting in the middle." Spotting alligators on the banks, he and Raleigh grabbed their rifles and tried to shoot them from the moving train.

The immensity of the landscape awed Jack, who occasionally sketched what he saw as if to help him comprehend it, a habit ingrained in him by his father. In a week, the men reached Corumbá, a frontier town near the Bolivian border, not far from where Fawcett had carried out much of his early exploration. This marked the end of the railroad line and the explorers' lavish accommodations, and that night they stayed in a squalid hotel. "The lavatory arrangements here are very primitive," Jack wrote his mother. "The combined [bathroom] and shower-room is so filthy that one must be careful where one treads; but Daddy says we must expect much worse in Cuyaba."

Jack and Raleigh heard a commotion outside the hotel and saw, in the moonlight, figures parading up and down the city's only good road, singing and dancing. It was the last night of Carnival. Raleigh, who liked to stay out late drinking "several excellent cocktails," joined in the revelry. "I am now by the way quite an enthusiastic dancer," he had earlier informed his brother. "You will probably think me reckless, eh, but still I figured I would have very few chances to dissipate in the next 20 months or so."

On February 23, Fawcett told Jack and Raleigh to load their equipment onto the *Iguatemi*, a small, dirty ship docked along the Paraguay River, which was bound for Cuiabá. Raleigh dubbed the ship "the little tub." It was supposed to hold twenty passengers, but more than twice that many crammed inside. The air reeked of sweat and burning wood from the boiler. There were no private quarters, and to hang their hammocks the men had to jostle for space on the deck. As the boat shoved off, winding northward, Jack practiced his Portuguese with the other passengers, but Raleigh lacked the ear and the patience to pick up more than *faz favor* ("please") and *obrigado* ("thank you"). "Raleigh is a funny chap," Jack wrote. "He calls Portuguese 'this damn jabbering language,' and makes no attempt to learn it. Instead he gets mad at everyone because they don't speak English."

In the evenings, the temperature dropped sharply, and the explorers slept in extra shirts, trousers, and socks. They decided not to shave, and their faces were soon covered with stubble. Jack thought Raleigh looked like "a desperate villain, such as you see in Western thrillers on the movies."

As the boat turned onto the São Lourenço River and then onto the Cuiabá River, the young men were introduced to the spectrum of Amazonian insects. "On Wednesday night they came aboard in clouds," Jack wrote. "The roof of the place where we eat and sleep was black—literally black—with them! We had to sleep with shirts drawn over our heads, leaving no breathing-hole, our feet wrapped in another shirt, and a mackintosh over the body. Termite ants were another pest. They invaded us for about a couple of hours, fluttering round the lamps till their wings dropped off, and then wriggling over floor and table in their millions." Raleigh insisted that the mosquitoes were "almost big enough to hold you down."

The *Iguatemi* crept along the river, moving so slowly that once even a canoe shot past it. The boys wanted to exercise, but there was no room on board, and all they could do was stare at the unending swamps. "Cuyaba will seem like Heaven after this!" Jack wrote his mother. Two days later he added, "Daddy says this is the dullest, most boring river journey he has ever made."

On March 3, eight days after leaving Corumbá, the *Iguatemi* drifted into Cuiabá, which Raleigh called "a God forsaken hole . . . best seen with the eyes closed!"

Fawcett wrote that they had reached the "stepping off point" into the jungle and were waiting several weeks for the rainy season to let up for "the attainment of the great purpose." Although Fawcett hated to linger, he didn't dare leave before the dry season had arrived, as he had done disastrously in 1920 with Holt. And there were still things to do—provisions to be collected and maps to be pored over. Jack and Raleigh tried to break in their new boots by trekking through the surrounding bush. "Raleigh's feet are covered with patches of Johnson's plaster, but he is keener than ever now [that] we are nearing the day of departure," Jack said. They carried their rifles and set up target practice, shooting at objects as if they were jaguars or monkeys. Fawcett had warned them to conserve ammunition, yet they were so excited that they spent twenty cartridges on their first attempt. "[What] a hell of a row!" Jack exclaimed of the noise.

Raleigh boasted that he was a fine shot—"even if I do say so myself."

During meals, the young men consumed additional portions. Jack even broke his vegetarian edict, eating chicken and beef. "We are feeding up now," he told his mother, "and I hope to put on ten pounds before leaving, as we need extra flesh to carry us over hungry periods during the expedition."

An American missionary who was staying in Cuiabá had several issues of *Cosmopolitan*, the popular monthly magazine owned by William Randolph Hearst. Raleigh and Jack swapped some of their books for them, which evoked a world the young men knew they would not see for at least two years. Issues from that period had advertisements for twelve-cent cans of Campbell's Tomato Soup and for the American Telephone & Telegraph Company ("Instead of speech through a partition, there is speech across a continent"), and such reminders of home seemed to make Raleigh "sentimental," as he put it. The magazines also contained several gripping adventure tales, including "The Thrill of Facing Eternity," in which the narrator asked, "What do I know about fear? What do I know about courage? . . . Until actually faced with a crisis no man knows how he will behave."

Rather than confronting their own reservoirs of courage, Jack and Raleigh seemed to prefer to dwell on what they would do after they returned from the expedition. They were sure that the journey would make them rich and famous, but their fantasies remained more those of boys than of men. "We intend to buy motor-cycles and really enjoy a good holiday in Devon, looking up all our friends and visiting the old haunts," Jack said.

One morning they went with Fawcett to purchase pack animals from a local rancher. Though Fawcett complained that he was "cheated" over everything, he acquired four horses and eight donkeys. "The horses being fairly good, but the mules very 'fraco' (weak)," Jack said in a letter home, showing off his newest Portuguese word. Jack and Raleigh immediately gave the animals names: an obstinate mule was Gertrude; another, with a bullet-shaped head, was Dumdum; and a third, forlorn-looking animal was Sorehead. Fawcett also obtained a pair of hunting dogs that were, as he put it, "rejoicing in the names of Pastor and Chulim."

By then, nearly everyone in the remote capital had heard of the famous Englishmen. Some inhabitants regaled Fawcett with legends of hidden cities. One man said that he had recently brought an Indian from the jungle who, upon seeing the churches in Cuiabá, remarked, "This is nothing, in my forest are buildings bigger and loftier by far than this. They have doors and windows of stone. The inside is lit by a great square crystal on a pillar. It shines so brightly as to dazzle the eyes."

Fawcett was grateful for any visions, however preposterous, that might confirm his own. "I have seen no reason to budge a hair's breadth" from the theory of Z, he wrote Nina.

AROUND THIS TIME, Fawcett heard the first news of Dr. Rice's expedition. For several weeks, there had been no reports of the party, which had been exploring a tributary of the Rio Branco, about twelve hundred miles north of Cuiabá. Many feared that the men had vanished. Then an amateur radio operator in Caterham, England, picked up on his wireless receiver Morse signals coming from deep in the Amazon. The operator jotted down the message:

> Progress slow, owing to extremely difficult physical conditions. Personnel expedition numbers over fifty. Unable use hydroplane at present due low water, objects expedition being attained. All well. This message sent by expedition's own wireless. Rice.

Another message reported that Dr. Theodor Koch-Grünberg, the noted anthropologist with the party, had contracted malarial fever and had died. Dr. Rice announced on the wireless that he was about to deploy the hydroplane, although it had to be swept clean of ants and termites and spiderwebs, which covered the control panel and cockpit like volcanic ash.

The men worried what would happen if they had to land in an emergency. Albert William Stevens, a noted balloonist and the expedition's aerial photographer, told the RGS, "If not over a waterway, parachuting would be advisable before the plane crashed in the massive trees of the forest; the only hope of the flyers would then be to find the wreck of their craft, and secure food. With machete and compass, they could perhaps cut their way to the nearest river, build a raft, and escape. A broken arm or leg would mean certain death, of course."

Finally, the men filled the tank with fuel—enough for about four hours—and three members of the expedition boarded the plane; the pilot started the propeller, and the machine roared down the river, hurtling into the sky. Stevens described the explorers' first vision of the jungle from five thousand feet up:

> The palms below, scattered through the forest, looked like hundreds of star-fish at the bottom of an ocean . . . Except for the spirals, blankets, and clouds of mist-like emanations ascending from numerous hidden streams of water, there was nothing in sight but the sombre, seemingly endless forest, premonitory in its silence and vastness.

Usually, the pilot and one other member of the party would fly for about three hours each morning, before the rising temperature outside might cause the engine to overheat. Over several weeks, Dr. Rice and his team surveyed thousands of square miles of the Amazon—an amount inconceivable on foot or even by boat. The men discovered, among other things, that the Parima and the Orinoco rivers did not, as had been suspected, share the same source.

Once, the pilot thought he saw something moving between the trees and dived toward the canopy. There was a cluster of "white" Yanomami Indians. When the plane landed, Dr. Rice tried to establish contact, offering the Indians beads and handkerchiefs; unlike on his previous expedition, the tribesmen accepted his overtures. After spending several hours with the tribe, Dr. Rice and his party began leaving the jungle. The RGS asked the Caterham operator to convey "the congratulations and good wishes of the Society."

The expedition, despite the unfortunate death of Koch-Grünberg, was a historic achievement. In addition to the cartographic discoveries, it had shifted the human vantage point in the Amazon from below the canopy to above, tilting the balance of power that had always favored the jungle over its trespassers. "Those regions where the natives are so hostile or the physical obstacles so great as to effectually bar" entering on foot, Dr. Rice declared, "the airplane passes over easily and quickly." Moreover, the wireless radio had allowed him to keep in contact with the outside world. ("The Brazilian jungle has ceased to be lonely," the *New York Times* proclaimed.) The RGS hailed in a bulletin the first-ever "communication by radio to the Society from an expedition in the field." At the same time, the Society recognized, wistfully, that a Rubicon had been crossed: "Whether it is an advantage to take off the glamour of an expedition into the unknown by reporting daily is a matter on which opinions will differ." Owing to the huge cost of the equipment, the bulkiness of radios, and the lack of safe landing places in most regions of the Amazon, Dr. Rice's methods would not be widely adopted for at least another decade, but he had shown the way.

To Fawcett, though, there was only one piece of news that mattered: his rival had not found Z.

BOUNDING OUT OF the hotel one April morning, Fawcett felt the blazing sun on his face. The dry season had arrived. After nightfall on April 19, he led Raleigh and Jack through the city, where outlaws carrying Winchester .44 rifles often lingered in the doorways of dimly lit cantinas. Bandits had earlier attacked a group of diamond prospectors staying in the same hotel as Fawcett and his party. "[A prospector] and one of the bandits were killed, and two others seriously wounded," Jack told his mother. "The police went to work on the case after a few days, and over a cup of coffee asked the murderers why they did it! Nothing more has happened."

The explorers stopped at the house of John Ahrens, a German diplomat in the region whom they had befriended. Ahrens offered his guests tea and biscuits. Fawcett asked the diplomat if he would relay to Nina and the rest of the world any letters or other news from the expedition that emerged from the jungle. Ahrens indicated that he was pleased to do so, and he later wrote Nina to say that her husband's conversations about Z were so rare and interesting that he had never been happier.

The next morning, under Fawcett's watchful eye, Jack and Raleigh put on their explorer outfits, including lightweight, tear-proof pants and Stetsons. They loaded their .30-caliber rifles and armed themselves with eighteen-inch machetes, which Fawcett had had designed by the best steelmaker in England. A report sent out by NANA was headlined "Unique Outfit for Explorer . . . Product of Years' Experience in Jungle Research. Weight of Utensils Reduced to Last Ounce."

Fawcett hired two native porters and guides to accompany the expedition until the more dangerous terrain, about a hundred miles north. On April 20, a crowd gathered to see the party off. At the crack of whips, the caravan jolted forward, Jack and Raleigh as proud as could be. Ahrens accompanied the explorers for about an hour on his own horse. Then, as he told Nina, he watched them march northward "into a world so far completely uncivilised and unknown by people."

The expedition crossed the *cerrado*, or "dry forest," which was the least difficult part of the journey—the terrain consisted mostly of short, twisting trees and savanna-like grass, where a few ranchers and prospectors had established settlements. Yet, as Fawcett told his wife in a letter, it was "an excellent initiation" for Jack and Raleigh, who picked their way slowly, unaccustomed to the rocky ground and the heat. It was so hot,

Fawcett wrote in a particularly fervid dispatch, that in the Cuiabá River "fish were literally cooked alive."

By twilight, they had trekked seven miles, and Fawcett signaled to set up camp. Jack and Raleigh learned that this meant a race, before darkness enveloped them and the mosquitoes devoured their flesh, to string their hammocks, clean their cuts to prevent infections, collect firewood, and secure the pack animals. Dinner was sardines, rice, and biscuits—a feast compared with what they would eat once they had to survive off the land.

That night, as they slept in their hammocks, Raleigh felt something brushing against him. He awoke in a panic, as if he were being attacked by a jaguar, but it was only one of the mules, which had broken free. After he tied it up, he tried to fall asleep again, but before long dawn broke and Fawcett was shouting for everyone to move out, each person wolfing down a bowl of porridge and half a cup of condensed milk, his rations until supper; then the men were off again, racing to keep up with their leader.

Fawcett increased the pace from seven miles a day to ten miles, then to fifteen. One afternoon, as the explorers approached the Manso River, some forty miles north of Cuiabá, the rest of the expedition became separated from Fawcett. As Jack later wrote to his mother, "Daddy had gone on ahead at such a speed that we lost sight of him altogether." It was just as Costin had feared: there was no one to stop Fawcett. The trail forked, and the Brazilian guides didn't know which way Fawcett had turned. Eventually, Jack noticed indentations from hooves on one of the trails, and gave the order to follow them. Darkness was descending, and the men had to be careful not to lose each other as well. They could hear a sustained roar in the distance. With each step it grew louder, and suddenly the men discerned the rush of water. They had reached the Manso River. Still, Fawcett was nowhere to be found. Jack, assuming command of the party, told Raleigh and one of the guides to fire their rifles in the air. There was no reply. *"Daddy,"* Jack yelled, but all he could hear was the screeching of the forest.

Jack and Raleigh hung their hammocks and made a fire, fearing that Fawcett had been seized by the Kayapó Indians, who inserted large round disks in their lower lips and attacked their enemies with wooden clubs. The Brazilian guides, who recalled vivid accounts of Indian raids, did nothing to calm Jack's and Raleigh's nerves. The men lay awake, listening to the jungle. When the sun rose, Jack ordered everyone to fire more gunshots and to search the surrounding area. Then, as the explorers were eating breakfast, Fawcett appeared on his horse. While looking for rock paintings, he had lost track of the group and had slept on the ground, using his saddle for a pillow. When Nina heard what had happened, she feared how "anxious" they all must have been. She had received a photograph of Jack looking unusually somber, which she had shown to Large. "[Jack] has evidently been thinking about the big job before him," Large told her. She noted later that Jack's pride would keep him going, for he would say to himself, "My father chose me for this."

Fawcett let the expedition remain in camp another day to recover from the ordeal. Huddling under his mosquito net, he composed his dispatches, which from that point on would be "relayed to civilization by Indian runners over a long and perilous route," as editors' notes later explained.

Fawcett described the area as "the tickiest place in the world"; the insects swarmed over everything, like black rain. Several bit Raleigh on his foot, and the irritated flesh became infected—"poisoned," in Jack's phrase. As they pressed on the next day, Raleigh grew more and more gloomy. "It is a saying that one only knows a man well when in the wilds with him," Fawcett told Nina. "Raleigh in place of being gay and energetic, is sleepy and silent."

Jack, in contrast, was gaining in ardor. Nina was right: he seemed to have inherited Fawcett's freakish constitution. Jack wrote that he had packed on several pounds of muscle, "in spite of far less food. Raleigh has lost more than I gained, and it is he who seems to feel most the effects of the journey."

Upon hearing about Jack from her husband, Nina told Large, "I think you will rejoice with me in the knowledge that Jack is turning out so capable, and keeping strong and well. I can see his father is very pleased with him, and needless to say *so am I!*"

Because of Raleigh's condition and the weakened animals, Fawcett, who was more careful not to get too far ahead again, stopped for several days at a cattle-breeding ranch owned by Hermenegildo Galvão, one of the most ruthless farmers in Mato Grosso. Galvão had pushed farther into the frontier than most Brazilians and reportedly had a posse of *bugueiros*, "savage hunters," who were charged with killing Indians who threatened his feudal empire. Galvão was not accustomed to visitors, but he welcomed the explorers into his large red-brick home. "It was quite obvious from his manners that Colonel Fawcett was a gentleman and a man of engaging personality," Galvão later told a reporter.

For several days, the explorers remained there, eating and resting. Galvão was curious about what had lured the Englishmen into such wilderness. As Fawcett described his vision of Z, he removed from his belongings a strange object covered in cloth. He carefully unwrapped it, revealing the stone idol Haggard had given to him. He carried it with him like a talisman.

The three Englishmen were soon on their way again, heading east, toward Bakairí Post, where in 1920 the Brazilian government had set up a garrison—"the last point of civilization," as the settlers referred to it. Occasionally, the forest opened up, and they could see the blinding sun and blue-tinged mountains in the distance. The trail became more difficult, and the men descended steep, mud-slicked gorges and traversed rock-strewn rapids. One river was too dangerous for the animals to swim across with the cargo. Fawcett noticed a canoe, abandoned, on the opposite bank and said that the expedition could use it to transport the gear, but that someone would need to swim over and get it—a feat involving, as Fawcett put it, "considerable danger, being made worse by a sudden violent thunderstorm."

Jack volunteered and began to strip. Though he later admitted that he was "scared stiff," he checked his body for cuts that might attract piranhas and dived in, thrashing his arms and legs as the currents tossed him about. When he emerged on the opposite bank, he climbed in the canoe and paddled back across—his father greeting him proudly.

A month after the explorers left Cuiabá, and after what Fawcett described as "a test of patience and endurance for the greater trials" ahead, the men arrived at Bakairí Post. The settlement consisted of about twenty ramshackle huts, cordoned off by barbed wire, to protect against aggressive tribes. (Three years later, another explorer described the outpost as "a pinprick on the map: isolated, desolate, primitive and God forsaken.") The Bakairí tribe was one of the first in the region that the government had tried to "acculturate," and Fawcett was appalled by what he called "the Brazilian methods of civilizing the Indian tribes." In a letter to one of his sponsors in the United States, he noted, "The Bakairís have been dying out ever since they became civilized. There are only about 150 of them." He went on, "They have in part been brought here to plant rice, manioc . . . which is sent to Cuiabá, where it fetches, at present, high prices. The Bakairís are not paid, are raggedly clothed, mainly in khaki govt. uniforms, and there is a general squalor and lack of hygiene which is making the whole of them sick."

Fawcett was informed that a Bakairí girl had recently fallen ill. He often tried to treat the natives with his medical kit, but, unlike Dr. Rice, his knowledge was limited, and there was nothing he could do to save her. "They say the Bacairys are dying off on account of fetish [witchcraft], for there is a fetish man in the village who hates them," Jack wrote. "Only yesterday a little girl died—of fetish, they say!"

The Brazilian in charge of the post, Valdemira, put the explorers up in the newly constructed schoolhouse. The men soaked themselves in the river, washing away the grime and sweat. "We have all clipped our beards, and feel better without them," Jack said.

Members of other remote tribes occasionally visited Bakairí Post to obtain goods, and Jack and Raleigh soon saw something that astonished them: "about eight wild Indians, absolutely stark naked," as Jack wrote to his mother. The Indians carried seven-foot-long bows with six-foot arrows. "To Jack's great delight we have seen the first of the wild Indians here—naked savages from the Xingu," Fawcett wrote Nina.

Jack and Raleigh hurried out to meet them. "We gave them some guava cheese," Jack wrote, and "they liked it immensely."

Jack tried to conduct a rudimentary *autopsis*. "They are small people, about five feet two inches in height, and very well built," he wrote of the Indians. "They eat only fish and vegetables—never meat. One woman had a very fine necklace of tiny discs cut from snail shells, which must have required tremendous patience to make."

Raleigh, whom Fawcett had designated as the expedition's photographer, set up a camera and took pictures of the Indians. In one shot, Jack stood beside them, to demonstrate "the comparative sizes"; the Indians came up to his shoulders.

In the evening, the three explorers went to the mud hut where the Indians were staying. The only light inside was from a fire, and the air was filled with smoke. Fawcett unpacked a ukulele and Jack took out a piccolo that they had brought from England. (Fawcett told Nina that "music was a great comfort 'in the wilds,' and might even save a solitary man from insanity.") As the Indians gathered around them, Jack and Fawcett played a concert late into the night, the sounds wafting through the village.

On May 19, a fresh, cool day, Jack woke up exhilarated—it was his twenty-second birthday. "I have never felt so well," he wrote to his mother. For the occasion, Fawcett dropped his prohibition against liquor, and the three explorers celebrated with a bottle of Brazilian-made alcohol. The next morning, they prepared the equipment and the pack animals. To the north of the post, the men could see several imposing mountains and the jungle. It was, Jack wrote, "absolutely unexplored country."

The expedition headed straight for terra incognita. Before them were no clear paths, and little light filtered through the canopy. They struggled to see not just in front of them but above them, where most predators lurked. The men's feet sank in mud holes. Their hands burned from wielding machetes. Their skin bled from mosquitoes. Even Fawcett confessed to Nina, "Years tell, in spite of the spirit of enthusiasm."

Although Raleigh's foot had healed, his other one became infected, and when he removed his sock a large patch of skin peeled off. He seemed to be unraveling; he had already suffered from jaundice, his arm was swollen, and he felt, as he put it, "bilious."

Like his father, Jack was prone to contempt for others' frailty, and complained to his mother that his friend was unable to share his burden of work—he rode on a horse, with his shoe off—and that he was always scared and sullen.

The jungle widened the fissures that had been evident since Raleigh's romance on the boat. Raleigh, overwhelmed by the insects, the heat, and the pain in his foot, lost interest in "the Quest." He no longer thought about returning as a hero: all he wanted, he muttered, was to open a small business and to settle down with a family. ("The Fawcetts can have all my share of the notoriety and be welcome to it!" he wrote his brother.) When Jack talked of the archaeological importance of Z, Raleigh shrugged and said, "That's too deep for me."

"I wish [Raleigh] had more brains, as I cannot discuss any of this with him as he knows nothing of anything," Jack wrote. "We can only converse about Los Angeles or Seaton. What he will do during a year at 'Z' I don't know."

"I wish to *hell* you were here," Raleigh told his brother, adding, "You know there is a saying which I believe is true: 'Two's company—three's none.' It shows itself quite often with me now!" Jack and Fawcett, he said, maintained a "sense of inferiority for others. Consequently at times I feel very 'out of everything.' Of course I do not outwardly show it . . . but still, as I have said before, I feel 'awful lonesome' for real friendship."

After nine days, the explorers hacked their way to Dead Horse

Camp, where the men could still see the "white bones" from Fawcett's old pack animal. The men were approaching the territory of the warlike Suyás and Kayapós. An Indian once described to a reporter a Kayapó ambush of his tribe. He and a few other villagers, the reporter wrote, fled across a river and "witnessed throughout the night the macabre dance of their enemies around their slaughtered brothers." For three days, the invaders remained, playing wooden flutes and dancing among the corpses. After the Kayapós finally departed, the few villagers who had escaped across the river rushed back to their settlement: not a single person was alive. "The women, who they thought would have been spared, lay face up, their lifeless bodies in an advanced state of putrefaction, their legs spread apart by wooden struts forced between the knees." In a dispatch, Fawcett described the Kayapós as an aggressive "lot of stick-throwers who cut off and kill wandering individuals . . . Their only weapon is a short club like a policeman's billy"—which, he added, they deploy very skillfully.

After passing through the territory of the Suyás and Kayapós, the expedition would turn eastward and confront the Xavante, who were perhaps even more formidable. In the late eighteenth century, many in the tribe had been contacted by the Portuguese and moved into villages, where they received mass baptisms. Devastated by epidemics and brutalized by Brazilian soldiers, they eventually fled back into the jungle near the River of Death. A nineteenth-century German traveler wrote that "from that time onwards [the Xavante] no longer trusted any white man . . . These abused people have therefore changed from compatriots into the most dangerous and determined enemies. They generally kill anyone they can easily catch." Several years after Fawcett's journey, members of the Indian Protection Service tried to make contact with the Xavante, only to return to their base camp and discover the naked corpses of four of their colleagues. One was still clutching in his hand gifts for the Indians.

In spite of the risks, Fawcett was confident—after all, he had always succeeded where others failed. "It is obviously dangerous to penetrate large hordes of Indians traditionally hostile," he wrote, "but I believe in my mission and in its purpose. The rest does not worry me, for I have seen a good deal of Indians and know what to do and what not to do." He added, "I believe our little party of three white men will make friends with them all."

The guides, who were already feverish, were reluctant to go any farther, and Fawcett decided that the time had come to send them back. He selected half a dozen or so of the strongest animals to keep for a few more days. Then the explorers would have to proceed with their few provisions on their backs.

Fawcett pulled Raleigh aside and encouraged him to return with the guides. As Fawcett had written to Nina, "I suspect constitutional weakness, and fear that we shall be handicapped by him." After this point, Fawcett explained, there would be no way to carry him out. Raleigh insisted that he would see it through. Perhaps he remained loyal to Jack, in spite of everything. Perhaps he didn't want to be seen as a coward. Or perhaps he was simply afraid to turn back without them.

Fawcett finished his last letters and dispatches. He wrote that he would try to get out other communiqués in the coming year or so, but added that it was unlikely. As he noted in one of his final articles, "By the time this dispatch is printed, we shall have long since disappeared into the unknown."

After folding up his missives, Fawcett gave them to the guides. Raleigh had earlier written to his "dearest Mother" and family. "I shall look forward to seeing you again in old Cal when I return," he said. And he told his brother bravely, "Keep cheerful and things will turn up alright as they have for me."

The explorers gave a final wave to the Brazilians, then turned and headed deeper into the jungle. In his last words to his wife, Fawcett wrote, "You need have no fear of any failure."

The Last
Eyewitness

"Can you get the GPS to work?" Paolo asked.

I was sitting in the backseat of a four-wheel-drive Mitsubishi truck, fiddling with a Global Positioning System in an attempt to obtain readings of our coordinates. We were heading north—that much I knew—with a driver whom we had hired when we rented the pickup. Paolo had told me that we would need a powerful truck and a professional driver if we were to have any chance of completing our journey, especially in the rainy season. "This is the worst time of year," he said. "The roads are—how do you say in English?—*shit.*"

When I explained my mission to our driver, he asked me when the British colonel had disappeared.

"Nineteen twenty-five," I said.

"And you want to find him in the jungle?"

"Not exactly."

"Are you one of his descendants?"

"No."

He seemed to think about this for a long moment, then said, "Very well," and began cheerfully to load our gear, which included hammocks, rope, mosquito netting, water-purifying tablets, a satellite phone, antibiotics, and malarial pills. On our way out of Cuiabá, we also picked up a friend of Paolo's, a descendant of a Bakairí chief named Taukane Bakairí. (In Brazil, the last names of Indians are typically the same as that of their tribe.) Taukane, who was in his mid-forties and had a handsome, round face, wore Levi's and a baseball cap. He had been educated by missionaries, and though he now lived mostly in Cuiabá, he continued to represent his tribe's political interests. "I am what you might call an ambassador," he told me. And, in exchange for a "gift" of two tires for a communal tractor, he had agreed to take us to his village, the last place that Fawcett had incontrovertibly been seen. ("If it were up to me, I would take you for free," Taukane said. "But all Indians must now be capitalists. We have no choice.")

Upon leaving the city, we entered the central plains of Brazil, which mark the transition from dry forest to rain forest. After a while, a plateau came into view: Martian red in color, it spanned more than two thousand square miles, an endless tabletop that reached into the clouds. We stopped at its base, and Paolo said, "Come, I show you something."

We left the truck and climbed a steep, rocky slope. The ground was moist from a recent rainstorm, and we used our hands and knees to ascend, crawling over holes where snakes and armadillos had burrowed.

"Where are we going?" I asked Paolo, who had another cigarette clamped between his teeth.

"You Americans are always impatient," he said.

Lightning streaked the sky and a thin mist descended, making the ground more slippery. Rocks gave way under our feet, clapping as they hit the ground, fifty yards below.

"Almost there," Paolo said.

He helped to pull me up a ledge, and as I got to my feet, covered in mud, he pointed at another ridge, a few yards away, and said, "Now you see!"

Jutting into the sky was a cracked stone column. I blinked in the rain—in fact, there was not just one but several columns in a row, as in a Greek ruin. There was also a large archway, both sides of it intact, and behind it was a dazzlingly large tower. They looked like what the *bandeirante* had described in 1753.

"What is it?" I asked.

"Stone city."

"Who built it?"

"It is—how do you say?—an illusion."

"That?" I said, pointing to one of the columns.

"It was made by nature, by erosion. But many people who see it think it is a lost city, like Z."

In 1925, Dr. Rice had seen similarly eroded cliffs, in Roraima, Brazil, and thought they looked like "ruined architecture."

As we returned to the car and headed north, toward the jungle, Paolo said we would find out soon if Z were such a mirage. We eventually turned onto BR-163, one of the most treacherous roads in South America. Built in 1970 by the Brazilian government in an effort to open up the country's interior, it extends more than a thousand miles, from Cuiabá to the Amazon River. It was designated on our map as a major highway, but almost all the asphalt from its two lanes had been washed away during the rainy season, leaving behind a combination of ditches and puddle-filled gullies. Our driver sometimes chose to ignore the road altogether and steer along the rocky banks and fields, where herds of cattle occasionally parted in our midst.

As we passed the Manso River, where Fawcett had gotten separated from the rest of the group and where Raleigh had been bitten by ticks, I kept looking out the window, expecting to see the first signs of a fearsome jungle. Instead, the terrain looked like Nebraska—perpetual plains that faded into the horizon. When I asked Taukane where the forest was, he said, simply, "Gone."

A moment later, he pointed to a fleet of diesel-belching trucks heading in the opposite direction, carrying sixty-foot logs.

"Only the Indians respect the forest," Paolo said. "The white people cut it all down." Mato Grosso, he went on, was being transformed into domesticated farmland, much of it dedicated to soybeans. In Brazil alone, the Amazon has, over the last four decades, lost some two hundred and seventy thousand square miles of its original forest cover—an area bigger than France. Despite government efforts to reduce deforestation, in just five months in 2007 as much as two thousand seven hundred square miles were destroyed, a region larger than the state of Delaware. Countless animals and plants, many of them with potential medicinal purposes, have vanished. Because the Amazon generates half its own rainfall through moisture that rises into the atmosphere, the devastation has begun to change the region's ecology, contributing to droughts that destroy the jungle's ability to sustain itself. And few places have been as ravaged as Mato Grosso, where the state governor, Blairo Maggi, is one of the largest soybean producers in the world. "I don't feel the slightest guilt over what we are doing here," Maggi told the *New York Times* in 2003. "We're talking about an area larger than Europe that has barely been touched, so there is nothing at all to get worried about."

The latest economic boom, meanwhile, has produced another of the Amazon's convulsions of violence. The Brazilian Transport Ministry has said that loggers along BR-163 employ "the highest concentration of slave labor in the world." Indians are frequently driven off their land, enslaved, or murdered. On February 12, 2005, while Paolo and I were making our journey into the jungle, several gunmen, allegedly on the payroll of a rancher in the state of Pará, approached a seventy-three-year-old American nun who defended the rights of Indians. As the men aimed their guns, she removed her Bible and began to read from the Gospel of Saint Matthew: "Blessed are those who hunger and thirst for justice, for they shall be satisfied." The gunmen unloaded six bullets into her, leaving her body facedown in the mud.

James Petersen, the distinguished scientist from the University of Vermont who had trained the archaeologist Michael Heckenberger and had been extremely helpful in planning my trip, told me when we had last spoken, a few months earlier, that he was excited because he was heading into the Amazon to conduct research near Manaus. "Maybe you can visit me after the Xingu," he said. That would be wonderful, I responded. But I soon discovered that in August, while he was with the Brazilian archaeologist Eduardo Neves at a restaurant in a village along the Amazon River, a pair of bandits, allegedly working for a former police officer, stormed in to rob the place. One of the thieves opened fire, hitting Petersen in the stomach. He fell to the ground and said, "I can't breathe." Neves told him he would be okay, but by the time they arrived at a hospital, Petersen had died. He was fifty-one years old.

From BR-163, we veered onto a smaller dirt road, which went east, toward Bakairí Post. We passed close to where Fawcett had stayed with the cattle rancher Galvão, and we decided to see if we could find his manor. In letters, Fawcett had said that the ranch was known as Rio Novo, and that name was marked on several current maps. After nearly four hours of bone-jarring bumps, we came upon a rusty sign at a fork in the road—"Rio Novo"—with an arrow pointing left.

"Look at that," Paolo said.

We crossed a wobbly, wooden-slatted bridge over a river. The bridge creaked under the weight of the truck, and we looked down at the torrent of water, fifty feet below.

"How many mules and horses did the *coronel* have?" Paolo asked, trying to picture Fawcett's crossing.

"A dozen or so," I said. "According to his letters, Galvão replaced some of the weakest animals and gave him a dog . . . which supposedly returned to the farm, several months after Fawcett vanished."

"It wandered back on its own?" Paolo asked.

"That's what Galvão said. He also said something about some swallows he saw rise from the forest in the east, which he thought had to be some kind of sign from Fawcett."

For the first time, we entered a swath of dense forest. Though there was no farm in sight, we came across a mud hut with a thatched roof. Inside was an old Indian sitting on a tree stump with a wooden cane in his hand. He was barefoot and wore dusty slacks without a shirt. Behind him, hanging on the wall, was the skin of a jaguar and a picture of the Virgin Mary. Taukane asked him, in the Bakairí language, if there was a cattle-breeding ranch known as Rio Novo. The man spit when he heard the name and waved his cane toward the door. "That way," he said.

Another Indian, who was younger, appeared and said that he would show us the way. We got back in the car and drove down an overgrown path, the branches clapping against the windshield. When we couldn't drive any farther, our guide hopped out, and we followed him through the forest as he slashed at the creepers and vines with a machete. Several times he paused, studied the tops of the trees, and took a few paces east or west. Finally, he stopped.

We looked around—there was nothing but a cocoon of trees. "Where's Rio Novo?" Paolo asked.

Our guide lifted his machete over his head and slammed it into the ground. It hit something hard. "Right here," he said.

We looked down and, to our disbelief, saw a row of cracked bricks.

"This is where the entrance to the manor used to be," the guide said, adding, "It was very big."

We began to fan out in the forest, as rain started to fall again, looking for signs of the great Galvão farm.

"Over here!" Paolo cried. He was a hundred feet away, standing by a crumbling brick wall nestled in vines. The farm had been consumed by jungle in just a few decades, and I wondered how actual ancient ruins could possibly survive in such a hostile environment. For the first time, I had some sense of how it might be possible for the remnants of a civilization simply to disappear.

WHEN WE RETURNED to the road, the sun had begun to set. In our excitement, we had lost track of the time. We hadn't eaten since five-thirty in the morning and had nothing in the truck except a warm bottle of water and some crackers. (Earlier in the trip we had devoured my packets of freeze-dried food, Paolo saying, "Astronauts really eat this stuff?") As we drove through the night, lightning flashed in the distance, illuminating the emptiness around us. Taukane eventually nodded off, and Paolo and I became engaged in what had become our favorite diversion—trying to imagine what had happened to Fawcett and his party after they left Dead Horse Camp.

"I can see them starving to death," Paolo, who seemed focused on his own hunger, said. "Very slowly and very painfully."

Paolo and I were not alone in trying to conjure a denouement to the Fawcett saga. Dozens of writers and artists had imagined an ending where none existed, like the earlier cartographers who had conceived of much of the world without ever seeing it. There were radio and stage plays about the mystery. There was the screenplay "Find Colonel Fawcett," which was later the extremely loose basis for the 1941 movie *Road to Zanzibar*, with Bing Crosby and Bob Hope. There were comic books, including one in the *Adventures of Tintin* series; in the story, a missing explorer based on Fawcett rescues Tintin from a poisonous snake in the jungle. ("Everybody thinks you're dead," Tintin tells the explorer, who says, "I've decided never to return to civilization. I'm happy here.")

Fawcett also continued to inspire quest novelists. In 1956, the popular Belgian adventure author Charles-Henri Dewisme, who used the pseudonym Henry Verne, wrote *Bob Moran and the Fawcett Mystery*. In the novel, the hero Moran investigates the Amazon explorer's disappearance, and although he fails to reveal what happened to him, he uncovers the lost City of Z, making "Fawcett's dream come true."

Fawcett even appears in the 1991 novel *Indiana Jones and the Seven Veils*, one of a series of books written to capitalize on the success of the 1981 blockbuster movie *Raiders of the Lost Ark*. In the novel's convoluted plot, Indiana Jones—though insisting, "I'm an archeologist, not a private detective"—sets out to find Fawcett. He uncovers fragments of Fawcett's journal from his last expedition, which says, "My son, lame from a bad ankle and feverish from malaria, turned back some weeks ago, and I sent our last guide with him. God save them. I followed a river upstream . . . I ran out of water, and for the next two or three days my only source of liquid was the dew I licked from leaves. How I questioned myself over and over about my decision to go on alone! I called myself a fool, an idiot, a madman." Jones locates Fawcett and discovers that the Amazon explorer has found his magical city. After the two amateur archaeologists are taken prisoner by a hostile tribe, Jones, whip in hand, and Fawcett escape by plunging into the River of Death.

Paolo and I went through several more fantastical scenarios—Fawcett and his party had their bodies taken over by worms like Murray, contracted elephantiasis, were poisoned by lethal frogs—before we both fell asleep in the car. The next morning, we drove up a small mountainside to reach Bakairí Post. It had taken Fawcett a month to get here from Cuiabá. It took us two days.

Bakairí Post had grown, and more than eight hundred Indians now lived in the area. We went to the largest village, where several dozen one-story houses were organized in rows around a dusty plaza. Most of the houses were made of clay and bamboo and had thatched roofs, though some of the newer ones had concrete walls and tin roofs that clinked in the rain. The village, while still unmistakably poor, now had a well, a tractor, satellite dishes, and electricity.

When we arrived, nearly all the men, young and old, were away hunting, in preparation for a ritual to celebrate the corn harvest. But Taukane said that there was someone we had to meet. He took us to a house abutting the plaza, near a row of fragrant mango trees. We entered a small room with a single electric lightbulb hanging overhead and several wooden benches along the walls.

Before long, a tiny, stooped woman appeared through a back door. She held a child's hand for support and moved slowly toward us, as if leaning into a strong wind. She wore a floral cotton dress and had long gray hair, which framed a face so wizened that her eyes were almost invisible. She had a wide smile, revealing a majestic set of white teeth. Taukane explained that the woman was the oldest member of the village and had seen Fawcett and his expedition come through. "She is probably the last living person to have encountered them," he said.

She sat down on a chair, her bare feet hardly reaching the floor. Using Taukane and Paolo to translate from English into Portuguese and then into Bakairi, I asked her how old she was. "I don't know my exact age," she said. "But I was born around 1910." She continued, "I was just a little girl when the three outsiders came to stay in our village. I remember them because I had never seen people so white and with such long beards. My mother said, 'Look, the Christians are here!' "

She said that the three explorers had set up camp inside the village's new school, which no longer exists. "It was the nicest building," she said. "We didn't know who they were, but we knew they must be important because they slept in the school." In a letter, I recalled, Jack Fawcett had mentioned sleeping in a school. She added, "I remember that they were tall, so tall. And one of them carried a funny pack. He looked like a tapir."

I asked her what the village was like then. She said that by the time Fawcett and his men had arrived everything was changing. Brazilian military officials, she recalled, "told us we had to wear clothes, and they gave us each a new name." She added, "My real name was Comaeda Bakairi, but they told me I was now Laurinda. So I became Laurinda." She recalled the widespread sickness that Fawcett had described in his letters. "Bakairi people would wake up with coughs and go to the river to clean themselves, but it didn't help," she said.

After a while, Laurinda got up and stepped outside. Accompanying her, we could see, in the distance, the mountains that Jack had stared at with such wonder. "The three went in that direction," she said. "Over those peaks. People said there were no white people over those mountains, but that is where they said they were going. We waited for them to come back, but they never did."

I asked her if she had heard of any cities on the other side of the mountains that the Indians may have built centuries ago. She said she didn't know of any, but she pointed to the walls of her house and said that her ancestors had spoken of Bakairí houses that had been much bigger and more spectacular. "They were made of palm leaves from the *buriti* trees and were twice as high and so beautiful," she said.

Some of the hunters returned, carrying the carcasses of deer and anteaters and boars. In the plaza, a government official was setting up a large outdoor movie screen. I was told that a documentary would be shown teaching the Bakairís the meaning of the corn-harvest ritual that they were about to celebrate, which was part of their creation myth. Whereas the government had once tried to strip the Bakairís of their traditions, it was now attempting to preserve them. The old woman watched the proceedings from her doorstep. "The new generation still performs some of the old ceremonies, but they are not as rich or as beautiful," she said. "They do not care about the crafts or the dances. I try to tell them the old stories, but they are not interested. They do not understand that this is who we are."

Before we said goodbye, she remembered something else about Fawcett. For years, she said, other people came from far away to ask about the missing explorers. She stared at me, her narrow eyes widening. "What is it that these white people did?" she asked. "Why is it so important for their tribe to find them?"

22

DEAD OR ALIVE

The world waited for news. "Any day now may bring a cable from my husband announcing that he is safe and is returning with" Jack and Raleigh, Nina Fawcett told a reporter in 1927, two years after the party was last heard from. Elsie Rimell, who corresponded frequently with Nina, echoed her sentiments: "I believe firmly that my boy and those he is with will come back out of that wilderness."

Nina, who was living in Madeira with her sixteen-year-old daughter, Joan, beseeched the Royal Geographical Society not to lose confidence in her husband and proudly circulated one of Jack's last letters describing his journey into the wilderness. "I think it is quite interesting, as being the first experience of the kind as seen by a boy of twenty-two," she said. Once, when Joan was competing in a long-distance swimming race in the ocean, she told Nina, "Mother! I feel I must succeed, because if I succeed today Daddy will succeed in finding what he is searching for, and if I fail—they will fail." To everyone's astonishment, she won. Brian, who was then twenty and working at the railroad company in Peru, assured his mother that there was no reason to worry. "Father has got to his goal," he said, "and is staying there as long as possible."

By the spring of 1927, however, anxieties had become widespread; as a North American Newspaper Alliance bulletin declared, "Fear of Fawcett Fate Grows." Theories abounded over what might have happened to the explorers. "Have they been killed by the warlike savages, some of them cannibals?" one newspaper asked. "Did they perish in the rapids . . . or have they starved to death in this all but foodless region?" A popular theory was that the explorers were being held hostage by a tribe—a relatively common practice. (Several decades later, when Brazilian authorities approached the Txukahamei tribe for the first time, they found half a dozen white captives.)

In September 1927, Roger Courteville, a French engineer, announced that while traveling near the source of the Paraguay River, in Mato Grosso, he had discovered Fawcett and his companions living not as hostages but as hermits. "Explorer Called Dupe of Jungle's Sorcery: Fawcett Forgetting World in Paradise of Birds, Wild Cattle and Game," the *Washington Post* reported. Though some sympathized with Fawcett's apparent desire to "escape from a mechanical age and . . . from dank subway platforms and sunless tenements," as one American newspaper editorial put it, others alleged that the explorer had perpetrated one of the greatest hoaxes in history.

Brian Fawcett, who had rushed to meet with Courteville, thought he "described Daddy exactly." Yet, with each new telling, Courteville changed both his story and the spelling of his own name, and Nina ferociously defended Fawcett's reputation. "I was boiling over with indignation at the slur cast on my husband's honour," she wrote to the RGS, and informed Courteville, "As the story grew and changed, there came an element of evil and malice into it. But thank God, I, [Fawcett's] wife, saw the discrepancies of the published statements." By the time she had finished her campaign against the Frenchman, almost no one placed any credence in him or his story.

Still, the question remained: Where were Fawcett and his young companions? Nina was confident that her husband, having survived for years in the jungle, was alive. But, like Elsie Rimell, she realized now that something terrible must have happened to the expedition—most likely that the men had been kidnapped by Indians. "One cannot tell what hopelessness and despair might do with those boys," Nina said.

Just as her concerns were mounting, a tall, impeccably dressed man appeared at her doorstep in Madeira. It was Fawcett's longtime rival Dr. Alexander Hamilton Rice. He had come to console her, and assured her that even if the expedition had been taken hostage Fawcett would find a way to escape. The one person you need not worry about in the jungle is the colonel, Dr. Rice said.

Nina had so far resisted sending a rescue team, insisting that Fawcett and her son would rather die than have others lose their lives, but now, in her growing panic, she asked the doctor if he would be willing to go. "No better man could be selected to lead such an expedition," she later said. To the shock of many of his colleagues, however, Dr. Rice decided to retire from exploring. Perhaps, at the age of fifty, he felt too old, especially after seeing what had happened to his seemingly invulnerable rival. Perhaps Dr. Rice's wife, who had lost her first husband and son in a tragic accident, prevailed upon him not to go back. Or perhaps he simply felt that he had accomplished everything he could as an explorer.

The Royal Geographical Society, meanwhile, declared in 1927 that "we hold ourselves in readiness to help any competent and well-accredited" search party. Though the Society warned that if Fawcett "could not penetrate and push through, much less can anyone else," it was deluged with hundreds of letters from volunteers. One wrote, "I am thirty-six years of age. Practically Malaria-proof. Stand 5′11″ in my socks and am as hard as nails." Another said, "I am prepared to sacrifice all, including my life."

A few volunteers sought to escape a dreary home life. ("My wife and I have . . . decided that separation for a couple of years will do us both worlds of good.") Some hoped to attain fame and fortune, like Henry Morton Stanley, who had located Livingstone five decades earlier. Others were simply drawn to the heroic nature of the quest—to see, as one put it, "whether there is the making of a man in me, or just clay." A young Welshman, who offered to enlist with his friends, wrote, "We consider that there is a greater measure of heroism in this quiet adventure than, for example, in Lindbergh's spectacular triumph."

In February 1928, George Miller Dyott, a forty-five-year-old member of the Royal Geographical Society, launched the first major rescue effort. Born in New York—his father was British and his mother American—he had test piloted airplanes not long after the Wright brothers and was among the first ever to fly at night. After serving as a squadron commander during World War I, he had given up flying to become an explorer, and though he did not quite fit the image of a rugged adventurer—he was five feet seven and weighed only a hundred and forty pounds—he had trekked across the Andes more than a half-dozen times and ventured through parts of the Amazon. (He had navigated the River of Doubt to confirm Teddy Roosevelt's once-disputed claims.) He had also been held captive for several weeks by an Amazonian tribe that shrank its enemies' heads.

For the media, Fawcett's disappearance had only contributed to what one writer called a "romantic story which builds newspaper empires"— and few were as adept at keeping the story ablaze as Dyott. A former managing director of a company called Travel Films, he was one of the earliest explorers to bring along motion-picture cameras, and he knew instinctively how to strike a pose and talk like a character in a B movie.

The North American Newspaper Alliance sponsored his rescue effort, which it advertised as "an adventure that makes the blood race . . . Romance, mystery—and Peril!" Despite protests from the RGS that the publicity was threatening the expedition's objective, Dyott planned to file daily dispatches with a shortwave radio and to film his journey. To succeed, Dyott, who had once met Fawcett, claimed that he would need "the intuition of Sherlock Holmes" and "the skill of a big-game hunter." He pictured Fawcett and his companions "camped in some remote corner of the primeval forest, unable to come or go. Their reserve food supply must long since have been exhausted; their clothing torn to shreds or rotted to pieces." In such a prolonged "hand-to-hand" combat with the wilderness, Dyott added, it was only Fawcett's "supreme courage that will have held his party together and instilled in them the will to live."

Like Fawcett, Dyott had developed over the years his own idiosyncratic methods of exploring. He believed, for instance, that diminutive men—men, that is to say, built like himself—were best able to endure in the jungle. "A big man has to exert so much energy to carry his bulk that he has no surplus," Dyott told reporters, and he would be "difficult to stow in a canoe."

Dyott posted an advertisement in several American newspapers seeking a volunteer who was "small, spare, of wiry build." The *Los Angeles Times* broadcast his appeal under the headline "Dyott Needs Young Unmarried Man for Perilous Jungle Trip in Search for Scientist: Applicant Must Be Single, Quiet and Youthful." Within days, he received offers from twenty thousand people. "They have come from all over the world," Dyott told reporters. "England, Ireland, France, Germany, Holland, Belgium, Sweden, Norway, Denmark, Peru, Mexico—all are represented. Letters have come from Alaska, too." He noted, "There are applicants in all ranks of society . . . There are letters from lawyers, physicians, real estate dealers, steeplejacks . . . From Chicago an acrobat wrote, and a wrestler." Dyott hired three secretaries to help him sift through the applications. The *Independent*, an American weekly newspaper, marveled, "Perhaps if there were a sufficient number of jungles available and enough expeditions to go round, we would see the spectacle of our whole population marching off in search of lost explorers, ancient civilizations, and something which it vaguely felt was missing in its life." Nina told the RGS that the outpouring was a "great compliment" to the enduring reputation of Colonel Fawcett.

One of those who applied to join the expedition was Roger Rimell,

Raleigh's brother, who was now thirty years old. "I am *most* anxious naturally," he informed Dyott, "and do consider I am as entitled to go as much as anyone." Elsie Rimell was so desperate to find Raleigh that she consented, saying, "I know of no greater help I can give them than to offer the services of my one remaining son."

Dyott, however, not wanting to take someone with so little experience, politely declined. Several adventurous ladies also applied, but Dyott said, "I can't take a woman." In the end, he chose four hardened outdoorsmen who could operate a wireless radio and a movie camera in the jungle.

Dyott had strictly enforced a ban on married men, insisting that they were accustomed to "creature comforts" and "always thinking about their wives." But, on the eve of the party's departure from New York, he violated his own edict and married a woman nearly half his age, Persis Stevens Wright, whom the newspapers portrayed as a "Long Island society girl." The couple planned to honeymoon during the expedition's voyage to Rio. New York City's mayor, Jimmy Walker, who came to bid the expedition farewell, told Dyott that his bride's consent to his risking his life in order to save the lives of others was "a display of unselfish courage of which the whole nation should be proud."

On February 18, 1928, in the midst of a blizzard, Dyott and his party drove to the same piers in Hoboken, New Jersey, where Fawcett had departed with Jack and Raleigh three years earlier. Dyott's group was preparing to board the SS *Voltaire* when an anxious middle-aged woman appeared, bundled against the storm. It was Elsie Rimell. She had flown from California to meet with Dyott, whose expedition, she said, "fills me with new hope and courage." She handed him a small package—a present for her son Raleigh.

During the voyage to Brazil, the ship's crew dubbed the explorers the "Knights of the Round Table." A banquet was held in their honor, and special menus were printed that listed each of the explorers by nicknames, such as "King Arthur" and "Sir Galahad." The ship's purser declared, "On behalf of your noble band of knights allow me to wish you Cheerio, good luck and Godspeed."

After the *Voltaire* reached Rio, Dyott bade his wife farewell and headed with his men to the frontier. There he recruited a small army of Brazilian helpers and Indian guides, and the party soon grew to twenty-six members and required seventy-four oxen and mules to transport more than three tons of food and gear. A reporter later described the party as a "Cecil B. DeMille safari." Brazilians began to refer to it as the "suicide club."

In June, the expedition arrived at Bakairí Post, where a group of Kayapós had recently attacked and killed several inhabitants. (Dyott described the outpost as "the dregs of civilization mixing with the scum of the wilds.") While camping there, Dyott made what he considered a breakthrough: he met an Indian named Bernardino, who said that he had served as Fawcett's guide down the Kurisevo River, one of the headwaters of the Xingu. In exchange for gifts, Bernardino agreed to lead Dyott as far as he had taken Fawcett's party, and, shortly after they departed, Dyott spotted Y-shaped marks carved into the trunks of trees—a possible sign of Fawcett's former presence. "Fawcett's trail loomed largely before us and, like a pack of hounds on the scent, we were in full cry," Dyott wrote.

At night, Dyott sent his dispatches over the radio, and they were often passed on to NANA by the Radio Relay League, a network of amateur operators in the United States. Each new item was trumpeted in international bulletins: "Dyott Nearing Jungle Ordeal"; "Dyott Picks Up Fawcett Trail"; "Dyott Finds New Clew." John J. Whitehead, a member of the expedition, wrote in his diary, "How different would the story of Stanley and Livingstone been written, if they had possessed radio." Many people around the world tuned in, mesmerized. "I first heard of [the expedition] on my crystal set when I was only eleven years old," Loren McIntyre, an American who went on to become an acclaimed Amazon explorer himself, later recalled.

Listeners vicariously faced the sudden terrors that confronted the party. One night Dyott reported:

We came across tracks in the soft ground, tracks of human feet. We stopped and examined them. There must have been thirty or forty persons in a single band. After a few moments one of our Bakairí Indians turned and said in an expressionless voice, "Kayapós."

After trekking nearly a month northward from Bakairí Post, the party reached the settlement of the Nahukwá, one of many tribes that had sought sanctuary in the jungles around the Xingu. Dyott wrote of the Nahukwá, "These new denizens of the forest were as primitive as Adam and Eve." Several in the tribe greeted Dyott and his men warmly, but the chief, Aloique, seemed hostile. "He regarded us impassively with his small eyes," Dyott wrote. "Cunning and cruelty lurked behind their lids."

Dyott was surrounded by Aloique's children, and he noticed something tied to a piece of string around the neck of one boy—a small brass plate engraved with the words "W. S. Silver and Company." It was the name of the British firm that had supplied Fawcett with gear. Slipping into the chief's dark hut, Dyott lit a flare. In the corner, he spied a military-style metal trunk.

Without the benefit of translators, Dyott tried to interrogate Aloique, using elaborate sign language. Aloique, also gesturing, seemed to suggest that the trunk was a gift. He then indicated that he had guided three white men to a neighboring territory. Dyott was skeptical and urged Aloique and some of his men to take him along the same route. Aloique warned that a murderous tribe, the Suyás, lived in that direction. Each time the Nahukwás said the word "Suyá," they would motion to the backs of their heads, as if they were being decapitated. Dyott persisted and Aloique, in exchange for knives, agreed to guide them.

That night, as Dyott and his men slept among the Indians, many in the party were uneasy. "We cannot predict the actions of [the Indians] for we know nothing about them except—and this is important—from these regions the Fawcett party disappeared," Whitehead wrote. He slept with a .38 Winchester and a machete under his blanket.

As the expedition pushed on through the forest the following day, Dyott continued to question Aloique, and before long the chief seemed to add a new element to his story. Fawcett and his men, he now intimated, had been killed by the Suyás. "Suyás! *Bung-bung-bung!*" the chief yelled, falling to the ground, as if he were dead. Aloique's shifting explanations aroused Dyott's suspicions. As he later wrote, "The finger of guilt seemed to point to Aloique."

At one point, as Dyott was reporting his latest findings over the radio, the machine stopped working. "Jungle Cry Strangled," a NANA bulletin declared. "Dyott Radio Cut Off in Crisis." The prolonged silence unleashed dire speculation. "I am so afraid," Dyott's wife told reporters.

The expedition, meanwhile, was short of food and water, and some of the men were so ill that they could barely walk. Whitehead wrote that he "couldn't eat, my fever is too bad." The cook's legs had swollen and were oozing a gangrenous pus. Dyott decided to press on with only two of his men, in the hope of finding Fawcett's remains. "Remember," Dyott told Whitehead, "if anything happens to me, all my effects go to my wife."

The night before the small contingent left, one of the men in Dyott's expedition party, an Indian, reported that he had overheard Aloique plotting with tribesmen to murder Dyott and steal his equipment. By then, Dyott had no doubt that he had found Fawcett's killer. As a deterrent, Dyott told Aloique that he now intended to take his entire party with him. The next morning Aloique and his men had vanished.

Soon afterward, scores of Indians from various tribes in the Xingu region emerged from the forest, carrying bows and arrows, and demanding gifts. With every hour a new canoe arrived with more tribesmen. Some of the Indians wore striking jewelry and had in their possession exquisite pottery, which made Dyott think that Fawcett's stories of an ancient sophisticated civilization might be true. But it was impossible to make further inquiries. As Whitehead put it, "Natives from tribes all over the territory, possibly two thousand of them, gradually were hemming us in from all sides."

Dyott had exhausted his supply of gifts, and the Indians were growing hostile. He promised them that the next morning he would give each of them an ax and knives. After midnight, when the Indians appeared to be asleep, Dyott quietly gathered his men and set out in the expedition's boats. The men pushed off and floated with the currents. No one dared to strike a paddle. A moment later, they heard a group of canoes upriver coming toward them with more Indians, apparently heading to their camp. Dyott signaled to his men to pull their boats to the side of the river and lie down. The men held their breath as the Indians paddled past them.

At last, Dyott gave the order to row, and the explorers began to paddle furiously. One of the technicians got the wireless radio to work long enough to relay a brief message: "Am sorry to report Fawcett expedition perished at the hands of hostile Indians. Our position is critical . . . Can't even afford time to send full details by wireless. Must descend the Xingu without delay or we ourselves will be caught." The expedition then dumped the radio, along with other heavy gear, to hasten its exit. Newspapers debated the team's odds. "Dyott's Chance to Escape Even," one headline ran. When Dyott and his men finally emerged from the jungle, months later—sick, emaciated, bearded, mosquito pocked—they were greeted as heroes. "We want to luxuriate in the pleasant and heady atmosphere of notoriety," said Whitehead, who was subsequently hired as a pitchman for a laxative called Nujol. ("You can be sure that no matter what important equipment I have to discard, my next adventure will see me taking plenty of Nujol along.") Dyott published a book, *Man Hunting in the Jungle*, and starred in a 1933 Hollywood film about his adventures called *Savage Gold*.

But by then Dyott's story had begun to collapse. As Brian Fawcett pointed out, it is hard to believe that his father, who was so wary of anyone knowing his path, would have left Y marks on trees. The gear that

Dyott found in Aloique's house may well have been a gift from Fawcett, as Aloique insisted, or it may have come from Fawcett's 1920 expedition, when he and Holt had been forced to dump much of their cargo. Indeed, Dyott's case rested on his assessment of Aloique's "treacherous" disposition—a judgment based largely on interactions conducted in sign language and on Dyott's purported expertise in "Indian psychology."

Years later, when missionaries and other explorers entered the region, they described Aloique and the Nahukwá as generally peaceful and friendly. Dyott had ignored the likelihood that Aloique's evasiveness, including his decision to flee, stemmed from his own fears of a white stranger who was leading an armed brigade. Finally, there was Bernardino. "Dyott . . . must have swallowed hook, line and sinker what he was told," Brian Fawcett wrote. "I say this because there was no Bernardino with my father's party in 1925." According to Fawcett's last letters, he had brought with him from Bakairí Post only two Brazilian helpers: Gardenia and Simão. Not long after the expedition, Nina Fawcett released a statement declaring, "There is consequently still no proof that the three explorers are dead."

Elsie Rimell insisted that she would "never give up" believing that her son would return. Privately, though, she was despairing. A friend wrote her a letter saying that it was natural that she was so "down," but pleaded with her, "Do not lose hope." The friend assured her that the true fate of the explorers would soon be made known.

ON MARCH 12, 1932, a man with brooding eyes and a dark mustache appeared outside the British Embassy in São Paulo, demanding to see the consul general. He wore a sports jacket, striped tie, and baggy pants tucked into knee-high riding boots. He said it was an urgent matter concerning Colonel Fawcett.

The man was led in to see the consul general, Arthur Abbott, who had been a friend of Fawcett's. For years, Abbott had held out faith that the explorers might materialize, but only a few weeks earlier he had destroyed his last letters from Fawcett, believing that "all hope of ever seeing him again had gone."

In a later sworn statement, the visitor said, "My name is Stefan Rattin. I am a Swiss subject. I came to South America twenty-one years ago." He explained that, nearly five months earlier, he and two companions had been hunting near the Tapajós River, in the northwest corner of Mato Grosso, when he encountered a tribe holding an elderly white man with long yellowish hair. Later, after many of the tribesmen had got drunk, Rattin said, the white man, who was clad in animal skins, quietly approached him.

"Are you a friend?" he asked.

"Yes," Rattin replied.

"I am an English colonel," he said, and he implored Rattin to go to the British consulate and tell "Major Paget" that he was being held captive.

Abbott knew that the former British ambassador to Brazil, Sir Ralph Paget, had been a confidant of Fawcett's. Indeed, it was Paget who had lobbied the Brazilian government to fund Fawcett's 1920 expedition. These facts, Abbott noted in a letter to the Royal Geographical Society, were "only known to me and a few personal friends."

When Nina Fawcett and Elsie Rimell first heard Rattin's account, they thought it sounded credible. Nina said that she "dare not build my hopes too high"; still, she sent a telegram to a news outlet in Brazil saying that she was now convinced that her husband was "ALIVE."

Others remained skeptical. General Rondon, after interviewing Rattin for three hours, noted in a report that the place the Swiss trapper indicated that he had found Fawcett was five hundred miles from where the expedition was last sighted. Paget himself, when he was reached in England, wondered why Rattin would have been allowed to leave the tribe while Fawcett was forced to remain a prisoner.

Abbott, however, was convinced of Rattin's sincerity, especially since he vowed to rescue Fawcett without seeking a reward. "I promised

Colonel Fawcett I would bring aid and that promise will be fulfilled," Rattin said. The Swiss trapper soon set out with two men, one of them a reporter, who filed articles for the United Press syndicate. After walking through the jungle for weeks, the three men arrived at the Arinos River, where they built canoes out of bark. In a dispatch dated May 24, 1932, as the expedition was about to enter hostile Indian territory, the reporter wrote, "Rattin is anxious to get away. He calls, 'All aboard!' Here we go." The men were never heard from again.

Not long after, a fifty-two-year-old English actor named Albert de Winton arrived in Cuiabá, vowing to find Fawcett, dead or alive. He had recently had minor roles in several Hollywood films, including *King of the Wild*. According to the *Washington Post*, Winton had "given up the imitation thrills of the movies for the real ones of the jungle." Wearing a crisp safari uniform, a gun strapped to his waist, and smoking a pipe, he hurried into the wilderness. A woman from Orange, New Jersey, referring to herself as Winton's "American Representative," released updates to the RGS on stationery that was embossed *"Albert De Winton* EXPEDITION INTO UNEXPLORED BRAZILIAN JUNGLE IN SEARCH OF COLONEL P. H. FAWCETT." Nine months after Winton entered the jungle, he emerged with his clothes in tatters, his face shrunken. On February 4, 1934, a photograph of him appeared in newspapers with the caption "Albert Winton, Los Angeles actor, is not made up for a role in a film drama. This is what nine months in a South American wilderness did for him." After a brief rest in Cuiabá, where he visited a museum that had an exhibit devoted to Fawcett, Winton returned to the Xingu region. Months elapsed without any word from him. Then, in September, an Indian runner emerged from the forest with a crumpled note from Winton. It said that he had been taken prisoner by a tribe and entreated, "Please send help." Winton's daughter notified the RGS about "this grave turn of events," and prayed that someone at the Society would save her father. But Winton, too, was never seen again. Only years later did Brazilian officials learn from Indians in the region that two members of the Kamayurá tribe had found Winton floating, naked and half-mad, in a canoe. One of the Kamayurás smashed his head in with a club, then took his rifle.

Such stories did little to dissuade scores of additional explorers from trying to find Fawcett or the City of Z. There were German-led expeditions, and Italian ones, and Russian ones, and Argentine ones. There was a female graduate student in anthropology from the University of California. There was an American soldier who had served with Fawcett on the western front. There was Peter Fleming, the brother of Ian Fleming, the creator of James Bond. There was a band of Brazilian bandits. By 1934, the Brazilian government, overwhelmed by the number of search parties, had issued a decree banning them unless they received special permission; nonetheless, explorers continued to go, with or without permission.

Although no reliable statistics exist, one recent estimate put the death toll from these expeditions as high as one hundred. The University of California graduate student, who, in 1930, was one of the first female anthropologists to venture into the region to conduct research, made it out only to die a few years later from an infection she had contracted in the Amazon. In 1939, another American anthropologist hanged himself from a tree in the jungle. (He left a message that said, "The Indians are going to take my notes . . . They are very valuable and can be disinfected and sent to the museum. I want my family to imagine I died in an Indian village of natural causes.") One seeker lost his brother to fever. "I tried to save" him, he told Nina. "But unfortunately I could do nothing and so we buried him at the edge of the Araguaya."

Like Rattin and Winton, other explorers seemed to drop off the face of the earth. In 1947, according to the Reverend Jonathan Wells, a missionary in Brazil, a carrier pigeon flew out of the jungle with a note written by a thirty-two-year-old schoolteacher from New Zealand, Hugh McCarthy, who had become fixated on finding Z. Wells said that he had met McCarthy at his Christian mission, on the eastern fringe of the frontier in Mato Grosso, and had warned him that he would die if he proceeded alone into the forest. When McCarthy refused to turn back, Wells said, he gave the schoolteacher seven carrier pigeons to deliver messages, which McCarthy placed in wicker baskets in his canoe. The first note arrived six weeks later. It said, "I am still quite ill from my accident, but the swelling in my leg is gradually receding . . . Tomorrow I leave to continue my mission. I am told that the mountains which I seek are only five days away. God keep you. Hugh." After a month and a half, a second carrier reached Wells with a new message. "I . . . am in dire circumstances," McCarthy wrote. "Long ago I abandoned my canoe and threw away my rifle as it is impractical in the jungle. My food supply has been exhausted and I am living on berries and wild fruits." A last trace of McCarthy was in a third note that read, "My work is over and I die happily, knowing that my belief in Fawcett and his lost City of Gold was not in vain."

NINA CAREFULLY FOLLOWED all of these developments in what she called "The Fawcett Mystery." She had transformed herself into a kind of detective, sifting through documents and poring over Fawcett's old log-books with a magnifying glass. A visitor described her sitting in front of a map of Brazil, a pencil in her hand; scattered about her were her husband's and son's last letters and photographs, as well as a shell necklace that Jack had sent back from Bakairí Post. At her request, the RGS shared any reported sightings or rumors concerning the party's fate. "You have always taken the courageous view that you yourself can judge better than any one the value of such evidence," an RGS official told her. Insisting that she had "trained" herself to remain impartial, she acted, in case after case, as an arbiter of any evidence. Once, after a German adventurer claimed to have seen Fawcett alive, she wrote bitterly that the man had "more than one passport, at least three aliases, and a sheaf of Press cuttings was found on him!"

Despite her efforts to remain detached, she confessed to her friend Harold Large, after rumors spread that Indians had massacred the party, "My heart is lacerated by the horrible accounts I'm obliged to read and my imagination conjures up gruesome pictures of what might have happened. It takes all my strength of will to push these horrors out of my thoughts, the brutal wear and tear is great." Another friend of Nina's informed the Royal Geographical Society that "Lady Fawcett is suffering with heart and soul."

Nina discovered in her files a packet of letters that Fawcett had written to Jack and Brian when he was on his first expedition, in 1907. She gave them to Brian and Joan, she told Large, "so that they shall each and all know the real ego of the man from whom they are descended." She added, "He is much in my thoughts today—his birthday."

By 1936, most people, including the Rimells, had concluded that the party had perished. Fawcett's older brother, Edward, told the RGS, "I shall act on the conviction, long held, that they died years ago." But Nina refused to accept that her husband might not be coming back and that she had agreed to send her son to his death. "I am one of the few who *believe*," she said. Large referred to her as "Penelope" waiting for "the return of Ulysses."

Like Fawcett's quest for Z, Nina's search for the missing explorers became an obsession. "The return of her husband is all that she lives for nowadays," a friend told the consul general in Rio. Nina had almost no money, except for the fraction of Fawcett's pension and a small stipend that Brian sent her from Peru. As the years wore on, she lived like a nomadic pauper, wandering, with her stack of Fawcett-related papers, from Brian's home in Peru to Switzerland, where Joan had settled with her husband, Jean de Montet, who was an engineer, and four children, including Rolette. The more people who doubted the explorers' perseverance, the more wildly Nina seized upon evidence to prove her case. When one of Fawcett's compasses turned up in Bakairí Post, in 1933, she insisted that her husband had recently placed it there as a sign that he was alive, even though, as Brian pointed out, it was clearly something that his father had left behind before he departed. "I get the impression," Nina wrote a contact in Brazil, "that on more than one occasion Colonel Fawcett has tried to give signs of his presence, and no one—except myself—has understood his meaning." Sometimes she signed her letters, *"Believe me."*

In the 1930s, Nina began to receive reports from a new source: missionaries who were pushing into the Xingu area, vowing to convert what one of them called "the most primitive and unenlightened of all South American Indians." In 1937, Martha L. Moennich, an American missionary, was trekking through the jungle, her eyelids swollen from ticks, and reciting the Lord's promise—"Lo, I am with you always, even unto the end of the world"—when she claimed to make an extraordinary discovery: at the Kuikuro village, she met a boy with pale skin and bright-blue eyes. The tribe told her that he was the son of Jack Fawcett, who had fathered him with an Indian woman. "In his dual nature there are conspicuous traits of British reserve and of a military bearing, while on his Indian side, the sight of a bow and arrow, or a river, make him a little jungle boy," Moennich later wrote. She said that she had proposed taking the boy back with her so that he could be given the opportunity "not only to learn his father's language but to live among his father's race." The tribe, however, refused to relinquish him. Other missionaries brought back similar tales of a white child in the jungle—a child who was, according to one minister, "perhaps the most famous boy in the whole Xingu."

In 1943, Assis Chateaubriand, a Brazilian multimillionaire who owned a conglomerate of newspapers and radio stations, dispatched one of his tabloid reporters, Edmar Morel, to find "Fawcett's grandson." Months later, Morel returned with a seventeen-year-old boy with moon white skin named Dulipé. He was hailed as the grandson of Colonel Percy Harrison Fawcett—or, as the press called him, "the White God of the Xingu."

The discovery sparked an international frenzy. Dulipé, shy and nervous, was photographed in *Life* and paraded around Brazil like a carnival attraction—a "freak," as *Time* magazine put it. People packed into movie theaters, the lines curling around the block, to see footage of him in the wild, naked and pale. (When the RGS was asked about Dulipé, it responded phlegmatically that such "matters are rather outside the scientific scope of our Society.") Morel phoned Brian Fawcett in Peru and asked if he and Nina wanted to adopt the young man. When they examined photographs of Dulipé, however, Nina was taken aback. "Do you notice anything about the child's eyes?" she asked Brian.

"They are all screwed up, as though hurt by the glare."

"That child looks to me like an albino," she said. Tests later confirmed her assessment. Many legends of white Indians, in fact, stemmed from cases of albinism. In 1924, Richard O. Marsh, an American explorer who later searched for Fawcett, announced that on an expedition in Panama he not only had spotted "white Indians" but was bringing back three "living specimens" as proof. "They are golden haired, blue-eyed and white-skinned," Marsh said. "Their bodies are covered with long downy white hair. They . . . look like very primitive Nordic whites." After his ship landed in New York, Marsh led the three children—two startled white Indian boys, ten and sixteen years old, and a fourteen-year-old pale Indian girl named Marguerite—before a crush of onlookers and photographers. Scientists from around the country—from the Bureau of American Ethnology, the Museum of the American Indian, the Peabody Museum, the American Museum of Natural History, and Harvard University—soon gathered in a room at the Waldorf-Astoria Hotel to see the children on display, poking and prodding their bodies. "Feel the girl's neck," one of the scientists said. Marsh surmised that they were a "relic of the Paleolithic type." Afterward the *New York Times* said, "Scientists Declare White Indians Real." The Indians were kept in a house in a rural area outside Washington, D.C., so that they could be "closer to nature." Only later was it revealed conclusively that the children were, like many San Blas Indians in Panama, albinos.

Dulipé's fate was tragic. Seized from his tribe and no longer a commercial attraction, he was abandoned on the streets of Cuiabá. There the "White God of the Xingu" reportedly died of alcoholism.

By the end of 1945, Nina, now seventy-five years old, was suffering from debilitating arthritis and anemia. She needed a cane, and sometimes two, to get around, and described herself as having "no home, no one to help me or meet me and crippled!"

Brian had earlier written her a letter, saying, "You've been through enough to bust the spirit of a dozen people but whatever you felt you . . . have smiled through it all and taken the rough stuff that Fate has ladled out to you for such a long time in a manner that makes me feel awfully proud to be your son. You must be rather an advanced being, or the Gods wouldn't have put you through such a test, and your reward will undoubtedly be very Great."

In 1946, when yet another account surfaced that the three explorers were alive in the Xingu—this time it was claimed that Fawcett was both "a prisoner and a chief of the Indians"—Nina was sure her reward had finally come. She vowed to lead an expedition to rescue them, even though "it means certain death for me!" The report, however, turned out to be another fabrication.

As late as 1950, Nina insisted that it would not surprise her if the explorers walked through the door at any moment—her husband now eighty-two, her son forty-seven. But in April 1951, Orlando Villas Boas, a government official revered for his defense of the Amazonian Indians, announced that the Kalapalos had admitted that members of their tribe had killed the three explorers. What's more, Villas Boas claimed that he had proof: the bones of Colonel Fawcett.

THE COLONEL'S
BONES

T he chief of the Kalapalos will meet with us," Paolo told me, relaying a message that had been radioed in from the jungle. The negotiations, he said, would take place not far from Bakairí Post, in Canarana, a small frontier town on the southern border of Xingu National Park. When we arrived that evening, the city was in the midst of a dengue-fever epidemic, and many of the phone lines were down. It was also Canarana's twenty-fifth anniversary, and the city was celebrating with fireworks, which sounded like sporadic gunshots. In the early 1980s, the Brazilian government, as part of its continuing colonization of Indian territories, had sent in planes filled with cowboys—many of German descent—to settle the remote area. Though the town was desolate, the main roads were bafflingly wide, as if they were superhighways. Only when I saw a photograph of a guest parking his airplane in front of a local hotel did I understand the reason: for years, the city had been so inaccessible that the streets doubled as runways. Even today, I was told, it was possible for a plane to land in the middle of the road, and in the main square sat a passenger airplane, the town's only apparent monument.

The Kalapalo chief, Vajuvi, showed up at our hotel accompanied by two men. He had a tanned, deeply lined face and appeared to be in his late forties. Like his two companions, he was about five feet six, with muscular arms. His hair was trimmed in a traditional bowl cut high above the ears. In the Xingu region, tribesmen often dispensed with clothes, but for this visit to the city Vajuvi wore a cotton V-neck shirt and sun-bleached jeans that hung loosely around his hips.

After we introduced ourselves and I explained why I wanted to visit the Xingu, Vajuvi asked, "Are you a member of the colonel's family?"

I was accustomed to the question, though this time it seemed more loaded: the Kalapalos had been accused of killing Fawcett, an act that could require a family member to avenge his death. When I explained that I was a reporter, Vajuvi seemed accommodating. "I will tell you the truth about the bones," he said. He then added that the village wanted the sum of five thousand dollars.

I explained that I didn't have that kind of money and tried to extol the virtues of cultural exchange. One of the Kalapalos stepped toward me and said, "The spirits told me that you were coming and that you are rich." Another Kalapalo added, "I've seen pictures of your cities. You have too many cars. You should give us a car."

One of the Indians left the hotel and returned moments later with three more Kalapalos. Every few minutes another Kalapalo appeared, and the room was soon crowded with more than a dozen men, some old, some young, all of them surrounding Paolo and me. "Where are they coming from?" I asked Paolo.

"I don't know," he said.

Vajuvi let the other men argue and haggle. As the negotiations continued, many of the Kalapalos grew hostile. They pressed against me and called me a liar. Finally, Vajuvi stood and said, "You talk to your chief in the United States, and then we'll talk again in a few hours."

He walked out of the room, the members of his tribe following him.

"Do not worry," Paolo said. "They are pushing and we are pushing back. This is the way it happens."

Dispirited, I went up to my room. Two hours later, Paolo called on the hotel phone. "Please come downstairs," he said. "I think I reach an agreement for us."

Vajuvi and the other Kalapalos were standing at the entryway. Paolo told me that Vajuvi had agreed to take us into Xingu National Park if we paid for transportation and for several hundred dollars' worth of supplies. I shook the chief's hand, and, before I knew it, his men were patting me on the shoulders, asking about my family, as if we were meeting for the first time. "Now we talk and eat," Vajuvi said. "All is good."

The next day we prepared to leave. To reach one of the largest head-waters of the Xingu, the Kuluene River, we needed an even more power-ful truck, and so after lunch we said farewell to our driver, who seemed relieved to be going home. "I hope you find this Y you are looking for," he said.

After he departed, we rented a flatbed truck with tractor-size wheels. As word spread that a truck was heading into the Xingu, Indians emerged from all quarters, carrying children and bundles of goods, hurrying to climb on board. Every time the truck seemed full, another person squeezed on, and as the afternoon rains poured down we began our journey.

According to the map, the Kuluene was only sixty miles away. But the road was worse than any that Paolo and I had traveled: pools of water reached as high as the floorboards, and at times the truck, with all its weight, tipped perilously to one side. We drove no faster than fifteen miles an hour, sometimes coming to a halt, reversing, then pressing forward again. The forests had been denuded here as well. Some areas had recently been burned, and I could see the remnants of trees scattered for miles, their blackened limbs reaching into the open sky.

Finally, as we neared the river, the forest began to reveal itself. Trees gradually closed around us, their branches forming a net that covered the windshield. There was a constant clattering as the wood drummed against the sides of the truck. The driver flicked on the headlights, which bobbed over the terrain. After five hours, we reached a wire fence: the boundary of Xingu National Park. Vajuvi said that it was only half a mile to the river, and then we would travel by boat to the Kalapalo village. Yet the truck soon got stuck in the mud, forcing us to remove our equipment temporarily to lighten the weight, and by the time we reached the river it was pitch-black under the canopy of trees. Vajuvi said that we would have to wait to cross. "It's too dangerous," he said. "The river is filled with logs and branches. We must not disrespect it."

Mosquitoes pricked my skin, and macaws and cicadas chanted. Above our heads, some creatures howled. "Do not worry," Paolo said. "They are only monkeys."

We walked a bit farther and arrived at a shack: Vajuvi pushed the door, which creaked as it opened. He led us inside and fumbled around until he lit a candle, which revealed a small room with a corrugated-tin roof and a mud floor. There was a wooden pole in the middle of the room, and Vajuvi helped Paolo and me string our hammocks. Though my clothes were still damp with sweat and mud from the journey, I lay down, trying to shield my face from the mosquitoes. After a while, the candle went out, and I swung gently in the darkness, listening to the murmurings of cicadas and the cawing of monkeys.

I fell into a light sleep, but woke suddenly when I felt something by my ear. I opened my eyes with a start: five naked boys, carrying bows and arrows, were staring at me. When they saw me move, they laughed and ran off.

I sat up. Paolo and Vajuvi were standing around a wood fire, boiling water.

"What time is it?" I asked.

"Five thirty," Paolo said. He handed me some crackers and a tin cup filled with coffee. "It's still a long way," he said. "You must eat something."

After a quick breakfast, we walked outside, and in the light of day I could see that we were at a small encampment overlooking the Kuluene River. On the shore were two flat-bottom aluminum boats, into which we loaded our gear. Each boat was about twelve feet long and had an outboard motor—an invention that had been introduced into the Xingu only in recent years.

Paolo and I climbed into one boat with a Kalapalo guide, while Vajuvi and his family traveled in another. Both boats sped upriver, side by side. Farther north were rapids and waterfalls, but here the water was a calm, olive green expanse. Trees lined the banks, their boughs bent like old men, their leaves skimming the surface of the water. After several hours, we docked our boats along the shore. Vajuvi told us to gather our gear, and we followed him up a short path. He paused and waved his hand proudly in front of him. "Kalapalo," he said.

We stood at the edge of a circular plaza that was more than a hundred yards in circumference and dotted with houses much like those described by the old woman at Bakairí Post. Resembling the overturned hulls of ships, they appeared to be woven, rather than constructed, out of leaves and wood. Their exteriors were covered with thatch, except for a door in the back and the front—both low enough, I was told, to keep out evil spirits.

Several dozen people were walking across the plaza. Many of them were unclothed, and some had adorned their bodies with exquisite ornamentations: monkey-tooth necklaces, swirls of black pigment from the genipap fruit, and swaths of red pigment from the *uruku* berry. Women between the ages of thirteen and fifty wore loose cotton dresses, the upper half dangling around their waists. Most of the men who weren't naked had on spandex bathing suits, as if they were Olympic swimmers. Physical fitness was clearly a prized trait. Some of the babies, I noticed, had strips of cloth pulled tightly around their calves and biceps, like tourniquets, to accentuate their muscles. "For us, it is a sign of beauty," Vajuvi said. The tribe continued to commit infanticide against those who seemed unnatural or bewitched, although the practice was less common than previously.

Vajuvi led me into his house, a cavernous space filled with smoke from a wood-burning fire. He introduced me to two handsome women who had long jet-black hair that fanned down over their bare backs. The older woman had a tattoo of three vertical stripes on her upper arms, and the younger one wore a necklace with glittering white shells. "My wives," Vajuvi said.

Before long, more people stepped out of the shadows: children and grandchildren, sons-in-law and daughters-in-law, aunts and uncles, brothers and sisters. Vajuvi said that nearly twenty people lived in the house. It seemed less like a home than like a self-contained village. In the center of the room, near a pole supporting the roof, from which corn had been hung to dry, one of Vajuvi's daughters knelt in front of a large wooden loom, weaving a hammock, and next to her was a boy wearing a blue-beaded belt, holding fish in an elaborately detailed, brightly painted ceramic pot, and beside him an elderly hunter sat on a large hardwood bench carved in the shape of a jaguar, sharpening a five-foot-long arrow. Fawcett wrote of the southern basin of the Amazon, "The whole of this region is saturated with Indian traditions of a most interesting kind," which "cannot be founded upon nothing" and which suggest the prior presence of "a once-great civilization."

The village, which had about a hundred and fifty residents, was highly stratified. These people were not wandering hunter-gatherers. Chiefs were anointed by bloodlines, as with European kings. There were taboos on diet which forbade them to eat most red meats, including tapir, deer, and boar—dietary restrictions that were among the strictest of any in the world and seemed to contradict the notion that the Indians were threatened with a constant state of starvation. At puberty, boys and girls were held in extended seclusion, during which a designated elder taught them the rituals and the responsibilities of adulthood. (The son who was in line to become chief was sequestered for up to four years.) Dyott, during his journey in the Xingu with Aloique, passed through the Kalapalo village and was so impressed by the scene that he wrote, "There is reason to believe that Fawcett's stories of a forgotten civilization are based on fact."

I asked Vajuvi whether he knew if the people of this region, who were known as Xinguanos, had once descended from a larger civilization, or if there were any significant ruins in the surrounding jungle. He shook his head. According to legend, however, the spirit Fitsi-fitsi built giant moats in the area. ("Everywhere he went that seemed like a nice place to stay, Fitsi-fitsi would make long, deep ditches and leave part of his people there, and he himself would continue traveling.")

While Vajuvi, Paolo, and I were talking, a man named Vanite Kalapalo entered the house and sat down beside us. He seemed despondent. It was his job, he said, to guard one of the posts on the reservation. The other day, an Indian had come to him and said, "Listen, Vanite. You must come with me down the river. The white people are building something in Afasukugu." The word "Afasukugu" meant "the place of the big cats"; at this site, the Xinguanos believe, the first humans were created. Vanite picked up a stick and drew a map on the mud floor. "Here is Afasukugu," he said. "It is by a waterfall."

"It is outside the park," Vajuvi, the chief, added. "But it is sacred."

I remembered Fawcett had mentioned in one of his last letters that he had learned from the Indians of a sacred waterfall in the same area, which he hoped to visit.

Vanite continued with his story: "So I said, 'I will go with you to Afasukugu, but you are crazy. Nobody would build anything at the place of the jaguars.' But when I get there the waterfall is destroyed. They blew it up with thirty kilos of dynamite. The place was so beautiful, and now it is gone. And I ask a man working there, 'What are you doing?' He says, 'We are building a hydroelectric dam.' "

"It is in the middle of the Kuluene River," Vajuvi said. "All the water from there flows right into our park and into our territory."

Vanite, who was becoming agitated, didn't seem to hear the chief. He said, "A man from the Mato Grosso government comes to the Xingu and tells us, 'Do not worry. This dam will not hurt you.' And he offers each of us money. One of the chiefs from another tribe took the money, and the tribes are now fighting with each other. For me, the money means nothing. The river has been here for thousands of years. We don't live forever, but the river does. The god Taugi created the river. It gives us our food, our medicines. You see, we don't have a well. We drink water right from the river. How will we live without it?"

Vajuvi said, "If they succeed, the river will disappear and, with it, all our people."

Our search for Fawcett and the City of Z suddenly felt trivial—another tribe appeared to be on the verge of extinction. But later that night, after we bathed in the river, Vajuvi said that there was something he had to tell Paolo and me about the Englishmen. The next day, he promised, he would take us by boat to where the bones had been discovered. Before going to bed, he added, "There are many things about the Englishmen that only Kalapalo people know."

THE NEXT MORNING, as we got ready to depart, one of the girls in our house removed a piece of cloth from a large object in the corner of the room, near an array of masks. Underneath was a television set, which was powered by the village's sole generator.

The girl turned a knob, sat down on the mud floor, and began watching a cartoon featuring a raucous Woody Woodpecker–like bird. Within minutes, at least twenty other children and several adults from the village had gathered around the set.

As Vajuvi came to retrieve us, I asked him how long he had owned a television. "Only a few years," he said. "At first, all everyone did is stare at it in a trance. But now I control the generator, and it is on only a few hours a week."

Several of the men watching the television got their bows and arrows and went out to hunt. Meanwhile, Paolo and I followed Vajuvi and one of his sons, who was five years old, down to the river. "I thought we would catch our lunch, the way Kalapalos do," Vajuvi said.

We climbed into one of the motorboats and headed upriver. A mist that covered the forest slowly dissipated as the sun rose. The river, dark and muddy, occasionally narrowed into a chute so tight that tree branches hung over our heads like bridges. Eventually, we entered an inlet covered by a tangle of floating leaves. "The green lagoon," Vajuvi said.

He cut the engine, and the boat slid quietly through the water. Terns with yellow beaks fluttered amid the rosewood and cedar trees, and swallows zigzagged above the lagoon, shimmering white specks on the blanket of green. A pair of macaws cackled and screamed, and on the shore deer stood as still as the water. A small caiman scurried up the banks.

"You must always be careful in the jungle," Vajuvi said. "I listen to my dreams. If I have a dream of danger, then I stay in the village. Many accidents happen to white people because they don't believe their dreams."

The Xinguanos were famous for fishing with bows and arrows, their bodies perched silently on the fronts of canoes—a pose that Jack and Raleigh had excitedly caught on camera, sending the images back to the Museum of the American Indian. Vajuvi and his son, however, took out some fishing lines and baited the hooks. Then they spun the lines over their heads like lassos and sent the hooks sailing into the center of the lagoon.

As Vajuvi pulled in his line, he pointed to the shore and said, "Up that way is where the bones were dug up. But they were not Fawcett's bones—they were my grandfather's."

"Your grandfather's?" I asked.

"Yes. Mugika—that was his name. He was dead when Orlando Villas Boas began to ask about Fawcett. Orlando wanted to protect us from all the white people coming in, and he told the Kalapalo people, 'If you find a tall skeleton, I will give each of you a rifle.' My grandfather was one of the tallest men in the village. So several people in the village decide to dig up his bones and bury them out here by the lagoon and say they are Fawcett's."

As he spoke, his son's line went taut. He helped the boy pull it in, and a silvery white fish burst out of the water, flapping wildly on the hook. I leaned in to inspect it, but Vajuvi jerked me out of the way and began to club it with a stick.

"Piranha," he said.

I looked down at the fish, with its low-hung jaw, lying on the aluminum floor of the boat. Vajuvi opened its mouth with a knife, revealing a set of sharp interlocking teeth—teeth that the Indians sometimes used to scrape their flesh in purification rituals. After he removed the hook, he continued, "My father, Tadjui, was away at the time, and he was furious when he found out what the people did. But the bones had already been taken away."

Other evidence seemed to corroborate his story. As Brian Fawcett had noted at the time, many of the Kalapalos told contradictory versions of how the explorers had actually been killed: some said they were clubbed, others maintained that they were shot with arrows from afar. In addition, the Kalapalos insisted that Fawcett had been murdered because he had not brought any gifts and had slapped a young Kalapalo boy, yet this was at odds with Fawcett's long history of gentle behavior toward Indians. More significant, I later found an internal memo in the archives of the Royal Anthropological Institute, in London, which had examined the bones. It stated:

> The upper jaw provides the clearest possible evidence that these human remains were not those of Colonel Fawcett, whose spare upper denture is fortunately available for comparison . . . Colonel Fawcett is stated to have been six feet, one and a half inches tall. The height of the man whose remains have been brought to England is estimated at about five feet, seven inches.

"I would like to get the bones back and bury them where they belong," Vajuvi said.

After catching half a dozen piranhas, we glided to shore. Vajuvi gathered several sticks and built a fire. Without skinning the piranhas, he laid them on the wood, grilling one side, then the other. He put the blackened fish on a bed of leaves and tore several pieces off the bone. He wrapped the fish in *beiju*, a kind of pancake bread made from manioc flour, handing each of us a sandwich. As we ate, he said, "I will tell you what my parents told me really happened to the Englishmen. It is true that they were here. There were three of them, and no one knew who they were or why they had come. They had no animals and carried packs on their backs. One, who was the chief, was old, and the two others were young. They were hungry and tired from marching for so long, and the people in the village gave them fish and *beiju*. In return for their help, the Englishmen offered them fishhooks, which no one had seen before. And knives. Finally, the old man said, 'We must be going now.' The people asked them, 'Where are you going?' And they said, 'That way. To the east.' We said, 'Nobody goes that way. That's where the hostile Indians are. They will kill you.' But the old man insisted. And so they went." Vajuvi pointed eastward and shook his head. "In those days, nobody went that way," he said. For several days, he continued, the Kalapalos could see smoke above the trees—Fawcett's campfire—but on the fifth day it disappeared. Vajuvi said that a group of Kalapalos, fearing that something bad had happened to them, tried to find their camp. But there was no trace of the Englishmen.

I subsequently learned that what his parents had shared with him was an oral history, which had been passed down for generations with remarkable consistency. In 1931, Vincenzo Petrullo, an anthropologist who worked for the Pennsylvania University Museum, in Philadelphia, and who was one of the first whites to enter the Xingu, reported hearing a similar account, though amid all the sensationalist tales few had paid much attention to it. Some fifty years later, Ellen Basso, an anthropologist at the University of Arizona, recorded a more detailed version from a Kalapalo named Kambe, who was a boy when Fawcett and his party arrived in the village. She translated his account directly from the Kalapalo language, maintaining the epic rhythms of the tribe's oral histories:

> One of them remained by himself.
> While he sang, he played a musical instrument.
> His musical instrument worked like this, like this . . .
> He sang and sang.
> He put his arm around me this way.
> While he was playing we watched the Christians.
> While he was playing.
> Father and the others.
> Then, "I'll have to be going," he said.

Kambe also recounted how they could see their fire:

> "There's the Christians' fire," we said to one another.
> That was going on as the sun set.
> The next day as the sun set, again their fire rose up.
> The following day again, just a little smoke, spread out in the sky.
> On this day, *mbouk*, their fire had gone out . . .
> It looked as if the Englishmen's fire was no longer alive, as if it had
>   been put out.
> "What a shame! Why did he keep insisting they go away?"

When Vajuvi finished his version of the oral history, he said, "People always say the Kalapalos killed the Englishmen. But we did not. We tried to save them."

THE

OTHER WORLD

The room was dark. Nina Fawcett sat on one side of a table; on the other was a woman peering into a crystal ball. Nina, after years of searching for her husband and son in this world, had begun to look in another dimension.

She surrounded herself with psychics and soothsayers, many of whom sent her long letters detailing their attempts to contact the explorers. One medium told her that she was conscious of a presence in the room and, looking up, saw Fawcett standing by the window. The medium said that she asked him, "Are you alive or dead?" and Fawcett laughed and replied, "Can't you see that I am alive?" He added, "Give my love to Nina and tell her we are all right."

On another occasion, a medium reported that a young figure with a long beard floated before her. It was Jack. "We shall see you someday," he said. Then he vanished, leaving "a most beautiful scent behind."

Fawcett's brother, Edward, told the RGS of Nina's descent into the occult, "Her life flows more easily thus."

She was not the only one who turned to psychics to find answers to what the visible world stubbornly refused to reveal. Toward the end of his life, Reeves, Fawcett's mentor at the RGS, had shocked his colleagues by becoming a spiritualist—or what was sometimes called a "spiritual surveyor." In the 1930s, he attended séances, searching for clues to Fawcett's fate. So did Fawcett's friend Sir Ralph Paget, the former Brazilian ambassador. In the early 1940s, while attending a gathering in Seaford, England, at the house of the psychic Nell Montague, Paget placed a letter from Fawcett on the medium's crystal ball. Montague said that she saw three flickering white figures. One lay motionless on the ground. Another, who was older, was struggling to breathe and was clutching at a man with long hair and a beard. The crystal ball suddenly turned red, as if it were drenched in blood. Then Montague said she saw Indians with spears and arrows carrying off the three white men. The people in the room gasped. For the first time, Paget felt that his friend was dead.

In 1949, Geraldine Cummins, a celebrated practitioner of "automatism," whereby a person purportedly goes into a trance and writes down messages from spirits, described how Jack and Raleigh were massacred by Indians. "Pain—stop pain!" Raleigh gasped, before dying. Fawcett, Cummins reported, eventually collapsed in a state of delirium: "The voices and sounds became a distant murmur as I now faced the greyness of death. It is a moment of unearthly horror . . . a time when the universe seems implacable and abiding loneliness apparent as the destiny of man."

Although Nina dismissed such reports, she knew that she was facing her own mortality. Even before Cummins's prophecy, Brian Fawcett, who was caring for Nina in Peru, wrote to Joan, "I really don't think her days on earth will be many! . . . She herself would be the first to claim she was breaking up." Once, Nina woke at two in the morning and wrote to Joan that she had a vision that she "must be prepared for 'the Call' at any moment." She thought, "Have you really and truly asked yourself: Have I any fear of Death and the Hereafter?" She hoped her passing would be easy— "perhaps I would go to sleep and not wake up." Brian told his sister, "In a way it would be a good thing for her to go out here. There would be a rather pleasing thought in her leaving her remains in the same continent as her husband and . . . son."

With her health deteriorating, Nina told Brian that she needed to give him something important. She opened a trunk, revealing all of Fawcett's logbooks and diaries. "The time has come to hand over to you all the documents in my possession," she said.

Though Brian was only in his late thirties, his life had been scarred by death: not only had he lost his father and brother, but his first wife had died of diabetes when she was seven months pregnant. He had since re-married, yet there were no children, and he suffered spells of what he called "wild, despairing sorrows."

Brian now looked at his father's papers, which he described as "the pathetic relics of a disaster whose nature we had no means of knowing." Over the next several weeks, he carried the papers to work with him. After more than twenty years as a railroad engineer, he was bored and rest-less. "I feel that I am wasting my life, just going to a lousy office every day, signing a lot of stupid papers, and driving back again!" he confided to Joan. "It leads nowhere." He went on, "Others can find immortality in their children. That is denied me, and I want to seek it."

During his lunch break, he would read through his father's papers, picturing Fawcett "on his expeditions, sharing with him the hardships, seeing through his eyes the great objective." Resentful about not being chosen for the expedition, Brian had once professed little interest in his father's work. Now he was consumed by it. He decided to quit his job and stitch together the fragmentary writings into *Exploration Fawcett*. As he worked tirelessly on the manuscript, Brian told his mother, "Daddy seems very close to me, as though I were collaborating at his conscious direction. Naturally, there are times when it tugs at my heart strings a lot." When Brian completed a draft, in April 1952, he gave a copy to Nina, telling her, "It really is quite a 'monumental' work, and I think Daddy would have been proud of it." Lying in bed, Nina began to turn the pages. "I simply couldn't put it down!" she wrote to Joan. "I bundled into my night clothes after supper and read that book till 4 a.m." It was as if her husband were right beside her; all the memories of him and Jack flooded into her mind. Upon finishing the manuscript, she exclaimed, "Bravo! Bravo!"

The book, published in 1953, became an international sensation and was praised by Graham Greene and Harold Nicolson. Not long after, Nina died, at the age of eighty-four. Brian and Joan had no longer been able to care for her, and she had been staying in a run-down boardinghouse in Brighton, England, demented and virtually penniless. As one observer noted, she had "sacrificed" her life to her husband and his memory.

In the early 1950s, Brian decided to conduct his own expeditions in search of the missing explorers. He suspected that his father, who would be approaching ninety, was dead and that Raleigh, owing to his infirmities, had perished soon after leaving Dead Horse Camp. But Jack—he was the cause of Brian's gnawing doubt. What if he had survived? After all, Jack was strong and young when the party had disappeared. Brian sent a letter to the British Embassy in Brazil, asking for help in securing permission to carry out a search effort. He explained that no one had legally presumed his brother dead and that he could not do so "without satisfying myself that all has been done." Moreover, such a mission might bring about the "return to his own country of one who has been lost for thirty years." British officials thought Brian "just as mad as his father," as one diplomat put it in a private communiqué, and refused to facilitate his "suicide."

Still, Brian forged ahead with his plans and boarded a ship to Brazil; his arrival there touched off a media storm. "Briton to Hunt Dad, Brother Lost in Jungle," the *Chicago Daily Tribune* declared. Brian purchased an explorer's outfit and carried a sketchbook and logbook. A Brazilian who had been a friend of his father's gasped when he saw Brian. "But . . . but . . . I thought you were dead!" he said.

Brian told his sister that he was becoming an explorer in spite of himself, but he knew that he would never survive trekking in the wilderness. Instead, relying on the means that Dr. Rice had pioneered decades earlier and that were now more affordable, he rented a tiny propeller plane and, with a pilot, canvassed the jungle from the air. He dropped thousands of leaflets that fluttered over the trees like snow. The leaflets asked, "Are you Jack Fawcett? If your answer is yes, then make this sign holding arms above your head . . . Can you control the Indians if we land?"

He never received a response or found any evidence of Jack. But on another expedition he looked for the object of his brother and father's quest: the City of Z. "Fate must surely have guided my steps along this path for a purpose," Brian wrote. Peering through binoculars, he spied on a distant ridge a crumbling city with streets and towers and pyramids. "That looks like it!" the pilot shouted. But, as the plane got closer, they realized that it was simply an outcropping of freakishly eroded sandstone. "The illusion was remarkable—almost unbelievable," Brian said. And, as the days wore on, he began to fear what he had never allowed himself to consider—that there had never been a Z. As he later wrote, "The whole romantic structure of fallacious beliefs, already rocking dangerously, collapsed about me, leaving me dazed." Brian started questioning some of the strange papers that he had found among his father's collection, and never divulged. Originally, Fawcett had described Z in strictly scientific terms and with caution: "I do not assume that 'The City' is either large or rich." But by 1924 Fawcett had filled his papers with reams of delirious writings about the end of the world and about a mystical Atlantean kingdom, which resembled the Garden of Eden. Z was transformed into "the cradle of all civilizations" and the center of one of Blavatsky's "White Lodges," where a group of higher spiritual beings helped to direct the fate of the universe. Fawcett hoped to discover a White Lodge that had been there since "the time of Atlantis," and to attain transcendence. Brian wrote in his diary, "Was Daddy's whole conception of 'Z,' a spiritual objective, and the manner of reaching it a religious allegory?" Was it possible that three lives had been lost for "an objective that had never existed"? Fawcett himself had scribbled in a letter to a friend, "Those whom the Gods intend to destroy they first make mad!"

———•·•———

Z

T he cave is over in those mountains," the Brazilian businessman said. "That's where Fawcett descended into the subterranean city and is still alive."

Before Paolo and I headed into the jungle, we had stopped in Barra do Garças, a town near the Roncador Mountains, in the northeast corner of Mato Grosso. Many Brazilians had told us that, over the past few decades, religious cults had sprung up in the area that worshipped Fawcett as a kind of god. They believed that Fawcett had entered a network of underground tunnels and discovered that Z was, of all things, a portal to another reality. Even though Brian Fawcett had concealed his father's bizarre writings at the end of his life, these mystics had seized upon Fawcett's few cryptic references, in magazines such as the *Occult Review*, to his search for "the treasures of the invisible World." These writings, coupled with Fawcett's disappearance and the failure of anyone over the years to discover his remains, fueled the notion that he had somehow defied the laws of physics.

One sect, called the Magical Nucleus, was started, in 1968, by a man named Udo Luckner, who referred to himself as the High Priest of the

Roncador and wore a long white gown and a cylindrical hat with a Star of David. In the 1970s, scores of Brazilians and Europeans, including Fawcett's great-nephew, flocked to join the Magical Nucleus, hoping to find this portal. Luckner built a religious compound by the Roncador Mountains, where families were forbidden to eat meat or wear jewelry. Luckner predicted that the world would end in 1982 and said that his people must prepare to descend into the hollow earth. But, when the planet remained in existence, the Magical Nucleus gradually disbanded.

More mystics continued to come to the Roncador Mountains in search of this Other World. One was the Brazilian businessman whom Paolo and I had encountered in the small town. Short and pudgy, and in his late forties, he told us that he had been at "a loss for my purpose in life," when he had met a psychic who taught him about spiritualism and the underground portal. He said that he was now training to purify himself, in the hopes of eventually going down.

Amazingly, others were making similar preparations. In 2005, a Greek explorer had announced plans on an Internet site—the Great Web of Percy Harrison Fawcett, which requires a secret code to access—for an expedition to find "the same portal or the doorway to a Kingdom that was entered by Colonel Fawcett in 1925." The trek, which has yet to take place, will include psychic guides and is billed as an "Expedition of No Return in the Ethereal Place of the Unbelief." It promises participants they will be no longer humans but "beings from another dimension, which means that we shall never die, we shall never get sick, we shall never grow up." Just as the world's blank spaces were disappearing, these people had constructed their own permanent dreamscape.

Before Paolo and I left, the businessman warned us, "You will never find Z as long as you look for it in this world."

NOT LONG AFTER Paolo and I had met with the Kalapalos, I contemplated for the first time ending our search. Paolo and I were both tired and pocked with mosquito bites and had begun to quarrel. I had also come down with a severe stomach ailment, most likely from a parasite. One morning, I slipped away from the Kalapalo village with the satellite phone that I had brought. Paolo had advised me not to advertise that I had it, and I carried it in a small bag into the jungle. Crouching amid the leaves and vines, I removed the phone, trying to get a signal. After several failed tries, I received one and dialed home. "David, is that you?" Kyra asked, picking up.

"Yes. Yes. It's me," I said. "How are you? How's Zachary?"

"I can't hear you very well. Where are you?"

I looked up at the canopy. "Somewhere in the Xingu."

"Are you okay?"

"A little sick, but I'm okay. I miss you."

"Zachary wants to say something to you."

A moment later I could hear my son babbling. "Zachary, it's Daddy," I said.

"Dada," he said.

"Yes, Dada."

"He's started calling the phone Dada," my wife said, taking back the receiver. "When are you coming home?"

"Soon."

"It hasn't been easy."

"I know. I'm sorry." As I was talking, I heard someone approaching. "I gotta go," I said suddenly.

"What's going on?"

"Someone's coming."

Before she could reply, I hung up the phone and slipped it back in the bag. In the same moment, a young Indian appeared, and I followed him back to the village. That night, as I lay in my hammock, I thought about what Brian Fawcett had said of his second wife after his expedition. "I was all she had," he noted. "And this situation need not have arisen. I chose it deliberately—selfishly—forgetting what it might mean to her in my eagerness to pursue an idea to its end."

I knew that by then I had enough material to write a story. I had found out about the bones of Vajuvi's grandfather. I had heard the Kalapalos' oral history. I had reconstructed Fawcett's youth and training at the RGS and his last expedition. Yet there were gaps in the narrative that still haunted me. I had often heard about biographers who became consumed by their subjects, who, after years of investigating their lives, of trying to follow their every step and inhabit their world completely, were driven into fits of rage and despair, because, at some level, the people were unknowable. Aspects of their characters, parts of their stories, remained impenetrable. I wondered what had happened to Fawcett and his companions after the Kalapalos saw their campfire go out. I wondered if the explorers had been killed by Indians and, if so, which ones. I wondered if Jack had reached a point when he began to question his father, and whether Fawcett himself, perhaps seeing his son dying, had asked, "What have I done?" And I wondered, most of all, whether there really was a Z. Was it, as Brian Fawcett feared, just a concoction of his father's imagination, or perhaps of all our imaginations? The finished story of Fawcett seemed to reside eternally beyond the horizon: a hidden metropolis of words and paragraphs, my own Z. As Cummins, channeling Fawcett, put it, "My story is lost. But it is a human soul's vanity to endeavor to disinter it and convey it to the world."

The logical thing was to let go and return home. But there was one last person, I thought, who might know something more: Michael Heckenberger, the archaeologist from the University of Florida whom James Petersen had recommended I get in touch with. During our brief phone conversation, Heckenberger had told me that he would be willing to meet me in the Kuikuro village, which was north of the Kalapalo settlement. I had heard rumors from other anthropologists that Heckenberger had spent so much time in the Xingu that he had been adopted by the Kuikuro chief and had his own hut in the village. If anyone might have picked up some fragmentary evidence or legend regarding Fawcett's final days, it would be him. And so I decided to press on, even though Brian

Fawcett had warned others to stop "throwing away their lives for a mirage."

When I told Paolo, he gave me a quizzical look—it meant heading to the very place where James Lynch and his men had been kidnapped in 1996. Perhaps out of duty or resignation, Paolo said, "As you wish," and began to load our equipment in the Kalapalos' aluminum canoe. With Vajuvi serving as our guide, we set out along the Kuluene River. It had rained most of the night before, and the river spilled into the surrounding forest. Usually, Paolo and I talked animatedly about our quest, but now we simply sat in silence.

After several hours, the boat approached an embankment where a young Indian boy was fishing. Vajuvi steered the boat toward him and turned off the engine as the bow slid onto the shore.

"Are we here?" I asked Vajuvi.

"The village is inland," he said. "You'll have to walk from here."

Paolo and I unloaded our bags and our boxes of food, and said goodbye to Vajuvi. We watched as his boat disappeared behind a bend in the river. There was too much baggage for us to carry, and Paolo asked the boy if he could borrow his bicycle, which was propped against a tree. The boy agreed, and Paolo told me to wait while he went to find help. As he rode away, I sat under a *buriti* tree and observed the boy casting his line and pulling it in.

An hour passed without anyone from the village appearing. I stood and stared down the path—there was only a trail of mud surrounded by wild grass and bushes. It was past noon when four boys showed up on bicycles. They strapped the cargo on the backs of their bicycles, but they had no room for a large cardboard box, which weighed about forty pounds, or for my computer bag, and so I carried them myself. In a mixture of Portuguese, Kuikuro, and pantomime, the boys explained that they would meet me in the village, waved goodbye, and vanished down the path on their rickety bikes.

With the box resting on one shoulder and the bag in my hand, I followed on foot, alone. The path wound through a partially submerged mangrove forest. I wondered whether I should remove my shoes, but I had no place to carry them, so I left them on, my ankles sinking in the mud. The vestiges of the path soon disappeared underwater. I was unsure which way to go, and I veered to the right, where I thought I saw some trampled grass. I walked for an hour, and there was still no sight of anyone. The box on my shoulder had grown heavier, as had the bag for my laptop, which, among the mangroves, seemed like an absurdity of modern travel. I thought about leaving them behind, but there was no dry spot to be found.

Occasionally, I slipped in the mud, falling to my knees in the water. Thorny reeds tore the skin on my arms and legs, causing trickles of blood. I yelled out Paolo's name, but there was no response. Exhausted, I found a grassy knoll that was only a few inches below the waterline, and sat down. My pants filled with water as I listened to the frogs. The sun burned my face and hands, and I wiped muddy water on myself in a vain attempt to cool down. It was then that I removed from my pocket the map of the Xingu on which Paolo and I had sketched our route. The *Z* in the middle suddenly seemed ludicrous, and I began to curse Fawcett. I cursed him for Jack and Raleigh. I cursed him for Murray and Rattin and Winton. And I cursed him for myself.

After a while, I stood again and tried to find the correct path. I walked and walked; in one spot, the water rose to my waist, and I lifted the bag and the box onto my head. Each time I thought that I had reached the end of the mangrove forest, a new swath opened up before me—large patches of tall, damp reeds clouded with piums and mosquitoes, which ate into me.

I was slapping a mosquito on my neck when I heard a noise in the distance. I stopped but didn't see anything. As I took another step, the noise grew louder. I called out once more for Paolo.

Then I heard it again—a strange cackle, almost like laughter. A dark object darted in the tall grass, and another, and another. They were coming closer. "Who's there?" I asked in Portuguese.

Another sound reverberated behind me and I spun around: the grass was rustling, even though there was no wind. I walked faster, stumbling, trying to push through the reeds. The water deepened and widened until it resembled a lake. I was looking dumbfounded at the shore, some two hundred yards ahead, when I noticed, tucked in a bush, an aluminum canoe. Though there was no paddle, I rested the box and my bag in it and climbed in, short of breath. Then I heard the noise again and bolted upright. Out of the tall reeds burst dozens of naked children. They seized the edges of the canoe and began to swim me across the lake, screaming with laughter the entire way. When we reached the shore again, I stumbled out of the canoe, and the children followed me up a path. We had reached the Kuikuro village.

Paolo was sitting in the shade of the nearest hut. "I'm sorry I didn't go back for you," he said. "I didn't think I could make it." His vest was draped around his neck, and he was sipping water from a bowl. He handed the bowl to me, and though the water hadn't been boiled, I drank it greedily, letting it spill around my neck.

"Now you have some kind of real picture in your mind of what it was like for Fawcett," he said. "Now we go home, no?"

Before I could reply, a Kuikuro man came and told us to follow him. I paused for a moment uncertainly, then walked with him across the dusty central plaza, which was some two hundred and fifty yards in diameter— the largest one, I was told, in the Xingu. Two fires had recently swept through the huts along the plaza's perimeter, the flames leaping from one thatched roof to the next, leaving much of the settlement in ashes. The Kuikuro man paused outside one of the surviving homes and told us to enter. Near the door, I could see two magnificent clay sculptures—one of a frog, the other of a jaguar. I was admiring them when an enormous man stepped out of the shadows. He was built like Tamakafi, a mythical Xinguano fighter who, according to legend, had a colossal body, his arms as thick as thighs, his legs as big as a chest. The man wore only a thin bathing suit, and he had a bowl haircut that somehow made his stern face seem even more imposing.

"I am Afukaká," he said, in a surprisingly soft, measured voice. It was clear that he was the chief. He offered Paolo and me lunch—a bowl of fish and rice—which his two wives, who were sisters, served us. He seemed interested in the outside world and asked me many questions about New York, about the skyscrapers and restaurants.

As we spoke, a sweet serenading sound filtered into the hut. I turned to the door as a group of women dancers and men with bamboo flutes entered. The men, who were naked, had covered their bodies with elaborate painted images of fish and tortoises and anacondas, the shapes weaving along their arms and legs, the orange and yellow and red colors gleaming with sweat. Around the eyes of most of them were black circles of paint, which resembled masks at a costume party. Their heads were topped with large, colorful feathers.

Afukaká and Paolo and I stood as the group crowded into the hut. The men stepped forward twice, then back, then forward again, all the time blowing their flutes, some of which were ten feet long—beautiful pieces of bamboo that released humming tones, like wind catching an open bottle top. Several young girls with long black hair danced alongside the men, their arms slung over the shoulders of the person in front of them, forming a chain; they, too, were naked, except for strings of snail shells around their necks and a bark-cloth triangle, or *uluri*, that covered their pubic area. Some of the pubescent girls had recently been held in seclusion, and their bodies were paler than those of the men. Their necklaces rattled as they stamped their feet, adding to the insistent rhythm of the music. The group circled us for several minutes, then ducked under the doorway and disappeared into the plaza, the sound of the flutes fading as the musicians and the dancers entered the next hut.

I asked Afukaká about the ritual, and he said that it was a festival for fish spirits. "It is a way to commune with the spirits," he said. "We have hundreds of ceremonies—all beautiful."

After a while, I mentioned Fawcett. Afukaká echoed almost precisely what the Kalapalo chief had told me. "The fierce Indians must have killed them," he said. Indeed, it seemed likely that one of the more warlike tribes in the region—most likely the Suyás, as Aloique had suggested, or the Kayapós or the Xavante—had slaughtered the party; it was improbable that all three Englishmen would have starved to death, given Fawcett's talent for surviving in the jungle for long periods. But that was as far as the evidence led me, and I felt a sudden resignation. "Only the forest knows all," Paolo said.

While we were talking, a curious figure appeared. His skin was white, although parts of it had been scalded red from the sun, and he had scruffy blond hair. He wore baggy shorts and no shirt and carried a machete. It was Michael Heckenberger. "So you made it," he said with a smile, looking at my drenched, dirty clothes.

It was true what I had been told: he had been adopted by Afukaká, who had built him a hut right next to his own home. Heckenberger said that he had been doing research here on and off for the last thirteen years. During that time, he had battled everything from malaria to virulent bacteria that made his skin peel off. His body was also once invaded by maggots, like Murray's. "It was kind of horrifying," Heckenberger said. Because of the prevailing notion that the Amazon was a counterfeit paradise, most archaeologists had long ago abandoned the remote Xingu. "They assumed it was an archaeological black hole," Heckenberger said, adding that Fawcett was "the exception."

Heckenberger knew the story of Fawcett well and had even tried to conduct his own inquiry into his fate. "I'm fascinated by him and what he did in that time period," Heckenberger said. "He was one of these larger-than-life figures. Anyone who would jump in a canoe or march in here at a time when you know some of the Indians are going to try to—" He stopped in mid-sentence, as if contemplating the consequences.

He said that Fawcett was easy to dismiss as "a crank"; he lacked the tools and the discipline of a modern archaeologist, and he never questioned the shibboleth that any lost city in the Amazon had to have European origins. But even though Fawcett was an amateur, he went on, he was able to see things more clearly than many professional scholars.

"I want to show you something," Heckenberger said at one point.

Holding his machete in front of him, he led Paolo, Afukaká, and me into the forest, cutting away tendrils from trees, which shot upward, fighting for the glow of the sun. After walking for a mile or so, we reached an area where the forest thinned. Heckenberger pointed to the ground with his machete. "See how the land dips?" he asked.

Indeed, the ground seemed to slope downward for a long stretch, then tilt upward again, as if someone had carved out an enormous ditch.

"It's a moat," Heckenberger said.

"What do you mean, a moat?"

"A moat. A defensive ditch." He added, "From nearly nine hundred years ago."

Paolo and I tried to follow the moat's contours, which curved in a nearly perfect circle through the woods. Heckenberger said that the moat had originally measured between a dozen and sixteen feet deep, and about thirty feet wide. It was nearly a mile in diameter. I thought of the "long, deep ditches" that the spirit Fitsi-fitsi was said to have built around settlements. "The Kuikuros knew they existed, but they didn't realize that their own ancestors had built them," Heckenberger said.

Afukaká, who had helped with the excavation, said, "We thought they were made by the spirits."

Heckenberger walked over to a rectangular hole in the ground, where he had excavated part of the moat. Paolo and I peered over the edge with the chief. The exposed earth, in contrast to other parts of the forest, was dark, almost black. Using radiocarbon dating, Heckenberger had dated the trench to about A.D. 1200. He pointed the tip of his machete to the bottom of the hole, where there seemed to be a ditch within the ditch. "That's where they put the palisade wall," he said.

"A *wall*?" I asked.

Heckenberger smiled and went on, "All around the moat, you can see these funnel shapes, equally spread apart. There are only two explanations. Either they had traps at the bottom or they had something sticking into them, like tree trunks."

He said that the concept of traps for invading enemies to fall into was unlikely, since the people the moat was supposed to be protecting would have been in peril themselves. What's more, he said, when he examined the moats with Afukaká, the chief told him a legend about a Kuikuro who had escaped from another village by leaping over "a great palisade wall and ditch."

Still, none of it seemed to make sense. Why would anyone build a moat and a stockade wall in the middle of the wilderness? "There's nothing here," I said.

Heckenberger didn't respond; instead, he bent down and rooted through the dirt, picking up a piece of hardened clay with grooves along the edges. He held it up to the light. "Broken pottery," he said. "It's everywhere."

As I looked at other shards on the ground, I thought of how Fawcett had insisted that on certain high areas in the Amazon "very little scratching will produce an abundance" of ancient pottery.

Heckenberger said that we were standing in the middle of a vast ancient settlement.

"Poor Fawcett—he was so close," Paolo said.

The settlement was in the very region where Fawcett believed it would be. But it was understandable why he might not have been able to see it, Heckenberger went on. "There isn't a lot of stone in the jungle, and most of the settlement was built with organic materials—wood and palms and earth mounds—which decompose," he said. "But once you begin to map out the area and excavate it you are blown away by what you see."

He began walking once more through the forest, pointing out what were, clearly, the remains of a massive man-made landscape. There was not just one moat but three, arranged in concentric circles. There was a giant circular plaza where the vegetation had a different character from that of the rest of the forest, because it had once been swept clean. And there had been a sprawling neighborhood of dwellings, as evidenced by even denser black soil, which had been enriched by decomposed garbage and human waste.

As we walked around, I noticed an embankment that extended into the forest in a straight line. Heckenberger said that it was a road curb.

"They had roads, too?" I asked.

"Roads. Causeways. Canals." Heckenberger said that some roads had been nearly a hundred and fifty feet wide. "We even found a place where the road ends at one side of a river in a kind of ascending ramp and then continues on the other side with a descending ramp. Which can only mean one thing: there had to have been some kind of wooden bridge connecting them, over an area that was a half mile long."

They were the very same kinds of dreamlike causeways and settlements that the Spanish conquistadores had spoken of when they visited the Amazon, the ones in which Fawcett had so fervently believed and which twentieth-century scientists had dismissed as myths. I asked Heckenberger where the roads led, and he said that they extended to other, equally complex sites. "I just took you to the closest one," he said.

Altogether, he had uncovered twenty pre-Columbian settlements in the Xingu, which had been occupied roughly between A.D. 800 and A.D. 1600. The settlements were about two to three miles apart and were connected by roads. More astounding, the plazas were laid out along cardinal points, from east to west, and the roads were positioned at the same geometric angles. (Fawcett said that Indians had told him legends that described "many streets set at right angles to one another.")

Borrowing my notebook, Heckenberger began to sketch a huge circle, then another and another. These were the plazas and the villages, he said. He then drew rings around them, which he said were the moats. Finally, he added several parallel lines that jutted out from each of the settlements in precise angles—the roads, bridges, and causeways. Each form seemed to fit into an elaborate whole, like an abstract painting whose elements cohere only at a distance. "Once my team and I started to map everything out, we discovered that nothing was done by accident," Heckenberger said. "All these settlements were laid out with a complicated plan, with a sense of engineering and mathematics that rivaled anything that was happening in much of Europe at the time."

Heckenberger said that before Western diseases devastated the population, each cluster of settlements contained anywhere from two thousand to five thousand people, which means that the larger community was the size of many medieval European cities. "These people had a cultural aesthetic of monumentality," he said. "They liked to have beautiful roads and plazas and bridges. Their monuments were not pyramids, which is why they were so hard to find; they were horizontal features. But they're no less extraordinary."

Heckenberger told me that he had just published his research, in a book called *The Ecology of Power*. Susanna Hecht, a geographer at UCLA's School of Public Affairs, called Heckenberger's findings "extraordinary." Other archaeologists and geographers later described them to me as "monumental," "transformative," and "earth-shattering." Heckenberger has helped to upend the view of the Amazon as a counterfeit paradise that could never sustain what Fawcett had envisioned: a prosperous, glorious civilization.

Other scientists, I discovered, were contributing to this revolution in archaeology, which challenges virtually everything that was once believed about the Americas before Columbus. These archaeologists are often aided by gadgets that surpass anything Dr. Rice could have imagined. They include ground-penetrating radar, satellite imagery to map sites, and remote sensors that can detect magnetic fields in the soil to pinpoint buried artifacts. Anna Roosevelt, a great-granddaughter of Theodore Roosevelt's who is an archaeologist at the University of Illinois, has excavated a cave near Santarém, in the Brazilian Amazon, that was filled with rock paintings—renditions of animal and human figures similar to those that Fawcett had described seeing in various parts of the Amazon and that bolstered his theory of Z. Buried in the cave were remains of a settlement at least ten thousand years old—about twice as old as scientists had estimated the human presence in the Amazon. Indeed, the settlement is so ancient that it has cast doubt on the long-held theory of how the Americas were first populated. For years, archaeologists believed that the earliest American inhabitants were the Clovis—named for the spear points found in Clovis, New Mexico. It was thought that these big-game hunters had crossed the Bering Strait from Asia at the end of the Ice Age and settled in North America around eleven thousand years ago and then gradually migrated down to Central and South America. The Amazon settlement, however, may be as old as the first undisputed Clovis settlement in North America. Moreover, according to Roosevelt, the telltale signs of the Clovis culture—such as spears with distinctly fluted rock points—were not present in the Amazon cave. Some archaeologists now believe that there may have been a people that preceded the Clovis. Others, like Roosevelt, think that the same people from Asia simultaneously radiated throughout the Americas and developed their own distinct cultures.

In the cave and at a nearby riverbank settlement, Roosevelt made another astonishing discovery: seventy-five-hundred-year-old pottery, which predates by more than two thousand years the earliest pottery found in the Andes or Mesoamerica. This means that the Amazon may have been the earliest ceramic-producing region in all the Americas, and that, as Fawcett radically argued, the region was possibly even a wellspring of civilization throughout South America—that an advanced culture had spread outward, rather than vice versa.

Using aerial photography and satellite imaging, scientists have also begun to find enormous man-made earth mounds often connected by causeways across the Amazon—in particular in the Bolivian floodplains where Fawcett first found his shards of pottery and reported that "wherever there are 'alturas,' that is high ground above the plains, . . . there are artifacts." Clark Erickson, an anthropologist from the University of Pennsylvania who has studied these earthworks in Bolivia, told me that the mounds allowed the Indians to continue farming during seasonal floods and to avoid the leaching process that can deprive the soil of nutrients. To create them, he said, required extraordinary labor and engineering: tons of soil had to be transported, the course of rivers altered, canals excavated, and interconnecting roadways and settlements built. In many ways, he said, the mounds "rival the Egyptian pyramids."

Perhaps most startling is evidence that Indians transformed the landscape even where it *was* a counterfeit paradise—that is to say, where the soil was too infertile to sustain a large population. Scientists have uncovered throughout the jungle large stretches of *terra preta do Indio*, or "Indian black earth": soil that has been enriched with organic human waste and charcoal from fires, so that it is made exceptionally fertile. It is not clear if Indian black earth was an accidental by-product of human inhabitation or, as some scientists think, was created by design—by a careful and systematic "charring" of the soil with smoldering fires, like the Kayapós' practice in the Xingu. In either case, many Amazonian tribes appear to have exploited this rich soil to grow crops where agriculture was once thought inconceivable. Scientists have uncovered so much black earth from ancient settlements in the Amazon that they now believe the rain forest may have sustained millions of people. And for the first time scholars are reevaluating the El Dorado chronicles that Fawcett used to piece together his theory of Z. As Roosevelt put it, what Carvajal described was without question "no mirage." Scientists have admittedly not found evidence of the fantastical gold that the conquistadores had dreamed of. But the anthropologist Neil Whitehead says, "With some caveats, El Dorado really did exist."

Heckenberger told me that scientists were just beginning the process of understanding this ancient world—and, like the theory of who first populated the Americas, all the traditional paradigms had to be reevaluated. In 2006, evidence even emerged that, in some parts of the Amazon, Indians built with stone. Archaeologists with the Amapa Institute of Scientific and Technological Research uncovered, in the northern Brazilian Amazon, an astronomical observatory tower made of huge granite rocks: each one weighed several tons, and some were nearly ten feet tall. The ruins, believed to be anywhere from five hundred to two thousand years old, have been called "the Stonehenge of the Amazon."

"Anthropologists," Heckenberger said, "made the mistake of coming into the Amazon in the twentieth century and seeing only small tribes and saying, 'Well, that's all there is.' The problem is that, by then, many Indian populations had already been wiped out by what was essentially a holocaust from European contact. That's why the first Europeans in the Amazon described such massive settlements that, later, no one could ever find."

As we walked back into the Kuikuro village, Heckenberger stopped at the edge of the plaza and told me to examine it closely. He said that the civilization that had built the giant settlements had nearly been annihilated. Yet a small number of descendants had survived, and we were no doubt among them. For a thousand years, he said, the Xinguanos had maintained artistic and cultural traditions from this highly advanced, highly structured civilization. He said, for instance, that the present-day Kuikuro village was still organized along east and west cardinal points and its paths were aligned at right angles, though its residents no longer knew why this was the preferred pattern. Heckenberger added that he had taken a piece of pottery from the ruins and shown it to a local maker of ceramics. It was so similar to present-day pottery, with its painted exterior and reddish clay, that the potter insisted it had been made recently.

As Paolo and I headed toward the chief's house, Heckenberger picked up a contemporary ceramic pot and ran his hand along the edge, where there were grooves. "They're from boiling the toxins out of manioc," he said. He had detected the same feature in the ancient pots. "That means that a thousand years ago people in this civilization had the same staple of diet," he said. He began to go through the house, finding parallels between the ancient civilization and its remnants today: the clay statues, the thatched walls and roofs, the cotton hammocks. "To tell you the honest-to-God truth, I don't think there is anywhere in the world where there isn't written history where the continuity is so clear as right here," Heckenberger said.

Some of the musicians and dancers were circling through the plaza, and Heckenberger said that everywhere in the Kuikuro village "you can see the past in the present." I began to picture the flutists and dancers in one of the old plazas. I pictured them living in mound-shaped two-story houses, the houses not scattered but in endless rows, where women wove hammocks and baked with manioc flour and where teenage boys and girls were held in seclusion as they learned the rites of their ancestors. I pictured the dancers and singers crossing moats and passing through tall palisade fences, moving from one village to the next along wide boulevards and bridges and causeways.

The musicians were coming closer to us, and Heckenberger said something about the flutes, but I could no longer hear his voice over the sounds. For a moment, I could see this vanished world as if it were right in front of me. Z.

ACKNOWLEDGMENTS

I AM GRATEFUL to so many people who contributed to this project. Fawcett's granddaughter Rolette de Montet-Guerin and his great-granddaughter Isabelle generously allowed me access to Fawcett's diaries, letters, and photographs. Percy Fawcett's ninety-five-year-old nephew, Dr. Peter Fortescue, gave me a copy of his unpublished memoir; he vividly recalled when he was a boy and saw Percy and Jack Fawcett at a farewell dinner before they journeyed to the Amazon. Two of Henry Costin's children, Michael and Mary, shared reminiscences of their father and let me read his private letters. Ann Macdonald, Raleigh Rimell's cousin once removed, provided me with his last letters home. Robert Temple, who is Edward Douglas Fawcett's literary executor, and Robert's wife, Olivia, shed light on the marvelous life of Percy Fawcett's older brother. Commander George Miller Dyott's son Mark and Dr. Alexander Hamilton Rice's nephew John D. Farrington each furnished crucial details about their relatives. James Lynch told me about his own harrowing journey.

I am also indebted to a number of research institutions and their incredible staffs. Particularly, I want to thank Sarah Strong, Julie Carrington, Jamie Owen, and everyone else at the Royal Geographical Society; Maurice Paul Evans at the Royal Artillery Museum; Peter Lewis at the American Geographical Society; Vera Faillace at the National Library of Brazil; Sheila Mackenzie at the National Library of Scotland; Norwood Kerr and Mary Jo Scott at the Alabama Department of Archives and History; and Elizabeth Dunn at the Rare Book, Manuscript, and Special Collections Library at Duke University.

I could never have made it out of the jungle without my wonderful and good-humored guide, Paolo Pinage. I am also grateful to the Bakairí, Kalapalo, and Kuikuro Indians for welcoming me into their settlements and talking to me not only about Fawcett but their own rich cultures and history as well.

To learn about Amazonian archaeology and geography, I drew on the wisdom of several scholars—Ellen Basso, William Denevan, Clark Erickson, Susanna Hecht, Eduardo Neves, Anna Roosevelt, and Neil Whitehead, among them—though they should not be held accountable for my words. I would like to pay special tribute to James Petersen, who was murdered in the Amazon not long after we spoke, depriving the world of one of its finest archaeologists and most generous souls. And, needless to say, this book would have had a much different ending had it not been for the archaeologist Michael Heckenberger, a brilliant and fearless scholar who has done so much to illuminate the ancient civilizations of the Amazon.

William Lowther, Misha Williams, and Hermes Leal have all done prodigious research on Fawcett and patiently answered my questions.

In the United States, several terrific young journalists assisted me at various stages as researchers, including Walter Alarkon, David Gura, and Todd Neale. In Brazil, Mariana Ferreira, Lena Ferreira, and Juliana Lottmann helped me to track down a host of documents, while in England Gita Daneshjoo volunteered to retrieve an important paper. Nana Asfour, Luigi Sofio, and Marcos Steuernagel contributed first-rate translations; Ann Goldstein deciphered an ancient Italian script. Andy Young was an amazing help both with fact-checking and with Portuguese translations. Nandi Rodrigo was an industrious fact-checker and made wonderful editorial suggestions.

I can never thank enough Susan Lee, a remarkable young journalist who has worked on this project as a reporter, researcher, and fact-checker for months on end. She embodies all the best qualities of the profession— passion, intelligence, and tenacity.

Many friends came to my aid, lending their editorial insights while pushing me across the finish line. I especially want to thank Burkhard Bilger, Jonathan Chait, Warren Cohen, Jonathan Cohn, Amy Davidson, Jeffrey Frank, Lawrence Friedman, Tad Friend, David Greenberg, Raffi Khatchadourian, Larissa MacFarquhar, Katherine Marsh, Stephen Metcalf, Ian Parker, Nick Paumgarten, Alex Ross, Margaret Talbot, and Jason Zengerle.

It is also my good fortune to be surrounded by such talented editors at *The New Yorker*. Daniel Zalewski is one of the smartest and most gifted editors in the business, and painstakingly edited the piece that appeared in the magazine and then made invaluable contributions to the book. Dorothy Wickenden, who took the manuscript even on her vacation, provided her usual scrupulous edits and flourishes, improving the text immeasurably. Elizabeth Pearson-Griffiths is one of those editors who quietly make each writer they work with better, and every page benefited from her infallible eye and her ear for language. And I can never fully express my gratitude to David Remnick, who agreed to send me into the jungle in pursuit of Z and who, when the project began to grow and envelop my life, did everything he could to ensure that I finished it. This book would not have happened without him.

Kathy Robbins and David Halpern at the Robbins Office and Matthew Snyder at CAA are more than great agents; they are sage advisors, fierce allies, and, most of all, friends. I also want to thank everyone else at the Robbins Office, especially Kate Rizzo.

One of the best things in writing this book has been the opportunity to work with the extraordinary team at Doubleday. William Thomas has been what every book author dreams of finding: an incisive and meticulous editor as well as indefatigable champion, who has given everything to this project. Stephen Rubin, who ushered this book from its inception to its publication, has done so with his indomitable spirit and wisdom. Indeed, the entire team at Doubleday—including Bette Alexander, Maria Carella, Melissa Danaczko, Todd Doughty, Patricia Flynn, John Fontana, Catherine Pollock, Ingrid Sterner, and Kathy Trager—has been a marvel.

In John and Nina Darnton, I have not only perfect in-laws but also first-rate editors. My sister, Alison, along with her family, and my brother, Edward, have been a constant source of encouragement. So has my mother, Phyllis, who has been an amazing writing tutor over the years. My father, Victor, not only has supported me in every way but continues to show me the wonders of an adventurous life.

I hope that one day my son, Zachary, and my daughter, Ella, who was born after my trip, will read this book and think that perhaps their father wasn't such an old bore after all. Finally, I want to thank my wife, Kyra, who has given to this book more than words can describe, and is, and will always be, everything to me. Together, she, Zachary, and Ella have provided the most rewarding and unexpected journey of all.

A Note
on the Sources

DESPITE FAWCETT'S once-enormous fame, many details of his life, like those of his death, have been shrouded in mystery. Until recently, Fawcett's family kept the bulk of his papers private. Moreover, the contents of many of the diaries and correspondence of his colleagues and companions, such as Raleigh Rimell, have never been published.

In trying to excavate Fawcett's life, I have drawn extensively on these materials. They include Fawcett's diaries and logbooks; the correspondence of his wife and children, as well as those of his closest exploring companions and his most bitter rivals; the journals of members of his military unit during World War I; and Rimell's final letters from the 1925 expedition, which had been passed down to a cousin once removed. Fawcett himself was a compulsive writer who left behind an enormous amount of firsthand information in scientific and esoteric journals, and his son Brian, who edited *Exploration Fawcett*, turned out to be a prolific writer as well.

I also benefited from the tremendous research of other authors, particularly in reconstructing historical periods. I would have been lost, for instance, without John Hemming's three-volume history on the Brazilian

Indians or his book *The Search for El Dorado*. Charles Mann's *1491*, which was published not long after I returned from my trip, served as a wonderful guide to the scientific developments that are sweeping away so many previous conceptions about what the Americas looked like before the arrival of Christopher Columbus. I have listed these and other important sources in the bibliography. If I was especially indebted to a source, I tried to cite it in the notes as well.

Anything that appears in the text between quotation marks, including conversation in the jungle from vanished explorers, comes directly from a diary, a letter, or some other written document and is cited in the notes. In a few places, I found minor discrepancies in the quotations between published versions of letters, which had been edited, and their original; in these cases, I reverted to the original. In an effort to keep the notes as concise as possible, I do not include citations for well-established or uncontroversial facts, or when it is clear that a person is speaking directly to me.

ARCHIVAL AND UNPUBLISHED SOURCES

Alabama Department of Archives and History, ADAH

American Geographical Society, AGS

Costin Family Papers, private collection of Michael Costin and Mary Gibson

Fawcett Family Papers, private collection of Rolette de Montet-Guerin

Fundação Biblioteca Nacional, Rio de Janeiro, Brazil, FBN

Harry Ransom Center, The University of Texas at Austin, HRC

Imperial War Museum, IWM

National Library of Scotland, NLS

National Museum of the American Indian Archives, Smithsonian Institution, NMAI

Percy Harrison Fawcett Papers, Rare Book, Manuscript, and Special Collections Library, Duke University, PHFP

Rimell Family Papers, private collection of Ann Macdonald

Royal Anthropological Institute, RAI

Royal Artillery Historical Trust, RAHT

Royal Geographical Society, RGS

The National Archives, Kew, Surrey, TNA

NOTES

PREFACE

4   **"no Arts; no Letters"**: Hobbes, *Leviathan*, p. 186.

4   **"write a new"**: *Los Angeles Times*, Jan. 28, 1925.

CHAPTER 1: WE SHALL RETURN

8   **He was the last:** Though many of Fawcett's expeditions took place after the death of Queen Victoria in 1901, he is often categorized as a Victorian explorer. Not only did he come of age during the Victorian period, but he embodied, in almost every way, the Victorian ethos and spirit of exploration.

8   **"a man of indomitable"**: Dyott, "Search for Colonel Fawcett," p. 514.

8   **"outwalk and outhike"**: Loren McIntyre, in transcript of interview on National Public Radio, March 15, 1999.

8   **"Fawcett marked"**: K.G.G., "Review: Exploration Fawcett," *Geographical Journal*, Sept. 1953, p. 352.

8   **Among them was:** Doyle, notes to *Lost World*, p. 195; Percy Harrison Fawcett, *Exploration Fawcett*, p. 122. There is little known about the origins of the relationship between Percy Fawcett and Conan Doyle. *Exploration Fawcett* notes that Conan Doyle had attended one of Fawcett's lectures delivered before the Royal Geographical Society. Once, in a letter to Conan Doyle, Fawcett remembered how the author had tried to contact him during the writing of *The Lost World*, but because Fawcett was off in the jungle Nina had been forced to respond. In *The Annotated Lost World*,

285

published in 1996, Roy Pilot and Alvin Rodin point out that Fawcett was "well known to Conan Doyle" and catalog the many similarities between Fawcett and the novel's fictional explorer John Roxton. Interestingly, Percy Fawcett may not have been the only member of his family to influence Conan Doyle's famous literary work. In 1894, nearly two decades before Conan Doyle came out with *The Lost World,* Fawcett's brother, Edward, published *Swallowed by an Earthquake*—a novel that similarly tells of men discovering a hidden world of prehistoric dinosaurs. In an article in the *British Heritage* in 1985, Edward Fawcett's literary executor and the author Robert K. G. Temple accused Conan Doyle of borrowing "shamelessly" from Edward's now largely forgotten novel.

8   **"disappear into the unknown"**: Doyle, *Lost World*, p. 63.

9   **"Something there was"**: Ibid., p. 57.

9   **The ship:** My descriptions of the *Vauban* and life on board ocean liners come from, among other places, the Lamport & Holt brochure "South America: The Land of Opportunity, a Continent of Scenic Wonders, a Paradise for the Tourist"; Heaton's *Lamport & Holt*; and Maxtone-Graham's *Only Way to Cross.*

9   **"the great discovery"**: Fawcett to John Scott Keltie, Feb. 4, 1925, RGS.

10   **"What is there"**: *Los Angeles Times*, April 16, 1925.

10   **"their eyes in"**: Ralegh, *Discoverie of the Large, Rich, and Bewtiful Empyre of Guiana*, pp. 177–78.

10   **"thorow hollow"**: Ibid., p. 114.

10   **"We reached"**: Carvajal, *Discovery of the Amazon*, p. 172.

11   **"Does God think"**: Quoted in Hemming, *Search for El Dorado*, p. 144.

11   **"Commend thyself"**: Simón, *Expedition of Pedro de Ursua & Lope de Aguirre*, p. 227.

11   **"I swear to"**: Quoted in Hemming, *Search for El Dorado*, p. 144.

11   **"It is perhaps"**: *Atlanta Constitution*, Jan. 12, 1925.

11   **"The central place"**: Brian Fawcett, *Ruins in the Sky*, p. 48.

12   **"Not since"**: Colonel Arthur Lynch, "Is Colonel Fawcett Still Alive?" *Graphic* (London), Sept. 1, 1928.

12   **"I cannot say"**: Fawcett to Keltie, Aug. 18, 1924, RGS.

12   **"is about the only"**: Quoted in Fawcett to Isaiah Bowman, April 8, 1919, AGS.

13   **"it would be hopeless"**: Arthur R. Hinks to Captain F. W. Dunn-Taylor, July 6, 1927, RGS.

13   **"If with all"**: Fawcett, epilogue to *Exploration Fawcett*, p. 304.

13   **"will be no pampered"**: Ibid., pp. 14–15.

13   **"We will have to suffer"**: *Los Angeles Times*, Jan. 28, 1925.

13   **"to harass and"**: Ibid.

13   **"the reflection of"**: Williams, introduction to *AmaZonia*, p. 24.

13   **"six feet three"**: Fawcett, epilogue to *Exploration Fawcett*, p. 277.

13   **"He is . . . absolutely"**: Ibid., p. 15.

14   **"fine physique"**: Percy Harrison Fawcett, "General Details of Proposed Expedition in S. America" (proposal), n.d., RGS.

14 "He was a born": Fawcett, epilogue to *Exploration Fawcett*, p. 277.

14 "Now we have Raleigh": Williams, introduction to *AmaZonia*, p. 10.

14 "utterly impracticable": Dickens, *American Notes*, p. 13.

15 "hearse with windows": Ibid., p. 14.

15 "perfect ventilation": Lamport & Holt brochure, "South America."

15 "rather tiresome": Fawcett, epilogue to *Exploration Fawcett*, p. 278.

16 "Jack has": Ibid., p. 15.

16 "Raleigh will follow": Ibid.

16 "We shall return": *Los Angeles Times*, Jan. 28, 1925.

CHAPTER 2: THE VANISHING

17 It begins as barely: My descriptions of the Amazon River are drawn from several sources. They include Goulding, Barthem, and Ferreira, *Smithsonian Atlas of the Amazon*; Revkin, *Burning Season*; Haskins, *Amazon*; Whitmore, *Introduction to Tropical Rain Forests*; Bates, *Naturalist on the River Amazons*; and Price, *Amazing Amazon*.

19 The expedition was: My descriptions of the 1996 expedition are based on my interviews with James Lynch and members of his team as well as on information from Leal's *Coronel Fawcett*.

19 "among the most": Temple, "E. Douglas Fawcett," p. 29.

19 "captured the imagination": *Daily Mail* (London), Jan. 30, 1996.

19 Evelyn Waugh's: Heath, *Picturesque Prison*, p. 116.

20 "Enough legend": Fleming, *Brazilian Adventure*, p. 104.

20 "than those launched": *New York Times*, Feb. 13, 1955.

21 "Our route": Percy Harrison Fawcett, *Exploration Fawcett*, p. 269.

21 Even today: *New York Times*, Jan. 18, 2007.

21 "These forests are": Hemming, *Die If You Must*, p. 635.

22 "No one knows": Ibid.

22 In 2006, members: *New York Times*, May 11, 2006.

22 "only one and all": Percy Harrison Fawcett, "Case for an Expedition in the Amazon Basin" (proposal), RGS.

23 "a corpse piece": Quoted in Millard, *River of Doubt*, p. 168.

CHAPTER 3: THE SEARCH BEGINS

29 many archaeologists and geographers: For a much more detailed discussion of the academic debate over advanced civilizations in the Amazon, see Mann's *1491*.

30 "counterfeit paradise": See Meggers, *Amazonia*.

30 "cultural substitutes": Ibid., p. 104.

30 "This is the jungle": Cowell, *Tribe That Hides from Man*, p. 66.

30 As Charles Mann notes: Mann, *1491*, p. 9.

30 "the most culturally": Holmberg, *Nomads of the Long Bow*, p. 17.

30 "No records": Ibid., p. 122.

30   **"concept of romantic"**: Ibid., p. 161.

30   **"man in the"**: Ibid., p. 261.

30   **a more sophisticated**: Mann, *1491*, p. 328.

Chapter 4: Buried Treasure

33   **"the callowest"**: Percy Harrison Fawcett, "Passing of Trinco," p. 110.

34   **"Beneath these rocks"**: Percy Harrison Fawcett, "Gold Bricks at Badulla," p. 223.

34   **"As an impecunious"**: Ibid., p. 232.

34   **"possessed great abilities"**: From a self-published article by Timothy Paterson, "Douglas Fawcett and Imaginism," p. 2.

35   **"Her unhappy married"**: Ibid.

35   **"hateful"**: Fawcett to Doyle, March 26, 1919, HRC.

35   **"Perhaps it was all"**: Percy Harrison Fawcett, *Exploration Fawcett*, p. 15.

35   **"did nothing to"**: Ibid., p. 16.

35   **notion of a gentleman**: For details on the Victorian customs and ethos, see the 1865 manual *The Habits of Good Society*; Campbell, *Etiquette of Good Society*; and Bristow, *Vice and Vigilance*.

35   **"the memorable horror"**: Fawcett, *Exploration Fawcett*, p. 211.

36   **"craving for sensual"**: Percy Harrison Fawcett, "Obsession," p. 476.

36   **"a natural leader"**: Girouard, *Return to Camelot*, p. 260.

36   **"it takes something"**: From a newspaper article in Fawcett's scrapbook, Fawcett Family Papers.

36   **Royal Military Academy at Woolwich**: See Guggisberg, *Shop*.

36   **"The fashion of torture"**: Ibid., p. 57.

37   **"to regard the risk"**: Hankey, *Student in Arms*, p. 87.

37   **Now, as Fawcett**: Details of Sri Lanka in the 1890s come from various books of the time, including Ferguson, *Ceylon in 1893*; Willis, *Ceylon*; and Cave, *Golden Tips*.

37   **"Dear me"**: Twain, *Following the Equator*, p. 336.

38   **"I'm afraid"**: Fawcett, "Gold Bricks at Badulla," p. 225.

38   **"Did the hound"**: Ibid., p. 231.

38   **"Ceylon is a very"**: Ibid., p. 232.

39   **"He obviously did"**: Williams, introduction to *AmaZonia*, p. 16.

39   **"the way the ladies"**: Quotation from a newspaper article found in Fawcett's scrapbook, Fawcett Family Papers.

39   **"the only one"**: *Curieux*, Sept. 26, 1951.

39   **"she always had"**: Williams, introduction to *AmaZonia*, p. 18.

40   **"I was very happy"**: *Curieux*, Sept. 26, 1951.

40   **"My life would"**: Ibid.

40   **"a silly old"**: Fawcett to Doyle, March 26, 1919, HRC.

40   **"You are not"**: Williams, introduction to *AmaZonia*, p. 3.

40   **"It took me"**: *Curieux*, Sept. 26, 1951.

40   **"Destiny cruelly"**: Ibid.

40   **"Go . . . and marry"**: Williams, introduction to *AmaZonia*, p. 3. A similar account can be found in Hambloch, *Here and There*.

40   **"begged her to"**: My interview with Fawcett's granddaughter, Rolette.

40   **"I thought I had"**: *Curieux*, Sept. 26, 1951.

41   **"A particularly beautiful"**: Percy Harrison Fawcett, letter to the editor, *Occult Review*, Feb. 1913, p. 80.

41   **"lone wolf"**: Fawcett, *Exploration Fawcett*, p. 16.

41   **Madame Blavatsky**: See Meade, *Madame Blavatsky*; Washington, *Madame Blavatsky's Baboon*; and Oppenheim, *Other World*.

41   **"a genius"**: Meade, *Madame Blavatsky*, p. 40.

42   **"She weighed more"**: Ibid., p. 8.

42   **"the most human"**: Kelly, *Collected Letters of W. B. Yeats*, p. 164.

42   **"addicted to table-rapping"**: Oppenheim, *Other World*, p. 28.

42   **"I suppose I am"**: Stashower, *Teller of Tales*, p. 405.

43   **"For those who"**: Oppenheim, *Other World*, p. 184.

43   **"The ceremony commenced"**: *Dublin Review*, July–Oct. 1890, p. 56.

44   **"At the very time"**: A. N. Wilson, *Victorians*, p. 551.

44   **"I transgressed again"**: Fawcett, "Passing of Trinco," p. 116.

44   **In the late 1860s**: See Stanley, *How I Found Livingstone*; and Jeal, *Livingstone*.

45   **"E. M. Forster once"**: Pritchett, *Tale Bearers*, p. 25.

45   **"wild-man that eats"**: Edward Douglas Fawcett, *Swallowed by an Earthquake*, p. 180.

45   **"most venturesome"**: Edward Douglas Fawcett, *Secret of the Desert*, p. 206.

46   **"possibly thinking"**: Ibid., p. 3.

46   **"strange ruins"**: Ibid., p. 49.

46   **"we would-be"**: Ibid., p. 146.

46   **"I was overcome"**: Ibid., p. 195.

46   **"He won't"**: Ibid., p. 237.

46   **"Everywhere about me"**: Fawcett, "Passing of Trinco," p. 116.

47   **"the city has vanished"**: Walters, *Palms and Pearls*, p. 94.

47   **"old Ceylon is"**: Fawcett to Esther Windust, March 23, 1924, PHFP.

47   **"a geography militant"**: Conrad, "Geography and Some Explorers," p. 6.

CHAPTER 5: BLANK SPOTS ON THE MAP

49   **One person who**: Steve Kemper's 1995 account, "Fawcett's Wake," provided to author.

49   **For ages, cartographers**: Information on the history of maps and geography is drawn largely from Wilford, *Mapmakers*; Brown, *Story of Maps*; Sobel, *Longitude*; Bergreen, *Over the Edge of the World*; and De Camp and Ley, *Lands Beyond*.

50   **"with every kind"**: Quoted in Brehaut, *Encyclopedist of the Dark Ages*, p. 244.

50   **"I, Prester John"**: Quoted in Bergreen, *Over the Edge of the World*, p. 77.

50   **"to the dearest son"**: Quoted in De Camp and Ley, *Lands Beyond*, p. 148.

51   **"the Discovery of"**: Wilford, *Mapmakers*, p. 153.

51   **Finally, in the nineteenth:** For information on the history of the RGS, see Mill, *Record of the Royal Geographical Society*; Cameron, *To the Farthest Ends of the Earth*; and Keltie, "Thirty Years' Work of the Royal Geographical Society."

52   **"collect, digest"**: Mill, *Record of the Royal Geographical Society*, p. 17.

52   **"There was not"**: Francis Younghusband, in "The Centenary Meeting: Addresses on the History of the Society," *Geographical Journal*, Dec. 1930, p. 467.

52   **"[It] was composed"**: Keltie, "Thirty Years' Work of the Royal Geographical Society," p. 350.

53   **Richard Burton espoused:** For information on Burton, see Kennedy, *Highly Civilized Man*; Farwell, *Burton*; and Lovell, *Rage to Live*.

53   **"I protest vehemently"**: Quoted in Farwell, *Burton*, p. 267.

53   **"looked as if a tiger"**: Quoted in Lovell, *Rage to Live*, p. 581.

53   **"Explorers are not"**: David Attenborough, foreword to Cameron, *To the Farthest Ends of the Earth*.

53   **"What you can"**: Quoted in Kennedy, *Highly Civilized Man*, p. 102.

54   **"who sit in carpet slippers"**: Ibid., p. 103.

54   **"B is one of those men"**: Ibid., p. 169.

54   **"gladiatorial exhibition"**: Ibid., p. 124.

54   **"By God, he's killed"**: Quoted in Moorehead, *White Nile*, pp. 74–75.

54   **A cousin of Charles Darwin's:** See Gillham, *Life of Sir Francis Galton*; Pickover, *Strange Brains and Genius*; and Brookes, *Extreme Measures*.

55   **"no man expressed"**: Quoted in Pickover, *Strange Brains and Genius*, p. 113.

55   **"A passion for travel"**: Ibid., p. 118.

55   **"from north and south"**: Quoted in Driver, *Geography Militant*, p. 3.

56   **"So great is the heat"**: Quoted in Cameron, *To the Farthest Ends of the Earth*, p. 53.

57   **"There is very little"**: Fawcett to Keltie, Dec. 14, 1921, RGS.

CHAPTER 6: THE DISCIPLE

58   **It was February 4, 1900:** The date was identified in a 1901 letter from the War Office to the secretary of the Royal Geographical Society, while the location of the hotel was mentioned in Reeves's *Recollections of a Geographer*, p. 96.

58   **Billboard men:** For descriptions of London at the turn of the century, see Cook, *Highways and Byways in London*; Burke, *Streets of London Through the Centuries*; Sims, *Living London*; Flanders, *Inside the Victorian Home*; and Larson, *Thunderstruck*.

59   **On the corner:** For details about the RGS building on Savile Row, see Mill, *Record of the Royal Geographical Society*.

59   **In his late thirties:** My descriptions of Reeves and his course are drawn largely from his memoir, *Recollections of a Geographer*, and his published lectures, *Maps and Map-Making*.

60   **"How well I"**: Reeves, *Recollections of a Geographer*, p. 17.

60   **"He had an innate"**: Francis Younghusband, foreword to ibid., p. 11.

60   "the society of men": Galton, *Art of Travel*, p. 2.

60   "If you could blindfold": Reeves, *Maps and Map-Making*, p. 84.

61   "He was extremely": Reeves, *Recollections of a Geographer*, p. 96.

61   what the Greeks called: Bergreen, *Over the Edge of the World*, p. 84.

61   There were two principal: For further information about the role that these manu-
     als played in shaping Victorian attitudes, see Driver, *Geography Militant*, pp. 49–67.

61   "It is a loss": Freshfield and Wharton, *Hints to Travellers*, p. 2.

61   "Remember that": Ibid., p. 5.

62   "Had we lived": *New York Times*, Feb. 11, 1913.

62   In 1896, Great Britain: McNiven and Russell, *Appropriated Pasts*, p. 66.

62   "savages, barbarians": Freshfield and Wharton, *Hints to Travellers*, p. 435.

62   "the prejudices with": Ibid., pp. 445–46.

62   "it is established": Ibid., p. 422.

62   As with mapping: Information on the "tools" used by early anthropologists is derived
     largely from the 1893 edition of *Hints to Travellers* and the 1874 handbook prepared by the
     British Association for the Advancement of Science, *Notes and Queries on Anthropology*.

62   "Where practicable": Freshfield and Wharton, *Hints to Travellers*, p. 421.

62   "It is hardly safe": Ibid.

62   "emotions are differently": Ibid., p. 422.

63   "Notwithstanding his inveterate": Ibid., p. 58.

63   "We, the undersigned": Ibid., p. 6.

63   "Promote merriment": Ibid., p. 309.

63   "A frank, joking": Ibid., p. 308.

63   "constantly pushing and pulling": Ibid., p. 17.

64   "Use soap-suds": Ibid., p. 18.

64   "Afterwards burn out": Ibid., p. 21.

64   "Pour boiling grease": Ibid., p. 20.

64   "This can be done": Ibid., p. 225.

64   "To prepare them": Ibid., p. 201.

64   "take your knife": Ibid., p. 317.

65   "If a man be lost": Ibid., p. 321.

65   "Choose a well-marked": Ibid.

65   "with great credit": Ibid., p. 96.

65   "The R.G.S. bred me": Fawcett to John Scott Keltie, Nov. 2, 1924, RGS.

CHAPTER 7: FREEZE-DRIED ICE CREAM AND ADRENALINE SOCKS

67   "There were the Prudent": Fleming, *Brazilian Adventure*, p. 32.

68   More feared than piranhas: Millard, *River of Doubt*, pp. 164–65.

69   "Many deaths result": Percy Harrison Fawcett, *Exploration Fawcett*, p. 50.

70   "hush-hush": Brian Fawcett to Brigadier F. Percy Roe, March 15, 1977, RGS.

CHAPTER 8: INTO THE AMAZON

71   **It was the perfect:** Details of Fawcett's time working for the British Intelligence Office are drawn from his Morocco diary, 1901, Fawcett Family Papers.

71   **"nature of trails":** Ibid.

71   **In the nineteenth century:** See Hefferman, "Geography, Cartography, and Military Intelligence," pp. 505–6.

71   **British authorities transformed:** My information on the Survey of India Department and its spies comes primarily from Hopkirk's books *The Great Game* and *Trespassers on the Roof of the World*.

72   **"some sort of Moorish":** Percy Harrison Fawcett, "Journey to Morocco City," p. 190.

72   **"The Sultan is":** Fawcett, Morocco diary.

72   **In early 1906:** Percy Harrison Fawcett, *Exploration Fawcett*, pp. 18–19.

72   **Famous for his keen:** See Flint, *Sir George Goldie and the Making of Nigeria*; and Muffett, *Empire Builder Extraordinary*.

73   **"[He] was lashed":** Muffett, *Empire Builder Extraordinary*, p. 19.

73   **"bore holes":** Ibid., p. 22.

73   **"Do you know":** For the conversation between Fawcett and Goldie, see Fawcett, *Exploration Fawcett*, pp. 18–20.

74   **"Destiny intended me":** Ibid., p. 20.

74   **"toughs, would be":** Ibid.

74   **a thirty-year-old:** Fawcett used a pseudonym for Chivers in *Exploration Fawcett*, calling him Chalmers.

74   **"They were all":** Ibid., p. 21.

74   **Since the canal's:** Enrique Chavas-Carballo, "Ancon Hospital: An American Hospital During the Construction of the Panama Canal, 1904–1914," *Military Medicine*, Oct. 1999.

75   **"How strange":** Fawcett, *Exploration Fawcett*, p. 26.

75   **"a marvelous effect":** Freshfield and Wharton, *Hints to Travellers*, p. 12.

76   **"A mule's load":** Fawcett, *Exploration Fawcett*, p. 159.

76   **Christopher Columbus had:** My descriptions of the Amazon rubber boom and the frontier come from several sources, including Furneaux, *Amazon*, pp. 144–66; Hemming, *Amazon Frontier*, pp. 271–75; and St. Clair, *Mighty, Mighty Amazon*, pp. 156–63.

76   **In 1912, Brazil alone:** Author's interview with Aldo Musacchio, co-author of "Brazil in the International Rubber Trade, 1870–1930," which was published in *From Silver to Cocaine: Latin American Commodity Chains and the Building of the World Economy, 1500–2000*, ed. Steven Topik, Carlos Marichal, and Zephyr Frank (Durham, N.C.: Duke University Press, 2006).

76   **"No extravagance":** Furneaux, *Amazon*, p. 153.

77   **"the most criminal":** Quoted in Hemming, *Amazon Frontier*, pp. 292–93.

77   **"My heart sank":** Fawcett, *Exploration Fawcett*, p. 41.

78   **"from 'nowhere' ":** Ibid., p. 89.

78   **"as proper as":** Price, *Amazing Amazon*, p. 147.

78   **"Government? What"**: Quoted in Fifer, *Bolivia*, p. 131.

78   **"Here come"**: Fawcett, *Exploration Fawcett*, pp. 95–96.

78   **In one instance**: See Hardenburg, *Putumayo*.

79   **"In some sections"**: Ibid., p. 204.

79   **"It is no exaggeration"**: U.S. Department of State, *Slavery in Peru*, p. 120.

79   **"so many of them"**: Ibid., p. 69.

79   **"the wretched policy"**: Percy Harrison Fawcett, "Survey Work on the Frontier Between Bolivia and Brazil," p. 185.

79   **"the great dangers"**: Percy Harrison Fawcett, "Explorations in Bolivia," p. 515.

79   **"He could smell"**: Ibid., p. 64.

80   **"He has his choice"**: Percy Harrison Fawcett, "In the Heart of South America," pt. 4, p. 91.

80   **"the most ferocious"**: Theodore Roosevelt, *Through the Brazilian Wilderness*, p. 40.

80   **"there was an unpleasant"**: Fawcett, *Exploration Fawcett*, p. 131.

80   **In addition to piranhas**: For descriptions of the animals and insects of the Amazon, see Forsyth and Miyata, *Tropical Nature*; Cutright, *Great Naturalists Explore South America*; Kricher, *Neotropical Companion*; and Millard, *River of Doubt*.

80   **The German explorer-scientist**: Humboldt, *Personal Narrative of Travels to the Equinoctial Regions of America*, pp. 112–16.

81   **"One shock is sufficient"**: Fawcett, *Exploration Fawcett*, p. 50.

81   **"carry no hope"**: Fawcett, "In the Heart of South America," pt. 3, p. 498.

81   **"It was one"**: Fawcett, *Exploration Fawcett*, p. 84.

82   **"We lived simply"**: Costin to daughter Mary, Nov. 10, 1946, Costin Family Papers.

82   **"Inactivity was what"**: Fawcett, *Exploration Fawcett*, p. 94.

82   **"Monkeys are looked"**: Ibid., p. 47.

82   **"is against man"**: Ibid.

83   **"[Mosquitoes] constitute"**: Price, *Amazing Amazon*, p. 138.

83   **"The piums settled"**: Fawcett, *Exploration Fawcett*, p. 59.

83   **"The *Tabana* came singly"**: Ibid., p. 49.

83   **"Attacked in hammocks"**: Ernest Holt diary, Oct. 20, 1920, ADAH.

84   **according to one estimate**: Millard, *River of Doubt*, p. 250.

85   **"a couple of crossed"**: Fawcett, *Exploration Fawcett*, p. 89.

85   **"When [the Kanichana]"**: Métraux, *Native Tribes of Eastern Bolivia and Western Matto Grosso*, p. 80.

85   **"The head and the intestines"**: Clastres, "Guayaki Cannibalism," pp. 313–15.

86   **"court assassination"**: C. Reginald Enock, letter to the editor, *Geographical Journal*, April 19, 1911, RGS.

87   **"It was trying"**: Fawcett, *Exploration Fawcett*, p. 73.

87   **"Their bodies [were] painted"**: Ibid., p. 87.

87   **"One ripped through"**: Ibid.

87   **"I had observed"**: Ibid., p. 83.

87   **Still, two of the men**: Fawcett, "Explorations in Bolivia," p. 523.

87   **"I was tempted"**: Ibid., p. 43.

87   "**Unless he had**": Keltie to Nina Fawcett, Dec. 1, 1913, RGS.

88   "**the healthy person**": Fawcett, *Exploration Fawcett*, p. 55.

Chapter 9: The Secret Papers

91   "**professional burglar**": Malcolm, *Silent Woman*, p. 9.

92   **Many of the diaries:** Quotations from diaries and logbooks come from the private papers of the Fawcett family.

Chapter 10: The Green Hell

94   "**Are you game?**": See Percy Harrison Fawcett, *Exploration Fawcett*, pp. 116–22. For further information on the journey, see Fawcett's "Explorations in Bolivia" and his four-part series "In the Heart of South America."

95   "**When . . . the enterprising traveler**": Fawcett, "In the Heart of South America," pt. 2, p. 491.

95   "**Time and the foot**": Fawcett, *Exploration Fawcett*, p. 122.

95   **Conan Doyle reportedly:** Doyle, notes to *Lost World*, p. 195. The other place commonly said to have inspired the novel's setting is Mount Roraima in Venezuela.

95   "**What'll we do**": For details of their conversation, see Fawcett, *Exploration Fawcett*, pp. 120–21.

96   "**Starvation sounds almost**": Fawcett, "In the Heart of South America," pt. 3, p. 549.

97   "**The rain forest**": Millard, *River of Doubt*, p. 148.

97   "**the aquatic equivalents**": Forsyth and Miyata, *Tropical Nature*, p. 93.

97   **Nearly a month after:** Thirty-eight years later, it was revealed that Fawcett and his men had actually been several miles from the principal source. Brian Fawcett noted that "my father would have been bitterly disappointed."

98   "**How long could**": Fawcett, *Exploration Fawcett*, p. 122.

98   "**The voices of**": Ibid., p. 121.

98   "**Starvation blunts one's**": Fawcett, "In the Heart of South America," pt. 4, p. 89.

98   "**[An ambush], in spite**": Fawcett, *Exploration Fawcett*, p. 110.

98   "**For God's sake**": Ibid., p. 124.

Chapter 11: Dead Horse Camp

101   "**the most remarkable**": Percy Harrison Fawcett, "Case for an Expedition in the Amazon Basin" (proposal), April 13, 1924, RGS.

101   "**This area represents**": Ibid.

101   "**get the survivors**": Ibid.

CHAPTER 12: IN THE HANDS OF THE GODS

102   **"glorious prospect"**: Percy Harrison Fawcett, *Exploration Fawcett*, p. 108.

102   **"I wanted to forget"**: Ibid., pp. 108–9.

103   **"Deep down"**: Ibid., p. 109.

103   **"prison gate"**: Ibid., p. 138.

103   **"a very uncertain"**: Nina Fawcett to Joan, Jan. 24, 1946, Fawcett Family Papers.

103   **"subject my wife"**: Fawcett to John Scott Keltie, Oct. 3, 1911, RGS.

103   **He had once shown**: Nina Fawcett to Joan, Sept. 6, 1946, Fawcett Family Papers.

103   **"I felt relieved"**: Williams, introduction to *AmaZonia*, p. 24.

104   **"riotous democracy"**: Brian Fawcett to Nina, Dec. 5, 1933, Fawcett Family Papers.

104   **"They have had"**: Nina Fawcett to Keltie, Nov. 30, 1913, RGS.

104   **"I, personally, am"**: Nina Fawcett to Harold Large, April 12, 1926, Fawcett Family Papers.

104   **She learned how**: Fawcett, *Exploration Fawcett*, p. 16.

104   **"interesting to those"**: Nina Fawcett, "The Transadine Railway," n.d., RGS.

104   **"equality . . . between man"**: Nina Fawcett to Large, Dec. 6, 1923, Fawcett Family Papers.

104   **"Some day perhaps"**: Nina Fawcett to Keltie, Jan. 6, 1911, RGS.

105   **"Daddy gave us"**: Williams, introduction to *AmaZonia*, p. 30.

105   **"By the look of it"**: Percy Harrison Fawcett, "Gold Bricks at Badulla," p. 234.

105   **"the real apple"**: Author's interview with Fawcett's granddaughter.

105   **"Never forget us"**: Percy Harrison Fawcett, "Jack Going to School," 1910, Fawcett Family Papers.

106   **"A leader of men"**: Fawcett to Nina Fawcett, April 12, 1910, Fawcett Family Papers.

106   **"He was probably"**: Stanley Allen, *New Haven Register*, n.d., RGS.

106   **"I have for years"**: Barclay to David George Hogarth, Sept. 1, 1927, RGS.

106   **60 percent of**: Larson, *Thunderstruck*, p. 271.

106   **"a *disease* bred"**: Edward Douglas Fawcett, *Hartmann the Anarchist*, p. 27.

106   **"Of the Houses"**: Ibid., p. 147.

107   **" 'The lure of' "**: Quotations from newspaper articles found in Fawcett's scrapbook, Fawcett Family Papers.

107   **"regions which have"**: Suarez, Lembcke, and Fawcett, "Further Explorations in Bolivia," p. 397.

107   **"a great seeker"**: Fawcett to Keltie, Dec. 24, 1910, RGS.

107   **"What I hope"**: Suarez, Lembcke, and Fawcett, "Further Explorations in Bolivia," pp. 396–97.

108   **"I must tell you"**: Ibid.

108   **"I am a rapid"**: Fawcett to Keltie, Dec. 5, 1914, RGS.

108   **"He was fever-proof"**: Thomas Charles Bridges, *Pictorial Weekly*, n.d.

108   **"a virtual immunity"**: Furneaux, *Amazon*, p. 214.

108   **"perfect constitution"**: Fawcett to Keltie, March 10, 1910, RGS.

108   "What amazed me": Fawcett, *Exploration Fawcett*, p. 178.

109   "the conviction that": Barclay to David George Hogarth, Sept. 1, 1927, RGS.

109   "I am in the hands": Fawcett to Esther Windust, March 24, 1923, PHFP.

109   "prepared to travel": "Colonel Fawcett's Expedition in Matto Grosso," *Geographical Journal*, Feb. 1928, p. 176.

109   "By the way": Nina Fawcett to Keltie, Oct. 9, 1921, RGS.

109   "Such journeys": Fawcett to Keltie, March 2, 1912, RGS.

109   "hopeless rotter": From scrapbook, Fawcett Family Papers.

109   "Why he would not": Dyott, *Man Hunting in the Jungle*, p. 120.

109   "The strain has": Percy Harrison Fawcett, "Bolivian Exploration, 1913–1914" (proposal), n.d., RGS.

110   "I have no mercy": Fawcett to Keltie, Dec. 24, 1913, RGS.

110   "I am very glad": Keltie to Fawcett, Jan. 29, 1914, RGS.

110   Born in Glasgow: For details about Murray, see Riffenburgh, *Nimrod*; Niven, *Ice Master*; "Captain Bartlett Has No Views," *Washington Post*, July 6, 1914; Shackleton, *Heart of the Antarctic*; and Murray and Marston, *Antarctic Days*.

110   "Pulling, you are": Murray and Marston, *Antarctic Days*, p. 88.

111   "He is an admirable man": Fawcett to Keltie, Oct. 3, 1911, RGS.

111   "I had had rheumatism": Murray and Marston, introduction to *Antarctic Days*, p. xvi.

111   "barren regions": Fawcett, letter to the editor, *Travel*, n.d., RGS.

112   "A tough bugger": Author's interview with Michael Costin.

112   "It's impossible": Fawcett, *Exploration Fawcett*, p. 144.

112   "Several mules with": James Murray diary, Oct. 2, 1911, NLS.

112   "We were all": Costin to daughter Mary, Nov. 10, 1946, Costin Family Papers.

113   "We awoke to find": Fawcett, *Exploration Fawcett*, p. 150.

113   "Surely an iron-bound": Ernest Holt diary, Nov. 10, 1920, ADAH.

113   "The animals themselves": Rice, "Further Explorations in the North-West Amazon Basin," p. 148.

113   "My strength quite": For this quotation and all others from Murray on the 1911 expedition, see his diary, part of the William Laird McKinlay Collection at the National Library of Scotland.

115   "I thought that": Holt diary, Nov. 22, 1920, ADAH.

116   As Costin warned: Costin to daughter Mary, Nov. 10, 1946, Costin Family Papers.

116   "greatest cruelty that faithless": Quoted in Hemming, *Search for El Dorado*, p. 114.

117   "Every party": Mrs. Letheran to Fawcett, Oct. 30, 1919, Fawcett Family Papers.

117   "the motive power": Percy Harrison Fawcett, "Occult Life," p. 93.

117   "There is no disgrace": Fawcett, *Exploration Fawcett*, p. 163.

117   "Civilization has": Percy Harrison Fawcett, "Renegades from Civilization," n.d., Fawcett Family Papers.

118   "On such an expedition": Theodore Roosevelt, *Through the Brazilian Wilderness*, p. 303.

118   "It develops into": Fawcett, *Exploration Fawcett*, p. 60.

119   "Being unarmed": Costin, *Daily Chronicle* (London), Aug. 27, 1928.

120   "By this time": Fawcett, *Exploration Fawcett*, p. 169.

121   "I will not detail": Costin, *Daily Chronicle* (London), Aug. 27, 1928.

121   "You know that": Murray diary, Nov. 17, 1911, NLS.

122   "Murray is": Fawcett to Keltie, Dec. 31, 1911, RGS.

123   "I understand that": Keltie to Fawcett, June 11, 1912, RGS.

123   "Everything that could": Fawcett to Keltie, March 2, 1912, RGS.

123   "did not neglect": Keltie to Hugh Mill, March 1, 1912, RGS.

123   "I am sure": Keltie to Fawcett, June 1, 1912, RGS.

123   "So far they": Fawcett to Keltie, May 10, 1912, RGS.

124   "What a dreadful": Keltie to Fawcett, March 7, 1912, RGS.

124   "It's hell": Fawcett, *Exploration Fawcett*, p. 153.

124   "He and Costin": Ibid., p. 154.

124   in June 1913: On Murray's disappearance, see Niven, *Ice Master*.

CHAPTER 14: THE CASE FOR Z

129   In 1910: Percy Harrison Fawcett, "Further Explorations in Bolivia," p. 387.

129   "The moment": Carvajal, *Discovery of the Amazon*, p. 438.

130   "Retire! Retire!": Percy Harrison Fawcett, "In the Heart of South America," pt. 3, p. 552.

130   "One of these": Costin to daughter Mary, n.d., Costin Family Papers.

130   Over the years: Costin's and Fawcett's recollections differ in some minor details. Fawcett, for instance, remembered one of his colleagues eventually taking him across the river in a canoe.

130   "The Major made": Costin to daughter Mary, n.d., Costin Family Papers.

130   "On climbing the opposite": Fawcett, "In the Heart of South America," pt. 3, p. 552.

130   "[Fawcett] disappeared": Costin to daughter Mary, n.d., Costin Family Papers.

131   "[They] helped us": Fawcett, "Further Explorations in Bolivia," p. 388.

131   "The men are": Ibid.

131   "After a few minutes": Costin to daughter Mary, n.d., Costin Family Papers.

131   "a most intelligent": Fawcett, "Further Explorations in Bolivia," p. 388.

131   "There are problems": Fawcett to RGS, Oct. 15, 1909, RGS.

132   "Without any hesitation": Costin to daughter Mary, Nov. 10, 1946, Costin Family Papers.

132   "Whenever he came": Costin, *Daily Chronicle* (London), Aug. 27, 1928.

132   "I know, from persons": Suarez, Lembcke, and Fawcett, "Further Explorations in Bolivia," p. 397.

132   "standing deliberately": Nina to Keltie, 1909, RGS.

133   "His encounter with": Nina Fawcett to John Scott Keltie, Jan. 11, 1911, RGS.

133   There was, however: Costin, *Daily Chronicle* (London), Aug. 27, 1928.

133   "He did not wish": Ibid.

133   **"we could see"**: Ibid.

134   **"Food problems"**: Percy Harrison Fawcett, *Exploration Fawcett*, p. 171.

134   **"[The Echojas] would"**: Ibid., p. 149.

134   **"I sucked, whistled"**: Fawcett, "In the Heart of South America," pt. 2, p. 495.

134   **"With illness and disease"**: Fawcett, *Exploration Fawcett*, pp. 168–69.

135   **"In 99 cases"**: Fawcett, "In the Heart of South America," pt. 4, p. 92.

135   **Though some of the first:** For details on the first encounter between Native Americans and Europeans and on the Las Casas and Sepúlveda debate, see Huddleston, *Origins of the American Indians*; Todorov, *Conquest of America*; Pagden, *European Encounters with the New World*; and Greenblatt, *Marvelous Possessions*.

135   **"The Spanish have"**: Quoted in Columbia University, *Introduction to Contemporary Civilization in the West*, pp. 526–27.

135   **"Are these not men?"**: Quoted in Pagden, *European Encounters with the New World*, p. 71.

135   **"pretending to be"**: Las Casas, *Short Account of the Destruction of the Indies*, p. 12.

135   **"the simplest people"**: Ibid., pp. 9–10.

136   **"Is there any notable"**: British Association for the Advancement of Science, *Notes and Queries on Anthropology*, pp. 10–13. These racist views toward Native Americans were by no means limited to the Victorians. In 1909, the scientific director of the São Paulo Museum, Dr. Hermann von Ihering, contended that because Indians contribute "neither to labour nor to progress," Brazil had "no alternative but to exterminate them."

136   **many Victorians now:** For my descriptions of Victorian attitudes on race, I've drawn on several excellent books. They include Stocking, *Victorian Anthropology*; Kuklick, *Savage Within*; Stepan, *Idea of Race in Science*; and Kennedy, *Highly Civilized Man*.

136   **"quasi-gorillahood"**: Quoted in Kennedy, *Highly Civilized Man*, p. 133.

137   **"sub-species"**: Ibid., p. 143.

137   **"these poor wretches"**: Quoted in Stocking, *Victorian Anthropology*, p. 105.

137   **"firmness"**: Quoted in A. N. Wilson, *Victorians*, pp. 104–5.

137   **eugenics, which once:** Victoria Glendinning, *Leonard Woolf: A Biography* (New York: Free Press, 2006), p. 149.

137   **"children in mind"**: Quoted in Stocking, *Victorian Anthropology*, p. 157.

137   **lost tribes of Israel:** According to the Bible, in 722 B.C., the Assyrian army carried away and dispersed ten tribes from the northern Israelite kingdom. What happened to them has long mystified scholars. In the middle of the seventeenth century, Antonio de Montezinos, a Sephardic Jew who had escaped the Inquisition, claimed that he had found the descendants of the tribes in the Amazon jungle—that land "where never mankind dwelt." Some of the Indians, he reported, had said to him in Hebrew, "Hear O Israel! The Lord Our God the Lord is One." The influential European rabbi and scholar Menasseh ben Israel later endorsed Montezinos's account, and many believed that the Indians of America, whose origins had long confounded Westerners, were in fact Jews. In 1683, the Quaker and founder of Pennsylvania,

William Penn, said that he was "ready to believe" that the Indians were indeed "of the stock of the Ten Tribes." These theories were also picked up by the Mormons, who believed the Indians had originated, in part, from a migration of Jews.

137 **"There are all sorts"**: *Los Angeles Times*, April 16, 1925.

137 **"jolly children"**: Fawcett, *Exploration Fawcett*, pp. 170, 201.

138 **"savages of"**: Ibid., p. 215.

138 **"My experience"**: Ibid., p. 49.

138 **"roasted over"**: Percy Harrison Fawcett, "Bolivian Exploration, 1913–1914," p. 225.

138 **"elaborate ritual"**: Fawcett, *Exploration Fawcett*, p. 203.

138 **"plain proof"**: Ibid., p. 170.

138 **"He knew the Indians"**: Thomas Charles Bridges, *Pictorial Weekly*, n.d.

138 **"He understood them"**: Costin, *Daily Chronicle* (London), Aug. 27, 1928.

138 **"mental maze"**: Kennedy, *Highly Civilized Man*, p. 143.

138 **"There are three"**: Fawcett, *Exploration Fawcett*, p. 95.

139 **"white as we"**: Quoted in Babcock, "Early Observations in American Physical Anthropology," p. 309.

139 **"men, women and"**: Quoted in Woolf, "Albinism (OCA2) in Amerindians," p. 121.

139 **"very white"**: Carvajal, *Discovery of the Amazon*, p. 214.

139 **"Nietzschean explorer"**: Hemming, *Die If You Must*, p. 78.

140 **"Probably none of us"**: Fawcett, "Bolivian Exploration, 1913–1914," p. 222.

140 **"They slipped in"**: Fawcett, *Exploration Fawcett*, pp. 199–200.

140 **"Don't move!"**: Costin, *Daily Chronicle* (London), Aug. 27, 1928.

140 **"I myself made"**: Ibid.

140 **"Our friendship"**: Fawcett, *Exploration Fawcett*, p. 199.

141 **They had befriended**: The renowned Swedish anthropologist Baron Erland Nordenskiöld later reported that Fawcett had "discovered an important indigenous tribe that . . . has never been visited by the white man."

141 **"We do not"**: Bowman, "Remarkable Discoveries in Bolivia," p. 440.

141 **"Perhaps this is why"**: Fawcett, *Exploration Fawcett*, p. 173.

141 **"The tribe is also"**: Fawcett, "Bolivian Exploration, 1913–1914," p. 224.

141 **"intractable, hopelessly brutal"**: Ibid., p. 228.

141 **"brave and intelligent"**: Fawcett, *Exploration Fawcett*, p. 200.

142 **"Wherever there are"**: Percy Harrison Fawcett, "Memorandum Regarding the Region of South America Which It Is Intended to Explore" (proposal), 1920, RGS.

142 **"roads" and "causeways"**: Ibid.

142 **There was, for instance**: For details on Henry Savage Landor, see Hopkirk's *Trespassers on the Roof of the World* and Landor's *Everywhere* and *Across Unknown South America*.

142 **"I did not masquerade"**: Landor, *Across Unknown South America*, vol. 1, p. 14.

143 **"In Xanadu"**: Quoted in Millard, *River of Doubt*, p. 3.

143 **"I am going very slowly"**: Church, "Dr. Rice's Exploration in the North-Western Valley of the Amazon," pp. 309–10.

143   "We look upon": H.E., "The Rio Negro, the Casiquiare Canal, and the Upper Orinoco," p. 343.

144   "probably the first surgical": Royal Geographical Society, "Monthly Record," June 1913, p. 590.

144   one occasion they mutinied: *New York Times*, Sept. 7, 1913.

144   "He is a medical": Keltie to Fawcett, Jan. 29, 1914, RGS.

144   "as much at home": *New York Times*, July 24, 1956.

144   "Explorers are not": Fawcett to RGS, Jan. 24, 1922, RGS.

145   "Keep your ears open": Keltie to Fawcett, March 10, 1911, RGS.

145   "I see he even": Quoted in Millard, *River of Doubt*, p. 338.

145   "a pure fake": Ibid., p. 339.

145   "no mountaineer can": Quoted in Hopkirk, *Trespassers on the Roof of the World*, p. 135.

145   "unintelligible": *New York Times*, Oct. 6, 1915.

145   "for an elderly man": Fawcett to Keltie, Feb. 3, 1915, RGS.

145   "I do not wish": Fawcett to Keltie, April 15, 1924, RGS.

145   "a humbug from": Fawcett to Keltie, Sept. 27, 1912, RGS.

146   "counted in with": Fawcett to Keltie, April 9, 1915, RGS.

146   In 1900, Rondon: Millard, *River of Doubt*, p. 77.

146   "gentlemen, owing to": Percy Harrison Fawcett, "Case for an Expedition in the Amazon Basin" (proposal), April 13, 1924, RGS.

146   "the idea of": Brian Fawcett, *Ruins in the Sky*, p. 231.

146   "I think you worry": Keltie to Fawcett, Jan. 29, 1914, RGS.

146   "sure to go out": Ibid.

147   "prove to be": Bingham, introduction to *Lost City of the Incas*, pp. 17–18.

147   "the pin-up of": Hugh Thomson, *Independent* (London), July 21, 2001.

CHAPTER 15: EL DORADO

148   "The great lord": Quoted in Hemming, *Search for El Dorado*, p. 97.

149   So, according to: For details, see Hemming's definitive account, *The Search for El Dorado*. Also see Wood, *Conquistadors*; Smith, *Explorers of the Amazon*; and St. Clair, *Mighty, Mighty Amazon*.

149   "gleaming like": Quoted in Hemming, *Search for El Dorado*, p. 101.

149   As fanciful as these: The theologian Sepúlveda would later dismiss the "ingenuity" of the Indians, such as the Aztecs and the Incas, by saying "animals, birds, and spiders" can also make "certain structures which no human accomplishment can competently imitate."

149   "Some of our soldiers": Quoted in Hemming, *Search for El Dorado*, p. 7.

149   "like something from": Ibid., p. 45.

149   "Because of many reports": Carvajal, appendix to *Discovery of the Amazon*, p. 245.

150   "Cinnamon of the most": Quoted in Hemming, *Search for El Dorado*, p. 111.

150   "The butcher Gonzalo": Ibid., p. 112.

151   **"like mad men"**: Carvajal, *Discovery of the Amazon*, p. 172.

151   **"either die or see"**: Ibid., p. 171.

151   **"went in as far"**: Ibid., p. 213.

152   **"as the brown waters"**: St. Clair, *Mighty, Mighty Amazon*, p. 47.

152   **"more rich and bewtifull cities"**: Ralegh, *Discoverie of the Large, Rich, and Bewtiful Empyre of Guiana*, p. 111.

152   **"more desirous"**: Quoted in Trevelyan, *Sir Walter Raleigh*, p. 494.

152   **"God knows"**: Ibid., pp. 504–5.

152   **His skull was**: Adamson and Folland, *Shepherd of the Ocean*, p. 449.

152   **"Some, contrary to nature"**: Quoted in Hemming, *Search for El Dorado*, p. 63.

152   **"Oh, diabolical plan!"**: Ibid., p. 42.

152   **"They marched like"**: Ibid., p. 172.

153   **"exaggerated romance"**: Fawcett to Arthur R. Hinks, n.d., RGS.

153   **"All that night"**: Carvajal, *Discovery of the Amazon*, p. 202.

153   **"many roads" and "fine highways"**: Ibid.

154   **"great quantity of maize"**: Ibid., p. 211.

154   **"cities that glistened"**: Ibid., p. 217.

154   **"there was a villa"**: Ibid., p. 201.

154   **"full of lies"**: Carvajal, introduction to *Discovery of the Amazon*, p. 25.

154   **"Both the General"**: Quoted in Hemming, *Search for El Dorado*, p. 134.

155   **"they had seen"**: Ibid., p. 133.

155   **"introduction of small-pox"**: Typed extracts from Fawcett's correspondence, Fawcett to Harold Large, Oct. 16, 1923, Fawcett Family Papers.

155   **"the greatest secrets"**: Percy Harrison Fawcett, *Exploration Fawcett*, p. 173.

CHAPTER 16: THE LOCKED BOX

158   **"incited by the insatiable"**: My translation of the document was checked against the more authoritative translation done by Richard Burton's wife, Isabel, which is included in his second volume of *Explorations of the Highlands of the Brazil*.

158   **"It was difficult"**: Percy Harrison Fawcett, *Exploration Fawcett*, p. 10.

159   **"It feels genuine!"**: Brian Fawcett to Nina and Joan, Feb. 6, 1952, Fawcett Family Papers.

CHAPTER 17: THE WHOLE WORLD IS MAD

161   **"Of course experienced"**: Keltie to Fawcett, Dec. 11, 1914, RGS.

161   **"finger on important"**: Fawcett to Keltie, Feb. 3, 1915, RGS.

161   **"Fear not"**: Quoted in *The New York Times Current History: The European War*, vol. 1, *August–December 1914*, p. 140.

161   **"in the thick"**: Fawcett to Keltie, Jan. 18, 1915, RGS.

161   **"one of the most"**: Cecil Eric Lewis Lyne, "My Participation in the Two Great Wars" (unpublished memoir), RAHT.

161 **"was probably the nastiest"**: Henry Harold Hemming, "My Story" (unpublished memoir), IWM.

161 **"Fawcett and I"**: Lyne, "My Participation in the Two Great Wars."

161 **One day Fawcett**: Ibid.

162 **wearing a long**: See John Ramsden's first American edition of *Man of the Century: Winston Churchill and His Legend Since 1945* (New York: Columbia University Press, 2002), p. 372.

162 **"queer garments"**: For Fawcett's encounter with Churchill, see Lyne, "My Participation in the Two Great Wars."

162 **"Filth & rubbish"**: Quoted in Gilbert, *Churchill*, p. 332.

162 **"He is very well"**: Nina Fawcett to Keltie, March 2, 1916, RGS.

162 **"So you can imagine"**: Nina Fawcett to Keltie, April 25, 1916, RGS.

163 **"If you only knew"**: Fawcett to Edward A. Reeves, Feb. 5, 1915, RGS.

163 **A bulletin**: "Monthly Record," *Geographical Journal*, Oct. 1916, p. 354.

163 **"the dream of his life"**: Nina Fawcett to Keltie, March 11, 1916, RGS.

163 **"I possess the medal"**: Fawcett to Keltie, Jan. 15, 1920, RGS.

164 **It was the Battle**: For descriptions of the war, see Gilbert, *Somme*; Ellis, *Eye-Deep in Hell*; Winter, *Death's Men*; and Hart, *Somme*.

164 **"at least provides"**: Percy Harrison Fawcett, *Exploration Fawcett*, p. 66.

164 **"Tell me"**: Huntford, *Shackleton*, p. 599.

165 **"Dante would never"**: Cecil Eric Lewis Lyne diary, RAHT.

165 **"burnt up"**: Ellis, *Eye-Deep in Hell*, pp. 66–67.

165 **"He was troubled"**: Nina Fawcett to Keltie, March 3, 1917, RGS.

165 **The war had claimed**: Mill, *Record of the Royal Geographical Society*, p. 204.

165 **"He was a good fellow"**: Fawcett to Keltie, n.d., 1917, RGS.

165 **"of purely unselfish"**: Davson, *History of the 35th Division*, p. 43.

165 **"If you can imagine"**: "British Colonel in Letter Here Tells of Enormous Slaughter," in Fawcett's scrapbook, n.d., n.p., Fawcett Family Papers.

166 **"Is that you, boy?"**: Stashower, *Teller of Tales*, p. 346.

166 **"She loved you so"**: Fawcett to Doyle, March 26, 1919, HRC.

167 **"He and his intelligence"**: Hemming, "My Story." Henry Harold Hemming was also the father of John Hemming, the celebrated historian who later became the director of the Royal Geographical Society.

167 **Or, as he told**: Fawcett to Doyle, March 26, 1919, HRC.

167 **"many times in France"**: *Washington Post*, March 18, 1934.

168 **"full of the hidden"**: Letter to the editor, *Times* (London), July 4, 1936.

168 **"It is a little"**: Keltie to Fawcett, April 7, 1915, RGS.

168 **"I am getting older"**: Fawcett to Keltie, Feb. 23, 1918, RGS.

168 **"Knowing what these"**: Fawcett, letter to the editor, *Travel*, 1918.

168 **"the whole business"**: Fawcett to Keltie, Feb. 23, 1918, RGS.

168 **"Many thousands must"**: Fawcett, *Exploration Fawcett*, p. 209.

168 **"now quite an inch"**: Nina Fawcett to Large, May 19, 1919, Fawcett Family Papers.

168 **"We all went"**: Ibid.

169 "I had a ripping": Jack Fawcett to Large, Oct. 2, 1924, Fawcett Family Papers.

169 "able and willing": Fawcett, epilogue to *Exploration Fawcett*, p. 277.

169 "This is mine": Ibid.

169 "At school it was": Ibid.

169 "hidden feeling": Nina Fawcett to Joan, Dec. 14, 1952, Fawcett Family Papers.

169 "no favourites": Brian Fawcett to Nina, Dec. 5, 1933, Fawcett Family Papers.

170 "My elder brother": Brian Fawcett to Brigadier F. Percy Roe, March 15, 1977, RGS.

171 "the general practitioner": Dyott, *On the Trail of the Unknown*, p. 141.

171 "I cannot induce": Fawcett, *Exploration Fawcett*, p. 260.

171 "one of the world's": Schurz, "Distribution of Population in the Amazon Valley," p. 206.

171 "an extremely original": Quoted in Rob Hawke, "The Making of a Legend: Colonel Fawcett in Bolivia" (thesis, University of Essex, n.d.), p. 41.

171 "He is a visionary": Arthur R. Hinks to Sir Maurice de Bunsen, Feb. 26, 1920, RGS.

171 "I do not expect": Hinks to Keltie, Dec. 31, 1923, RGS.

171 "Remember that I": Fawcett to Keltie, March 17, 1925, RGS.

172 "Never mind what": Keltie to Fawcett, Dec. 11, 1914, RGS.

172 "rather queer": Hinks to Keltie, Dec. 31, 1923, RGS.

172 "I don't lose": Fawcett to Keltie, April 15, 1924, RGS.

172 "an opportunity to grow": Fawcett, *Exploration Fawcett*, p. 209.

173 "the difficulty of": Rice, "Rio Negro, the Casiquiare Canal, and the Upper Orinoco," p. 324.

173 "The results": Swanson, "Wireless Receiving Equipment," p. 210.

174 "A large, stout": Rice, "Rio Negro, the Casiquiare Canal, and the Upper Orinoco," p. 340.

175 "dress, manners, and": Ibid., p. 325.

175 "There was no alternative": Rice, "Recent Expedition of Dr. Hamilton Rice," pp. 59–60.

175 "We could hear": *Los Angeles Times*, Dec. 22, 1920.

175 "skedaddled": Fawcett to Keltie, July 18, 1924, RGS.

175 "rather too soft": Fawcett to Keltie, April 9, 1924, RGS.

176 "it is quite": RGS to de Bunsen, March 10, 1920, RGS.

176 On February 26: My description of the meeting between Fawcett and Rondon is drawn largely from Leal's *Coronel Fawcett*, pp. 95–96.

176 "it is a matter": Fawcett to Secretary, War Office, Feb. 17, 1919, WO 138/51, TNA.

176 "The higher rank": Fawcett to the Secretary of the Army Council, Aug. 8, 1922, WO 138/51, TNA.

176 "instant attention": Quoted in Hemming, *Die If You Must*, p. 14.

177 Undeterred, Fawcett: In *Exploration Fawcett*, both Brown and Holt are given pseudonyms. The former is referred to as Butch Reilly and the latter as Felipe.

177   "I'm flesh and blood": Ibid., p. 214.

178   In the 1870s: Hobhouse, *Seeds of Wealth*, p. 138.

178   "The electric lights": Furneaux, *Amazon*, p. 159.

178   "impoverished and backward": Fawcett, *Exploration Fawcett*, pp. 212–13.

178   "Lat x+4 to x + 5": Nina Fawcett to Large, June 10, 1921, Fawcett Family Papers.

178   May "protection" be: Jack Fawcett to Fawcett, March 3, 1920, Fawcett Family Papers.

178   "get alarmed at": Fawcett to James Rowsell, June 10, 1921, TNA.

178   "I am going to": Fawcett to Keltie, Feb. 2, 1920, RGS.

179   "More than half ill": Holt diary, Oct. 24–26, 1920, ADAH.

179   "giving me": Fawcett, *Exploration Fawcett*, p. 218.

179   "It was rather": Ibid., p. 192.

179   "It is awful": Holt diary, Nov. 18, 1920.

179   "Never mind me": Fawcett, *Exploration Fawcett*, p. 217.

179   "There was nothing": Ibid.

180   "The exit from Hell": Holt diary, Nov. 17, 1920.

180   "What does it mean": Nina Fawcett to Large, Jan. 26, 1921, Fawcett Family Papers.

180   "Col. Fawcett's expedition": Cândido Mariano da Silva Rondon, *Anglo-Brazilian Chronicle*, April 2, 1932.

180   "You are a strong": Harriett S. Cohen to Holt, Jan. 28, 1921, ADAH.

181   "Unfortunately we live": Fawcett to Holt, Aug. 18, 1921, ADAH.

181   "After close association": Holt diary, Aug. 17, 1921.

181   "convinced I am": Fawcett to Esther Windust, March 5, 1923, PHFP.

181   "I longed for the day": Fawcett, *Exploration Fawcett*, p. 222.

181   "the prospects of returning": Fawcett to Keltie, Feb. 4, 1920, RGS.

182   "Loneliness is not": Fawcett, *Exploration Fawcett*, p. 238.

182   "I must return": Brian Fawcett, *Ruins in the Sky*, p. 235.

CHAPTER 18: A SCIENTIFIC OBSESSION

183   "It's up to you": Brian Fawcett, *Ruins in the Sky*, p. 16.

183   "[Lawrence] may be": Fawcett to Harold Large, March 26, 1919, Fawcett Family Papers.

184   "of faith, courage": Fawcett to Esther Windust, March 5, 1923, PHFP.

184   "I want to go": Fawcett, *Ruins in the Sky*, p. 16.

184   "unsatisfied and unsettled": Raleigh Rimell to Roger Rimell, March 5, 1925, Rimell Family Papers.

184   "both strong as": Fawcett to Large, Feb. 5, 1925, Fawcett Family Papers.

184   "I can only say": Fawcett to John Scott Keltie, April 4, 1924, RGS.

185   "All water has": Nina Fawcett to Large, Nov. 26, 1922, Fawcett Family Papers.

185   "The situation is": Fawcett to Large, Oct. 16, 1923, Fawcett Family Papers.

185   "My man actually": Nina Fawcett to Large, July 18, 1919, Fawcett Family Papers.

185   "I wish you": Fawcett to Keltie, Dec. 29, 1923, RGS.

185 **"P.H.F. was in"**: Nina Fawcett to Large, Aug. 14, 1922, Fawcett Family Papers.

185 **"My father's impatience"**: Percy Harrison Fawcett, epilogue to *Exploration Fawcett*, p. 275.

186 **"Archeological and ethnological"**: Fawcett to Large, Oct. 16, 1923, Fawcett Family Papers.

186 **"the money wasted"**: Fawcett to Keltie, Nov. 29, 1921, RGS.

186 **"men of science"**: Fawcett, *Exploration Fawcett*, p. 208.

186 **"all the skepticism"**: Fawcett to Keltie, Nov. 1, 1924, RGS.

186 **"going to see"**: Fawcett to Keltie, Dec. 18, 1922, RGS.

186 **"The valley and city"**: Mrs. Letheran to Fawcett, Oct. 9, 1919, Fawcett Family Papers.

186 **"the treasures of"**: Percy Harrison Fawcett, "Planetary Control," p. 347.

186 **"a trifle unbalanced"**: George Miller Dyott to Arthur R. Hinks, June 24, 1927, RGS.

186 **"scientific maniac"**: Stanley Allen, *New Haven Register*, n.d., RGS.

186 **"mental storms"**: Percy Harrison Fawcett, "Obsession."

186 **"The Mining Syndicate"**: Fawcett to Large, Oct. 19, 1923, Fawcett Family Papers.

186 **"It seemed as"**: Jack Fawcett to Windust, Dec. 2, 1924, PHFP.

187 **"A short time"**: Jack Fawcett to Windust, Oct. 28, 1924, PHFP.

187 **"The capacity for love"**: Fay Brodie-Junes to Nina Fawcett, n.d., Fawcett Family Papers.

187 **"the Gods will"**: Fawcett to Large, Oct. 19, 1923, Fawcett Family Papers.

188 **"a supply of bombs"**: *New York Times*, Oct. 4, 1924.

188 **"the whole method"**: *New York Times*, Aug. 12, 1924.

188 **"highly respectable man"**: Fawcett to Hinks, Dec. 23, 1924, RGS.

188 **"to get into touch"**: Jack Fawcett to Windust, Oct. 28, 1924, PHFP.

189 **"the finest exploration"**: Fawcett to Keltie, Feb. 4, 1925, RGS.

189 **"We have known"**: *Atlanta Constitution*, Jan. 12, 1925.

190 **"I judge from Lynch's"**: Fawcett to Keltie, Nov. 4, 1924, RGS.

190 **"a modern Columbus"**: Fawcett to Keltie, Oct. 10, 1924, RGS.

190 **"The R.G.S. bred me"**: Fawcett to Keltie, Nov. 2, 1924, RGS.

190 **"If they don't"**: Nina Fawcett to Large, March 31, 1927, Fawcett Family Papers.

190 **"Not a sum"**: Fawcett to Keltie, March 17, 1925, RGS.

190 **"In some ways"**: Fawcett to Keltie, Feb. 4, 1925, RGS.

190 **"a fine young fellow"**: Reeves, *Recollections of a Geographer*, p. 98.

190 **"I shall rejoice"**: Fawcett to Keltie, Nov. 10, 1924, RGS.

191 **"In two years' time"**: Fawcett, *Ruins in the Sky*, p. 46.

191 **"[He] succumbed"**: Fawcett to Hinks, Dec. 23, 1924, RGS.

191 **"must have suffered"**: Fawcett to Keltie, March 17, 1925, RGS.

191 **"the plan can"**: Isaiah Bowman to Rockefeller, Jan. 3, 1925, AGS.

192 **"He did precipitate"**: Fawcett to Keltie, March 17, 1925, RGS.

192 **"I am a great believer"**: Fawcett to Keltie, Dec. 25, 1924, RGS.

192 **"the honour of immortality"**: Fawcett to Bowman, Dec. 15, 1924, AGS.

CHAPTER 19: AN UNEXPECTED CLUE

194 **In 2004:** *New York Times*, Dec. 29, 2006.

196 **Although he made:** Nina Fawcett to Arthur R. Hinks, Nov. 17, 1927, RGS.

196 **"would preserve a higher":** Percy Harrison Fawcett, "Proposal for a S. American Expedition," April 4, 1924, RGS.

CHAPTER 20: HAVE NO FEAR

197 **"At least forty million":** Percy Harrison Fawcett, epilogue to *Exploration Fawcett*, p. 278.

197 **"No Olympic games":** *Los Angeles Times*, Jan. 28, 1925.

197 **"Aren't the reports":** Fawcett, epilogue to *Exploration Fawcett*, p. 280.

197 **Brazilian authorities:** Fawcett to John Scott Keltie, Feb. 4, 1925, RGS.

198 **"They do not want":** Ibid.

198 **"We have met":** Fawcett to Keltie, March 7, 1925, RGS.

198 **the daughter of:** Williams, introduction to *AmaZonia*, p. 22.

198 **"I became acquainted":** Fawcett, epilogue to *Exploration Fawcett*, p. 279.

198 **"[The colonel] and Jack":** Ibid.

198 **"[Raleigh] is much":** Jack Fawcett to Nina and Joan, May 16, 1925, RGS.

198 **"I suppose after":** Fawcett, epilogue to *Exploration Fawcett*, p. 279.

198 **"I don't intend":** Ibid.

199 **"A whole lot":** Ibid., p. 281.

199 **"A snake-bite which bleeds":** *Los Angeles Times*, Dec. 3, 1925. According to snake experts today, it is actually not possible to determine if a snake is poisonous simply based on whether the wound bleeds.

199 **"I saw some quite":** Fawcett, epilogue to *Exploration Fawcett*, p. 279.

199 **"The lavatory":** Ibid., p. 281.

200 **"I am now":** Raleigh Rimell to Roger Rimell, March 5, 1925, Rimell Family Papers.

200 **"Raleigh is a funny":** Fawcett, epilogue to *Exploration Fawcett*, p. 283.

200 **"a desperate villain":** Ibid., p. 281.

200 **"On Wednesday night":** Ibid., p. 282.

201 **"almost big enough":** Raleigh Rimell to Dulcie Rimell, March 11, 1925, Rimell Family Papers.

201 **"Cuyaba will seem":** Fawcett, epilogue to *Exploration Fawcett*, p. 281.

201 **"Daddy says":** Ibid., p. 282.

201 **"a God forsaken hole":** Raleigh Rimell to Roger Rimell, March 5, 1925, Rimell Family Papers.

201 **Fawcett wrote:** Fawcett to Harold Large, March 20, 1925, Fawcett Family Papers.

201 **"Raleigh's feet":** Fawcett, epilogue to *Exploration Fawcett*, p. 284.

201 **"[What] a hell":** Ibid., p. 283.

201 **Raleigh boasted that:** Raleigh Rimell to Roger Rimell, March 5, 1925, Rimell Family Papers.

202   **"We are feeding"**: Fawcett, epilogue to *Exploration Fawcett*, p. 283.

202   **"We intend to buy"**: Ibid., p. 280.

202   **"The horses being"**: Jack Fawcett to Nina and Joan, May 16, 1925, RGS.

203   **"This is nothing"**: *Los Angeles Times*, April 23, 1925.

203   **"I have seen no reason"**: Fawcett to Nina, March 6, 1925, RGS.

203   **"Progress slow"**: Royal Geographical Society, "Dr. Hamilton Rice on the Rio Branco," p. 241.

204   **"If not over"**: Stevens, "Hydroplane of the Hamilton Rice Expedition," pp. 42–43. Interestingly, in 1932, Stevens, while flying in a hot-air balloon, became the first photographer to capture the moon's shadow on the earth during a solar eclipse. In 1935, he also broke the world record for the highest ascent in a balloon—a record that wouldn't be surpassed for another twenty-one years.

204   **"The palms below"**: Ibid., pp. 35–36.

205   **"the congratulations"**: Royal Geographical Society, "Dr. Hamilton Rice on the Rio Branco," p. 241.

205   **"Those regions"**: *New York Times*, Aug. 24, 1924.

205   **"The Brazilian jungle"**: *New York Times*, July 11, 1925.

205   **"communication by radio"**: Royal Geographical Society, "Dr. Hamilton Rice on the Rio Branco," p. 241.

205   **"Whether it is"**: Ibid.

205   **"[A prospector] and"**: Fawcett, epilogue to *Exploration Fawcett*, p. 284.

206   **"into a world"**: Ahrens to Nina Fawcett, July 10, 1925, RGS.

206   **"an excellent initiation"**: Fawcett, epilogue to *Exploration Fawcett*, p. 289.

207   **"fish were literally"**: *Los Angeles Times*, Dec. 1, 1925.

207   **"Daddy had gone"**: Fawcett, epilogue to *Exploration Fawcett*, p. 286.

208   **"[Jack] has evidently"**: Large to Nina Fawcett, May 24, 1929, Fawcett Family Papers.

208   **"My father chose"**: *Los Angeles Times*, July 17, 1927.

208   **"the tickiest place"**: *Los Angeles Times*, Dec. 1, 1925.

208   **"It is a saying"**: Fawcett to Nina, May 20, 1925, Fawcett Family Papers.

208   **"in spite of"**: Jack Fawcett to Nina and Joan, May 16, 1925, RGS.

209   **"I think you"**: Nina Fawcett to Large, Aug. 30, 1925, Fawcett Family Papers.

209   **Galvão had pushed**: For details on Galvão, see Leal, *Coronel Fawcett*.

209   **"It was quite"**: Translation and extract from the newspaper *O Democrata*, n.d., RGS.

209   **"considerable danger"**: *Los Angeles Times*, Dec. 1, 1925.

210   **"a pinprick"**: John James Whitehead diary, June 8, 1928, RGS.

210   **"the Brazilian methods"**: Fawcett to Isaiah Bowman, May 20, 1925, NMAI.

210   **"The Bakairís have been"**: American Geographical Society, "Correspondence," p. 696.

210   **"They have in part"**: Fawcett to Bowman, May 20, 1925, NMAI.

210   **"They say the Bacairys"**: Jack Fawcett to Nina and Joan, May 19, 1925, RGS.

210   **"We have all clipped"**: Ibid.

211 **"about eight wild"**: Jack Fawcett to Nina and Joan, May 16, 1925, RGS.

211 **"To Jack's great delight"**: Fawcett, epilogue to *Exploration Fawcett*, p. 290.

211 **"We gave them"**: Jack Fawcett to Nina and Joan, May 16, 1925, RGS.

211 **"They are small"**: Ibid.

211 **"music was"**: Nina Fawcett to the Brazilian ambassador, Feb. 3, 1937, RGS.

211 **"I have never"**: Jack Fawcett to Nina and Joan, May 19, 1925, RGS.

211 **"absolutely unexplored"**: Jack Fawcett to Nina and Joan, May 16, 1925, RGS.

212 **"Years tell"**: Fawcett, epilogue to *Exploration Fawcett*, p. 291.

212 **"The Fawcetts can"**: Raleigh Rimell to Roger Rimell, March 17, 1925, Rimell Family Papers.

212 **"That's too deep"**: Jack Fawcett to Nina and Joan, May 19, 1925, Fawcett Family Papers.

212 **"I wish [Raleigh]"**: Ibid.

212 **"I wish to *hell*"**: Raleigh Rimell to Roger Rimell, March 17, 1925, Rimell Family Papers.

212 **"sense of inferiority"**: Raleigh Rimell to Roger Rimell, March 5, 1925, Rimell Family Papers.

213 **"witnessed throughout"**: Hemming, *Die If You Must*, p. 140.

213 **"lot of stick-throwers"**: *Los Angeles Times*, Dec. 2, 1925.

213 **In the late eighteenth century:** For information about the Xavante and the Kayapós, see Hemming, *Die If You Must*, pp. 86–132.

213 **"from that time"**: Quoted in ibid., p. 95.

213 **"It is obviously"**: Fawcett to Keltie, March 17, 1925, RGS.

214 **"I believe our"**: *Los Angeles Times*, Dec. 2, 1925.

214 **"I suspect constitutional"**: Fawcett to Nina, May 29, 1925, Fawcett Family Papers.

214 **"By the time"**: *Los Angeles Times*, Dec. 1, 1925.

214 **"I shall look"**: Raleigh Rimell to Roger Rimell, March 5, 1925, Rimell Family Papers.

214 **"You need have"**: Fawcett, epilogue to *Exploration Fawcett*, p. 291.

CHAPTER 21: THE LAST EYEWITNESS

217 **"ruined architecture"**: Rice, "Rio Branco, Uraricuera, and Parima," p. 218.

218 **"I don't feel"**: *New York Times*, Sept. 17, 2003.

218 **"the highest concentration"**: *Economist*, July 24, 2004.

218 **On February 12:** See *New York Times*, May 16, 2007; *Baltimore Sun*, March 14, 2005; and *Dayton Daily News*, Aug. 14, 2007.

219 **But I soon discovered:** My account of Petersen's death is based on my interviews with Eduardo Neves and on newspaper accounts.

221 **"Fawcett's dream"**: Verne, *Bob Moran and the Fawcett Mystery*, p. 76.

221 **"I'm an archeologist"**: MacGregor, *Indiana Jones and the Seven Veils*, p. 58.

222 **"My son, lame"**: Ibid., p. 2.

CHAPTER 22: DEAD OR ALIVE

225   "Any day now": *Los Angeles Times*, July 17, 1927.

225   "I believe firmly": *Los Angeles Times*, Jan. 1, 1928.

225   "I think it": Nina Fawcett to Arthur R. Hinks, July 11, 1927, RGS.

225   "Mother! I feel": Nina Fawcett to Harold Large, Nov. 23, 1925, Fawcett Family Papers.

226   "Father has got": *Los Angeles Times*, July 17, 1927.

226   "Have they been": Ibid.

226   Several decades later: Cowell, *Tribe That Hides from Man*, p. 93.

226   "Explorer Called Dupe": *Washington Post*, Sept. 12, 1927.

226   "escape from": *Independent*, Sept. 24, 1927.

226   "described Daddy exactly": Brian Fawcett to Nina, Sept. 23, 1927, RGS.

226   "I was boiling": Nina Fawcett to Hinks, Oct. 24, 1927, RGS.

226   "As the story grew": Nina Fawcett to Courteville, Aug. 1, 1928, RGS.

227   "One cannot tell": *Los Angeles Times*, July 17, 1927.

227   "No better man": Ibid.

227   "we hold ourselves": D. G. Hogarth, "Address at the Anniversary General Meeting, 20 June 1927," *Geographical Journal*, Aug. 1927, p. 100.

227   "I am thirty-six years": R. Bock to D. G. Hogarth, June 21, 1927, RGS.

227   "I am prepared": Robert Bunio to Hogarth, June 21, 1927, RGS.

227   "My wife and I": *Los Angeles Times*, Nov. 27, 1927.

228   "whether there is": Ibid.

228   "We consider that": Geoffrey Steele-Ronan to Hogarth, June 21, 1927, RGS.

228   "romantic story": St. Clair, *Mighty, Mighty Amazon*, p. 254.

228   To succeed, Dyott: *Los Angeles Times*, Jan. 28, 1929.

229   "camped in some": *Los Angeles Times*, Nov. 6, 1927.

229   "supreme courage": Ibid.

229   "A big man": *Los Angeles Times*, Nov. 13, 1927.

229   "They have come": *Los Angeles Times*, Dec. 14, 1927.

229   "There are applicants": *Los Angeles Times*, Nov. 27, 1927.

229   "Perhaps if there": *Independent*, Dec. 3, 1927.

230   "I am *most* anxious": Roger Rimell to RGS, 1933, RGS.

230   "I know of no": *Los Angeles Times*, Nov. 17, 1927.

230   "I can't take": *Los Angeles Times*, Nov. 27, 1927.

230   "creature comforts": Ibid.

230   "a display of unselfish": *Los Angeles Times*, March 28, 1928.

230   "fills me with": *Los Angeles Times*, Nov. 17, 1927.

230   "On behalf of": John James Whitehead diary, March 1, 1928, RGS.

231   "Cecil B. DeMille safari": Kigar, "Phantom Trail of Colonel Fawcett," p. 21.

231   "the dregs of civilization": Dyott, *Man Hunting in the Jungle*, p. 85.

231   "Fawcett's trail loomed": Ibid., p. 135.

231   "How different would": Whitehead diary, May 28, 1928, RGS.

231 **"I first heard"**: McIntyre, "The Commander and the Mystic," p. 5.

232 **"We came across"**: *Los Angeles Times*, Aug. 18, 1928.

232 **"These new denizens"**: Dyott, *Man Hunting in the Jungle*, p. 173.

232 **"He regarded us"**: Ibid., p. 177.

232 **"We cannot predict"**: Whitehead diary, July 24, 1928, RGS.

233 **"The finger of guilt"**: Dyott, *Man Hunting in the Jungle*, p. 236.

233 **"I am so afraid"**: *Los Angeles Times*, Aug. 16, 1928.

233 **"couldn't eat"**: Whitehead diary, Aug. 12, 1928, RGS.

233 **"Remember,"** Dyott: Ibid., July 25, 1928.

234 **"Natives from tribes"**: Stanley Allen, *New Haven Register*, n.d., RGS.

234 **"Am sorry to report"**: Dyott to NANA (radio dispatch), Aug. 16, 1928, RGS.

234 **"We want to"**: Whitehead diary, Sept. 28, 1928, RGS.

234 **"You can be"**: *Chicago Daily Tribune*, March 19, 1930.

235 **"Indian psychology"**: Dyott, *Man Hunting in the Jungle*, p. 264.

235 **"Dyott . . . must have"**: Brian Fawcett, *Ruins in the Sky*, p. 71.

235 **"There is consequently"**: Nina Fawcett to NANA, Aug. 23, 1928, RGS.

235 **"never give up"**: *Los Angeles Times*, Aug. 22, 1928.

235 **"Do not lose"**: Esther Windust to Elsie Rimell, Dec. 14, 1928, PHFP.

236 **"all hope of"**: Abbott to Charles Goodwin, March 22, 1932, FO 743/16, TNA.

236 **"My name is Stefan"**: Translated statement of Stefan Rattin, prepared by Charles Goodwin and sent to Sir William Seeds, March 18, 1932, FO 743/17, TNA.

236 **"only known to me"**: Abbott to Hinks, Dec. 8, 1932, RGS.

236 **"dare not build my"**: H. Kingsley Long, "The Faith of Mrs. Fawcett," *Passing Show*, Nov. 12, 1932.

236 **"I promised Colonel"**: *Chicago Daily Tribune*, March 20, 1932.

237 **"Rattin is anxious"**: *Washington Post*, May 28, 1932.

237 **"given up the imitation"**: *Washington Post*, Sept. 30, 1934.

237 **"Albert Winton, Los Angeles"**: *Los Angeles Times*, Feb. 4, 1934.

237 **"this grave turn"**: George W. Cumbler to British Consulate Office, Oct. 17, 1934, RGS.

237 **Only years later**: Hemming, *Die If You Must*, p. 700.

238 **"The Indians are going"**: *New York Times*, Aug. 12, 1939.

238 **"I tried to save"**: *O Globo*, Aug. 23, 1946.

238 **In 1947**: See Childress, *Lost Cities and Ancient Mysteries of South America*, pp. 303–5.

239 **"You have always"**: Hinks to Nina Fawcett, Oct. 25, 1928, RGS.

239 **"more than one passport"**: Nina Fawcett to A. Bain Mackie, June 20, 1935, RGS.

239 **"My heart is lacerated"**: Nina Fawcett to Large, May 6, 1929, Fawcett Family Papers.

240 **"Lady Fawcett is suffering"**: A. Bachmann to Hinks, Feb. 12, 1934, RGS.

240 **"so that they shall"**: Nina Fawcett to Large, Fawcett Family Papers.

240 **"I shall act on"**: Edward Douglas Fawcett to Hinks, 1933, RGS.

240 **"I am one"**: Nina Fawcett to Thomas Roch, March 10, 1934, RGS.

240 **Large referred to**: Large to Nina Fawcett, April 16, 1925, Fawcett Family Papers.

240 **"The return of her"**: Mackie to Goodwin, Nov. 21, 1933, TNA.

240 **"I get the impression"**: Nina Fawcett to Reverend Monseigneur Couturon, July 3, 1933, RGS.

241 **"the most primitive"**: Moennich, *Pioneering for Christ in Xingu Jungles*, p. 9.

241 **In 1937**: Ibid., pp. 17–18.

241 **"In his dual nature"**: Percy Harrison Fawcett, epilogue to *Exploration Fawcett*, p. 301.

241 **"not only to learn"**: Moennich, *Pioneering for Christ in Xingu Jungles*, pp. 124–26.

241 **"perhaps the most famous"**: *New York Times*, Jan. 6, 1935.

241 **a "freak"**: "The 'Grandson,' " *Time*, Jan. 24, 1944.

241 **"matters are rather"**: Hinks to Morel, Feb. 16, 1944, RGS.

242 **When they examined**: Fawcett, *Ruins in the Sky*, p. 123.

242 **"living specimens"**: Marsh, "Blond Indians of the Darien Jungle," p. 483.

242 **"They are golden"**: *Los Angeles Times*, June 15, 1924.

242 **"Feel the girl's neck"**: *New York Times*, July 9, 1924.

242 **"relic of the Paleolithic"**: *New York Times*, July 7, 1924.

242 **"closer to nature"**: *Washington Post*, Oct. 16, 1924.

243 **"no home"**: Nina Fawcett to Joan, Sept. 6, 1946, Fawcett Family Papers.

243 **"You've been"**: Brian Fawcett to Nina, Dec. 5, 1933, Fawcett Family Papers.

243 **"it means certain"**: Everild Young to Colonel Kirwan, Sept. 24, 1946, RGS.

CHAPTER 23: THE COLONEL'S BONES

249 **"The whole"**: Percy Harrison Fawcett, "Proposal for a S. American Expedition" (proposal), April 4, 1924, RGS.

249 **"There is reason"**: Dyott, *Manhunting in the Jungle*, p. 224.

250 **"Everywhere he went"**: Villas Boas and Villas Boas, *Xingu*, p. 165.

252 **"Up that way"**: In 1998, Vajuvi told a similar story to the British adventurer Benedict Allen, who made a film about his journey for the BBC entitled *The Bones of Colonel Fawcett*.

253 **"The upper jaw"**: "Report on the Human Remains from Brazil," 1951, RAI.

255 **"One of them"**: Basso, *Last Cannibals*, pp. 78–86.

CHAPTER 24: THE OTHER WORLD

256 **"Are you alive"**: Esther Windust to Nina Fawcett, Oct. 10, 1928, PHFP.

256 **"We shall see"**: Mrs. Mullins to Nina Fawcett, Feb. 9, 1928, Fawcett Family Papers.

256 **"Her life flows"**: Edward Douglas Fawcett to Arthur R. Hinks, 1933.

257 **Toward the end**: Reeves, *Recollections of a Geographer*, pp. 198–99.

257 **In the early 1940s**: Leal, *Coronel Fawcett*, pp. 213–15.

257 **In 1949**: Cummins, *Fate of Colonel Fawcett*, p. 143.

257 **"Pain—stop pain"**: Ibid., p. 58.

257 **"The voices and sounds"**: Ibid., p. 111.

257 **"I really don't":** Brian Fawcett to Joan, Sept. 3, 1945, Fawcett Family Papers.

257 **"Have you really":** Nina Fawcett to Joan, April 22, 1942, Fawcett Family Papers.

257 **"In a way":** Brian Fawcett to Joan, Sept. 3, 1945, Fawcett Family Papers.

258 **"The time has come":** Brian Fawcett, *Ruins in the Sky*, p. 124.

258 **"wild, despairing":** Brian Fawcett to Joan, Sept. 3, 1945, Fawcett Family Papers.

258 **"the pathetic relics":** Percy Harrison Fawcett, introduction to *Exploration Fawcett*, p. xiii.

258 **"I feel that":** Brian Fawcett to Joan, Sept. 3, 1945, Fawcett Family Papers.

258 **"on his expeditions":** Fawcett, introduction to *Exploration Fawcett*, p. xiii.

258 **"Daddy seems very":** Brian Fawcett to Nina, April 1, 1951, Fawcett Family Papers.

258 **"It really is":** Brian Fawcett to Nina, May 15, 1952, Fawcett Family Papers.

258 **"I simply couldn't":** Nina Fawcett to Joan, Dec. 14, 1952, Fawcett Family Papers.

259 **Brian and Joan:** Williams, introduction to *AmaZonia*, p. 20.

259 **"sacrificed":** Ibid.

259 **"without satisfying":** Brian Fawcett to Sir Geoffrey Thompson, May 20, 1955, FO 371/114106, TNA.

259 **"just as mad":** Thompson to I. F. S. Vincent, May 19, 1955, FO 371/114106, TNA.

259 **"But . . . but":** Fawcett, *Ruins in the Sky*, p. 217.

260 **"Fate must surely":** Ibid., p. 284.

260 **"That looks like":** Ibid., p. 245.

260 **"The whole romantic":** Ibid., p. 301.

260 **"I do not assume":** Percy Harrison Fawcett, "Memorandum Regarding the Region of South America Which It Is Intended to Explore" (proposal), 1919, RGS.

260 **"the cradle of":** Fawcett, *Ruins in the Sky*, p. 299.

260 **"the time":** "The Occult Interests of Col. P. H. Fawcett," n.d., n.p., PHFP.

260 **"Was Daddy's whole":** Williams, introduction to *AmaZonia*, p. 7.

260 **"an objective that":** Fawcett, *Ruins in the Sky*, p. 301.

260 **"Those whom the Gods":** Fawcett to Windust, March 5, 1923, PHFP.

CHAPTER 25: Z

261 **One sect, called:** Details about the sect come from Leal, *Coronel Fawcett*, and my interviews.

263 **"I was all she had":** Brian Fawcett, *Ruins in the Sky*, p. 307.

264 **"My story is lost":** Cummins, *Fate of Colonel Fawcett*, p. 43.

265 **"throwing away":** Fawcett, *Ruins in the Sky*, p. 301.

271 **"very little scratching":** Percy Harrison Fawcett, "Memorandum Regarding the Region of South America Which It Is Intended to Explore" (proposal), 1919, RGS.

273 **Heckenberger has helped:** For further information on Heckenberger's discoveries, see *The Ecology of Power*.

273 **Other scientists:** My descriptions of the revolution in archaeology in the Amazon

come from my interviews with many of the anthropologists and other scientists who are or were working in the field, including William Denevan, Clark Erickson, Susanna Hecht, Michael Heckenberger, Eduardo Neves, James Petersen, Anna Roosevelt, and Neil Whitehead. My information is also derived from many of these and other scholars' published research. See, for instance, "Secrets of the Forest" and *Moundbuilders of the Amazon*, by Roosevelt; "The Timing of *Terra Preta* Formation in the Central Amazon," by Neves; and *Time and Complexity in Historical Ecology*, edited by Balée and Erickson. For a general survey of the latest scientific developments that are overturning so much of what was once believed about the Americas before Columbus, see Mann's *1491*.

274   **Some archaeologists now:** A team of archaeologists claims that at a site in Monte Verde, Chile, there are indications of human presence from more than thirty-two thousand years ago, which, if true, would further shatter the traditional theory of how and when the Americas were first settled.

275   **"no mirage":** Roosevelt, "Secrets of the Forest," p. 26.

275   **"With some caveats":** Interview with author.

Selected
Bibliography

Adamson, Jack H., and H. F. Folland. *The Shepherd of the Ocean: An Account of Sir Walter Ralegh and His Times.* Boston: Gambit, 1969.

American Geographical Society. "Correspondence." *Geographical Review* 15, no. 4 (1925).

Babcock, William H. "Early Observations in American Physical Anthropology." *American Journal of Physical Anthropology* 1, no. 3 (1918).

Baker, Samuel White. *Eight Years in Ceylon.* Dehiwala: Tisara Prakasakayo, 1966.

Balée, William, and Clark L. Erickson, eds. *Time and Complexity in Historical Ecology: Studies in the Neotropical Lowlands.* New York: Columbia University Press, 2006.

Basso, Ellen B. *The Last Cannibals: A South American Oral History.* Austin: University of Texas Press, 1995.

Bates, Henry Walter. *The Naturalist on the River Amazons.* Santa Barbara, Calif.: Narrative Press, 2002.

Bergreen, Laurence. *Over the Edge of the World: Magellan's Terrifying Circumnavigation of the Globe.* New York: William Morrow, 2003.

Berton, Pierre. *The Arctic Grail: The Quest for the North West Passage and the North Pole, 1818–1909.* New York: Lyons Press, 2000.

Bingham, Hiram. *Across South America: An Account of a Journey from Buenos Aires to Lima by Way of Potosi, with Notes on Brazil, Argentina, Bolivia, Chile, and Peru.* New York: Da Capo Press, 1976.

————. *Lost City of the Incas: The Story of Machu Picchu and Its Builders.* New illustrated ed., with an introduction by Hugh Thomson. New York: Phoenix, 2003.

Bodard, Lucien. *Green Hell: Massacre of the Brazilian Indians.* Translated by Jennifer Monaghan. New York: Outerbridge & Dienstfrey, 1972.

Bowman, Isaiah. "Remarkable Discoveries in Bolivia." *Bulletin of the American Geographical Society* 47, no. 6 (1915).

Brantlinger, Patrick. *Rule of Darkness: British Literature and Imperialism, 1830–1914.* Ithaca, N.Y.: Cornell University Press, 1988.

Brehaut, Ernest. *An Encyclopedist of the Dark Ages: Isidore of Seville.* New York: Columbia University Press, 1912.

Brinton, Daniel Garrison. *The American Race: A Linguistic Classification and Ethnographic Description of the Native Tribes of North and South America.* Philadelphia: David McKay, 1901.

Bristow, Edward J. *Vice and Vigilance: Purity Movements in Britain Since 1700.* Totowa, N.J.: Rowman & Littlefield, 1977.

Bristow, Joseph. *Empire Boys: Adventures in a Man's World.* London: Unwin Hyman, 1991.

British Association for the Advancement of Science. *Notes and Queries on Anthropology, for the Use of Travellers and Residents in Uncivilized Lands.* London: Edward Stanford, 1874.

Brookes, Martin. *Extreme Measures: The Dark Visions and Bright Ideas of Francis Galton.* New York: Bloomsbury, 2004.

Brown, Lloyd A. *The Story of Maps.* New York: Dover, 1979.

Burke, Thomas. *The Streets of London Through the Centuries.* London: B. T. Batsford, 1940.

Burton, Richard Francis. *Explorations of the Highlands of the Brazil; with a Full Account of the Gold and Diamond Mines.* 2 vols. New York: Greenwood Press, 1969.

Cameron, Ian. *To the Farthest Ends of the Earth: 150 Years of World Exploration by the Royal Geographical Society.* New York: E. P. Dutton, 1980.

Campbell, Lady Colin. *Etiquette of Good Society.* London: Cassell, 1893.

Carvajal, Gaspar de. *The Discovery of the Amazon.* Edited by José Toribio Medina. Translated by Bertram T. Lee and H. C. Heaton. New York: Dover, 1988.

Cave, Henry. *Golden Tips: A Description of Ceylon and Its Great Tea Industry.* London: S. Low, Marston & Co., 1900.

Childress, David Hatcher. *Lost Cities and Ancient Mysteries of South America.* Stelle, Ill.: Adventures Unlimited Press, 1986.

Church, George Earl. "Dr. Rice's Exploration in the North-Western Valley of the Amazon." *Geographical Journal* 31, no. 3 (1908).

Clastres, Pierre. "Guayaki Cannibalism." In *Native South Americans: Ethnology of the Least Known Continent.* Edited by Patricia J. Lyon. Boston: Little, Brown, 1974.

Columbia University. *Introduction to Contemporary Civilization in the West.* New York: Columbia University Press, 1960.

Conklin, Beth A. *Consuming Grief: Compassionate Cannibalism in an Amazonian Society.* Austin: University of Texas Press, 2001.

Conrad, Joseph. "Geography and Some Explorers." In *The Collected Works of Joseph Conrad.* Vol. 22. London: Routledge, 1995.

Cook, Emily Constance Baird. *Highways and Byways in London.* London: Macmillan, 1903.

Cowell, Adrian. *The Heart of the Forest.* New York: Alfred A. Knopf, 1961.

———. *The Tribe That Hides from Man.* Briarcliff Manor, N.Y.: Stein & Day, 1974.

Crone, G. R. "Obituary: Alexander Hamilton Rice, A.M., M.D." *Geographical Journal* 122, no. 3 (1956).

Cummins, Geraldine. *The Fate of Colonel Fawcett.* London: Aquarian Press, 1955.

Cutright, Paul Russell. *The Great Naturalists Explore South America.* New York: Macmillan, 1940.

Davis, Shelton H. *Victims of the Miracle: Development and the Indians of Brazil.* Cambridge, U.K.: Cambridge University Press, 1977.

Davson, H. M. *The History of the 35th Division in the Great War.* London: Sifton Praed, 1926.

De Camp, L. Sprague, and Willy Ley. *Lands Beyond.* New York: Rinehart, 1952.

Denevan, William M. *Cultivated Landscapes of Native Amazonia and the Andes.* New York: Oxford University Press, 2001.

Diacon, Todd A. *Stringing Together a Nation: Cândido Mariano da Silva Rondon and the Construction of a Modern Brazil, 1906–1930.* Durham, N.C.: Duke University Press, 2004.

Diamond, Jared. *Guns, Germs, and Steel: The Fates of Human Societies.* New York: W. W. Norton, 1999.

Dickens, Charles. *American Notes; and Pictures from Italy.* New York: Macmillan, 1903.

Dillehay, Tom D., ed. *Monte Verde: A Late Pleistocene Settlement in Chile.* 2 vols. Washington, D.C.: Smithsonian Institution Press, 1989–97.

Doyle, Arthur Conan. *The Lost World: Being an Account of the Recent Amazing Adventures of Professor George E. Challenger, Lord John Roxton, Professor Summerlee, and Mr. E. D. Malone of the "Daily Gazette."* Edited by Ian Duncan. New York: Oxford University Press, 1998.

Driver, Felix. *Geography Militant: Cultures of Exploration and Empire.* Oxford, U.K.: Blackwell, 2001.

Dyott, George Miller. *Man Hunting in the Jungle: Being the Story of a Search for Three Explorers Lost in the Brazilian Wilds.* Indianapolis: Bobbs-Merrill, 1930.

———. *On the Trail of the Unknown: In the Wilds of Ecuador and the Amazon.* London: Thornton Butterworth, 1926.

———. "The Search for Colonel Fawcett." *Geographical Journal* 74, no. 6 (1929).

Ellis, John. *Eye-Deep in Hell: Trench Warfare in World War I.* New York: Pantheon, 1976.

Farwell, Byron. *Burton: A Biography of Sir Richard Francis Burton.* New York: Penguin, 1990.

Fawcett, Brian. *Ruins in the Sky.* London: Hutchinson, 1958.

Fawcett, Edward Douglas. *Hartmann the Anarchist; or, The Doom of the Great City.* New York: Arno Press, 1975.

————. *The Secret of the Desert; or, How We Crossed Arabia in the* Antelope. London: E. Arnold, 1895.

————. *Swallowed by an Earthquake*. London: E. Arnold, 1894.

Fawcett, Percy Harrison. "At the Hot Wells of Konniar." *Occult Review*, July 1925.

————. "Bolivian Exploration, 1913–1914." *Geographical Journal* 45, no. 3 (1915).

————. *Exploration Fawcett*. London: Hutchinson, 1953.

————. "Explorations in Bolivia." *Geographical Journal* 35, no. 5 (1910).

————. "Further Explorations in Bolivia: The River Heath." *Geographical Journal* 37, no. 4 (1911).

————. "Gold Bricks at Badulla." *Blackwood's Magazine*, March 1965.

————. "In the Heart of South America." Pts. 1–4. *Wide World Magazine*, July–Oct. 1912.

————. "Journey to Morocco City." *Geographical Journal* 19, no. 2 (1902).

————. "The Lost City of My Quest." *Blackwood's Magazine*, Jan. 1933.

————. "A New Touring Ground: Morocco, the Country of the Future." *Pall Mall Magazine*, Sept. 1902.

————. "Obsession." *Light*, July 29, 1922.

————. "The Occult Life." *Occult Review*, Aug. 1923.

————. "The Passing of Trinco." *Blackwood's Magazine,* Feb. 1959.

————. "The Planetary Control." *Occult Review*, Dec. 1922.

————. "The Source of the River Heath." *Geographical Journal* 47, no. 4 (1916).

————. "South American Forests." *Geographical Journal* 40, no. 6 (1912).

————. "Survey Work on the Bolivia-Brazil Boundary." *Geographical Journal* 35, no. 2 (1910).

————. "Survey Work on the Frontier Between Bolivia and Brazil." *Geographical Journal* 33, no. 2 (1909).

Ferguson, John. *Ceylon in 1893: Describing the Progress of the Island Since 1803, Its Present Agricultural and Commercial Enterprises, and Its Unequalled Attractions to Visitors, with Useful Statistical Information, Specially Prepared Map, and Upwards of One Hundred Illustrations.* London: John Haddon, 1893.

Fifer, J. Valerie. *Bolivia: Land, Location, and Politics Since 1825.* Cambridge, U.K.: Cambridge University Press, 1972.

————. "Bolivia's Boundary with Brazil: A Century of Evolution." *Geographical Journal* 132, no. 3 (1966).

————. "The Empire Builders: A History of the Bolivian Rubber Boom and the Rise of the House of Suárez." *Journal of Latin American Studies* 2, no. 2 (1970).

Flanders, Judith. *Inside the Victorian Home: A Portrait of Domestic Life in Victorian England.* New York: W. W. Norton, 2003.

Fleming, Peter. *Brazilian Adventure.* New York: Grosset & Dunlap, 1933.

Flint, John E. *Sir George Goldie and the Making of Nigeria.* London: Oxford University Press, 1960.

Forsyth, Adrian, and Kenneth Miyata. *Tropical Nature.* New York: Charles Scribner's Sons, 1984.

Fraser, Robert. *Victorian Quest Romance: Stevenson, Haggard, Kipling, and Conan Doyle*. Plymouth, U.K.: Northcote House, 1998.

Freshfield, Douglas W., and W. J. L. Wharton, eds. *Hints to Travellers, Scientific and General*. 7th ed. London: Royal Geographical Society, 1893.

Furneaux, Robin. *The Amazon: The Story of a Great River*. London: Hamish Hamilton, 1969.

Galton, Francis. *The Art of Travel; or, Shifts and Contrivances Available in Wild Countries*. Harrisburg, Pa.: Stackpole Books, 1971.

Gilbert, Martin. *Churchill: A Life*. New York: Henry Holt, 1991.

———. *The Somme: Heroism and Horror in the First World War*. New York: Henry Holt, 2006.

Gillham, Nicholas W. *A Life of Sir Francis Galton: From African Exploration to the Birth of Eugenics*. New York: Oxford University Press, 2001.

Girouard, Mark. *The Return to Camelot: Chivalry and the English Gentleman*. New Haven, Conn.: Yale University Press, 1981.

Glass, Frederick C. *Adventures with the Bible in Brazil*. New York: Loizeaux Brothers, 1943.

Glendinning, Victoria. *Leonard Woolf: A Biography*. New York: Free Press, 2006.

Gott, Richard. *Land Without Evil: Utopian Journeys Across the South American Watershed*. New York: Verso, 1993.

Goulding, Michael, Ronaldo Barthem, and Efrem Ferreira. *The Smithsonian Atlas of the Amazon*. Washington, D.C.: Smithsonian Institution Press, 2003.

Green, Martin Burgess. *Dreams of Adventure, Deeds of Empire*. New York: Basic Books, 1979.

Greenblatt, Stephen. *Marvelous Possessions: The Wonder of the New World*. Chicago: University of Chicago Press, 1991.

Guggisberg, F. G. *The Shop: The Story of the Royal Military Academy*. London: Cassell, 1900.

H.E. "The Rio Negro, the Casiquiare Canal, and the Upper Orinoco, September 1919–April 1920: Discussion." *Geographical Journal* 58, no. 5 (1921).

Haggard, H. Rider. *King Solomon's Mines*. New York: Oxford University Press, 1989.

Halstead, John P. *Rebirth of a Nation: The Origins and Rise of Moroccan Nationalism, 1912–1944*. Cambridge, Mass.: Harvard University Press, 1967.

Hambloch, Ernest. *Here and There: A Medley of Memories*. London: Johnson, 1968.

Hankey, Donald. *A Student in Arms*. New York: E. P. Dutton, 1917.

Hardenburg, W. E. *The Putumayo, the Devil's Paradise; Travels in the Peruvian Amazon Region and an Account of the Atrocities Committed upon the Indians Therein*. London: T. F. Unwin, 1912.

Hart, Peter. *The Somme*. London: Weidenfeld & Nicolson, 2005.

Haskins, Caryl. *The Amazon: The Life History of a Mighty River*. Garden City, NY: Doubleday, 1943.

Heath, Jeffrey M. *The Picturesque Prison: Evelyn Waugh and His Writing*. Kingston, Ont.: McGill-Queen's University Press, 1982.

Heaton, Paul Michael. *Lamport & Holt*. Newport, U.K.: Starling Press, 1986.

Hecht, Susanna. "Indigenous Soil Management and the Creation of Amazonian Dark Earths: Implications of Kayapó Practices." In *Amazonian Dark Earths: Origins, Properties, Management*, edited by J. Lehmann et al. The Netherlands: Kluwer Academic, 2004.

Hecht, Susanna, and Alexander Cockburn. *The Fate of the Forest: Developers, Destroyers, and Defenders of the Amazon*. New York: Verso, 1989.

Heckenberger, Michael J. *The Ecology of Power: Culture, Place, and Personhood in the Southern Amazon, A.D. 1000–2000*. New York: Routledge, 2005.

Heckenberger, Michael J., et al. "Amazonia 1492: Pristine Forest or Cultural Parkland?" *Science* 301 (2003).

———. "Of Lost Civilizations and Primitive Tribes, Amazonia: Reply to Meggers." *Latin American Antiquity* 12, no. 3 (2001).

———. "Village Size and Permanence in Amazonia: Two Archaeological Examples from Brazil." *Latin American Antiquity* 10, no. 4 (1999).

Hefferman, Michael. "Geography, Cartography, and Military Intelligence: The Royal Geographical Society and the First World War." *Transactions of the Institute of British Geographers* 21, no. 3 (1996).

Hemming, John. *Amazon Frontier: The Defeat of the Brazilian Indians*. Cambridge, Mass.: Harvard University Press, 1987.

———. *Die If You Must: Brazilian Indians in the Twentieth Century*. London: Macmillan, 2003.

———. *Red Gold: The Conquest of the Brazilian Indians*. Cambridge, Mass.: Harvard University Press, 1978.

———. *The Search for El Dorado*. London: Michael Joseph, 1978.

Hobbes, Thomas. *Leviathan*. Edited and introduced by C. B. Macpherson. London: Penguin, 1985.

Hobhouse, Henry. *Seeds of Wealth: Four Plants That Made Men Rich*. Washington, D.C.: Shoemaker & Hoard, 2004.

Holmberg, Allan R. *Nomads of the Long Bow: The Siriono of Eastern Bolivia*. Garden City, N.Y.: Natural History Press, 1969.

Honigsbaum, Mark. *The Fever Trail: In Search of the Cure for Malaria*. New York: Farrar, Straus & Giroux, 2002.

Hopkirk, Peter. *The Great Game: The Struggle for Empire in Central Asia*. New York: Kodansha International, 1992.

———. *Trespassers on the Roof of the World: The Secret Exploration of Tibet*. New York: Kodansha International, 1995.

Houghton, Walter E. *The Victorian Frame of Mind, 1830–1870*. New Haven, Conn.: Yale University Press, 1957.

Huddleston, Lee Eldridge. *Origins of the American Indians: European Concepts, 1492–1729*. Austin: University of Texas Press, 1967.

Humboldt, Alexander von, and Aimé Bonpland. *Personal Narrative of Travels to the Equinoctial Regions of America, During the Years 1799–1804*. Translated and edited by Thomasina Ross. 3 vols. Vol. 2. London: George Bell and Sons, 1885.

Huntford, Roland. *Shackleton*. New York: Carroll & Graf, 1998.

Huxley, Elspeth. *Scott of the Antarctic*. New York: Atheneum, 1978.

Jeal, Tim. *Livingstone*. New Haven, Conn.: Yale University Press, 2001.

Johnson, Donald S. *Phantom Islands of the Atlantic: The Legends of Seven Lands That Never Were*. New York: Walker, 1996.

Johnson, J. H. *Stalemate! The Great Trench Warfare Battles of 1915–1917*. London: Arms and Armour Press, 1995.

Kelly, John, ed. *The Collected Letters of W. B. Yeats*. Vol. 1. New York: Oxford University Press, 2005.

Keltie, J. Scott. "Thirty Years' Work of the Royal Geographical Society." *Geographical Journal* 49, no. 5 (1917).

Kennedy, Dane. *The Highly Civilized Man: Richard Burton and the Victorian World*. Cambridge, Mass.: Harvard University Press, 2005.

Kigar, Paul Donovan. "The Phantom Trail of Colonel Fawcett." *Americas* (April 1975).

Knox, Robert. *An Historical Relation of Ceylon*. Colombo: Tisara Prakasakayo, 1966.

Kricher, John C. *A Neotropical Companion: An Introduction to the Animals, Plants, and Ecosystems of the New World Tropics*. Princeton, N.J.: Princeton University Press, 1997.

Kuklick, Henrika. *The Savage Within: The Social History of British Anthropology, 1885–1945*. Cambridge, U.K.: Cambridge University Press, 1991.

Landes, David S. *The Wealth and Poverty of Nations: Why Some Are So Rich and Some So Poor*. New York: W. W. Norton, 1998.

Landor, A. Henry Savage. *Across Unknown South America*. 2 vols. London: Hodder & Stoughton, 1913.

————. *Everywhere: The Memoirs of an Explorer*. New York: Frederick A. Stokes, 1924.

Larson, Erik. *Thunderstruck*. New York: Crown, 2006.

Las Casas, Bartolomé de. *A Short Account of the Destruction of the Indies*. Translated and edited by Nigel Griffin. New York: Penguin, 1992.

Lathrap, Donald W. *The Upper Amazon*. London: Thames & Hudson, 1970.

Leal, Hermes. *Coronel Fawcett: A Verdadeira História do Indiana Jones*. São Paulo: Geração Editorial, 1996.

Lestringant, Frank. *Mapping the Renaissance World: The Geographical Imagination in the Age of Discovery*. Translated by David Fausett. Berkeley: University of California Press, 1994.

Lightman, Bernard V., ed. *Victorian Science in Context*. Chicago: University of Chicago Press, 1997.

Lovell, Mary S. *A Rage to Live: A Biography of Richard and Isabel Burton*. New York: W. W. Norton, 1998.

Lyon, Patricia J. *Native South Americans: Ethnology of the Least Known Continent*. Boston: Little, Brown, 1974.

MacGregor, Rob. *Indiana Jones and the Seven Veils*. New York: Bantam Books, 1991.

MacKenzie, John M., ed. *Imperialism and Popular Culture*. Manchester, U.K.: Manchester University Press, 1986.

Malcolm, Janet. *The Silent Woman: Sylvia Plath and Ted Hughes.* New York: Vintage Books, 1995.

Mann, Charles. "The Forgotten People of Amazonia." *Science* 297 (2002).

———. "1491." *Atlantic Monthly,* April 2002.

———. *1491: New Revelations of the Americas Before Columbus.* New York: Vintage Books, 2006.

———. "The Good Earth: Did People Improve the Amazon Basin?" *Science* 287 (2000).

———. "The Real Dirt on Rainforest Fertility." *Science* 297 (2002).

Marsh, Richard O. "Blond Indians of the Darien Jungle." *World's Work,* March 1925.

———. *White Indians of Darien.* New York: G. P. Putnam's Sons, 1934.

Matthiessen, Peter. *The Cloud Forest: A Chronicle of the South American Wilderness.* New York: Penguin, 1996.

Maxtone-Graham, John. *The Only Way to Cross.* New York: Macmillan, 1972.

McCullough, David. *The Path Between the Seas: The Creation of the Panama Canal, 1870–1914.* New York: Simon & Schuster, 1977.

McIntyre, Loren. "The Commander and the Mystic." *South American Explorer* (Spring 1996).

McNiven, Ian J., and Lynette Russell. *Appropriated Pasts: Indigenous Peoples and the Colonial Culture of Archaeology.* Lanham, Md.: AltaMira Press, 2005.

Meade, Marion. *Madame Blavatsky: The Woman Behind the Myth.* New York: G. P. Putnam's Sons, 1980.

Meggers, Betty J. *Amazonia: Man and Culture in a Counterfeit Paradise.* Washington, D. C.: Smithsonian Institution Press, 1996.

Meggers, Betty J., and Clifford Evans. *Archeological Investigations at the Mouth of the Amazon.* Smithsonian Institution. Bureau of American Ethnology. Washington, D.C.: Government Printing Office, 1957.

Métraux, Alfred. *The Native Tribes of Eastern Bolivia and Western Matto Grosso.* Washington, D.C.: Government Printing Office, 1942.

Mill, Hugh Robert. *The Record of the Royal Geographical Society, 1830–1930.* London: Royal Geographical Society, 1930.

Millard, Candice. *The River of Doubt: Theodore Roosevelt's Darkest Journey.* New York: Doubleday, 2005.

Moennich, Martha L. *Pioneering for Christ in Xingu Jungles.* Grand Rapids, Mich.: Zondervan, 1942.

Moorehead, Alan. *The White Nile.* New York: Harper's Perennial, 2000.

Muffett, D. J. M. *Empire Builder Extraordinary: Sir George Goldie.* Isle of Man, U.K.: Shearwater Press, 1978.

Murray, James, and George Marston. *Antarctic Days: Sketches of the Homely Side of Polar Life by Two of Shackleton's Men.* London: Andrew Melrose, 1913.

Neves, Eduardo G., et al. "Historical and Socio-Cultural Origins of Amazonian Dark Earths." In *Amazonian Dark Earths: Origins, Properties, and Management,* edited by J. Lehmann et al. The Netherlands: Kluwer Academic, 2004.

————. "The Timing of *Terra Preta* Formation in the Central Amazon: Archaeological Data from Three Sites." In *Amazonian Dark Earths: Explorations in Space and Time*, edited by Bruno Glaser and William I. Woods. New York: Springer, 2004.

Nicholl, Charles. *The Creature in the Map: A Journey to El Dorado*. London: J. Cape, 1995.

Niven, Jennifer. *The Ice Master: The Doomed 1913 Voyage of the* Karluk. New York: Hyperion, 2000.

Oppenheim, Janet. *The Other World: Spiritualism and Psychical Research in England, 1850–1914*. New York: Cambridge University Press, 1985.

Pagden, Anthony. *European Encounters with the New World*. New Haven, Conn.: Yale University Press, 1993.

Picchi, Debra. *The Bakairí Indians of Brazil: Politics, Ecology, and Change*. Prospect Heights, Ill.: Wareland Press, 2000.

Pickover, Clifford A. *Strange Brains and Genius: The Secret Lives of Eccentric Scientists and Madmen*. New York: HarperCollins, 1999.

Price, Willard. *The Amazing Amazon*. New York: John Day Co., 1952.

Pritchett, V. S. *The Tale Bearers: Literary Essays*. New York: Random House, 1980.

Ralegh, Walter. *The Discoverie of the Large, Rich, and Bewtiful Empyre of Guiana*. Transcribed, annotated, and introduced by Neil Whitehead. Manchester, U.K.: Manchester University Press, 1997.

Reeves, Edward Ayearst. *Maps and Map-Making*. London: Royal Geographical Society, 1910.

————. *The Recollections of a Geographer*. London: Seeley, Service & Company, 1935.

Revkin, Andrew. *The Burning Season: The Murder of Chico Mendes and the Fight for the Amazon Rain Forest*. Washington, D.C.: Island Press, 2004.

Rice, Alexander Hamilton. "Further Explorations in the North-West Amazon Basin." *Geographical Journal* 44, no. 2 (1914).

————. "The Recent Expedition of Dr. Hamilton Rice." *Geographical Journal* 56, no. 1 (1920).

————. "The Rio Branco, Uraricuera, and Parima." *Geographical Journal* 71, no. 2 (1928).

————. "The Rio Branco, Uraricuera, and Parima (Continued)." *Geographical Journal* 71, no. 3 (1928).

————. "The Rio Branco, Uraricuera, and Parima (Continued)." *Geographical Journal* 71, no. 4 (1928).

————. "The Rio Negro, the Casiquiare Canal, and the Upper Orinoco, September 1919–April 1920." *Geographical Journal* 58, no. 5 (1921).

Riffenburgh, Beau. *Nimrod: Ernest Shackleton and the Extraordinary Story of the 1907–1909 British Antarctic Expedition*. London: Bloomsbury, 2004.

Roosevelt, Anna C. "Dating a Paleoindian Site in the Amazon in Comparison with Clovis Culture." *Science* 275 (1997).

————. *Moundbuilders of the Amazon: Geophysical Archaeology on Marajó Island, Brazil*. San Diego, Calif.: Academic, 1991.

———. "Secrets of the Forest: An Archaeologist Reappraises the Past—and Future—of Amazonia." *Sciences* 32 (1992).

———, ed. *Amazonian Indians from Prehistory to the Present: Anthropological Perspectives.* Tucson: University of Arizona Press, 1994.

Roosevelt, Anna C., et al. "Paleoindian Cave Dwellers in the Amazon: The Peopling of the Americas." *Science* 272 (1996).

Roosevelt, Anna C., John Douglas, and Linda Brown. "The Migrations and Adaptations of the First Americans: Clovis and Pre-Clovis Viewed from South America." In *The First Americans: The Pleistocene Colonization of the New World*, edited by Nina G. Jablonski. San Francisco: California Academy of Sciences, 2002.

Roosevelt, Theodore. *Through the Brazilian Wilderness.* New York: Charles Scribner's Sons, 1914.

Royal Geographical Society. "Colonel Fawcett's Expedition in Matto Grosso." *Geographical Journal* 71, no. 2 (1928).

———. "Dr. Hamilton Rice on the Rio Branco." *Geographical Journal* 65, no. 3 (1925).

———. "The Monthly Record." *Geographical Journal* 54, no. 2 (1919).

———. "The Monthly Record." *Geographical Journal* 48, no. 4 (1916).

———. "The Monthly Record." *Geographical Journal* 41, no. 6 (1913).

Ryan, Simon. *The Cartographic Eye: How Explorers Saw Australia.* Cambridge, U.K.: Cambridge University Press, 1996.

Schurz, W. L. "The Distribution of Population in the Amazon Valley." *Geographical Review* 15, no. 2 (1925).

Semple, Ellen C. *Influences of Geographic Environment on the Basis of Ratzel's System of Anthropo-geography.* New York: Henry Holt, 1911.

Shackleton, Ernest Henry. *The Heart of the Antarctic: Being the Story of the British Antarctic Expedition, 1907–1909.* 2 vols. London: W. Heinemann, 1909.

Simón, Pedro. *The Expedition of Pedro de Ursua & Lope de Aguirre in Search of El Dorado and Omagua in 1560–1.* Edited by William Bollaert. London: Hakluyt Society, 1861.

Sims, George R., ed. *Living London: Its Work and Its Play, Its Humour and Its Pathos, Its Sights and Its Scenes.* 3 vols. London: Cassell, 1901–3.

Slater, Candace. *Entangled Edens: Visions of the Amazon.* Berkeley: University of California Press, 2002.

Smith, Anthony. *Explorers of the Amazon.* New York: Viking, 1990.

Sobel, Dava. *Longitude: The True Story of a Lone Genius Who Solved the Greatest Scientific Problem of His Time.* New York: Walker, 1995.

Staden, Hans. *Hans Staden: The True History of His Captivity.* Translated and edited by Malcolm Letts. London: George Routledge, 1928.

Stanley, Henry M. *How I Found Livingstone: Travels, Adventures, and Discoveries in Central Africa, Including Four Months' Residence with Dr. Livingstone.* London: Sampson Low, Marston, Low, & Searle, 1872.

Stashower, Daniel. *Teller of Tales: The Life of Arthur Conan Doyle.* New York: Henry Holt, 1999.

St. Clair, David. *The Mighty, Mighty Amazon*. London: Souvenir Press, 1968.

Stepan, Nancy. *The Idea of Race in Science: Great Britain, 1800–1960*. Hamden, Conn.: Archon Books, 1982.

Stevens, Albert William. "The Hydroplane of the Hamilton Rice Expedition, 1924–25." *Geographical Journal* 68, no. 1 (1926).

Steward, Julian H., ed. *Handbook of South American Indians*. Vol. 3, *The Tropical Forest Tribes*. Washington, D.C.: Smithsonian Institution, 1948.

Steward, Julian H., and Louis C. Faron. *Native Peoples of South America*. New York: McGraw-Hill, 1959.

Stocking, George, Jr. *Race, Culture, and Evolution: Essays in the History of Anthropology*. Chicago: University of Chicago Press, 1968.

———. *Victorian Anthropology*. New York: Free Press, 1987.

Suarez, Pedro, M. Eduardo Lembcke, and Percy Harrison Fawcett. "Further Explorations in Bolivia: The River Heath: Discussion." *Geographical Journal* 37, no. 4 (1911).

Swanson, John W. "The Radio-telegraphy of the Hamilton Rice Expedition, 1924–25." *Geographical Journal* 67, no. 6 (1926).

———. "The Wireless Receiving Equipment of the Hamilton Rice Expedition, 1919–20." *Geographical Journal* 60, no. 3 (1922).

Temple, Robert. "E. Douglas Fawcett: The English Jules Verne." *British Heritage*, Feb./March 1985.

Todorov, Tzvetan. *The Conquest of America*. Norman: University of Oklahoma Press, 1999.

Trevelyan, Raleigh. *Sir Walter Raleigh*. New York: Henry Holt, 2004.

Twain, Mark. *Following the Equator: A Journey Around the World*. Hartford, Conn.: American Publishing, 1897.

Ure, John. *Trespassers on the Amazon*. London: Constable, 1986.

U.S. Department of State. *Slavery in Peru: Message from the President of the United States Transmitting Report of the Secretary of State, with Accompanying Papers, Concerning the Alleged Existence of Slavery in Peru*. Washington, D.C.: Government Printing Office, 1913.

Verne, Henry. *Bob Moran and the Fawcett Mystery*. New York: Roy Publishers, 1956.

Villas Boas, Orlando, and Claudio Villas Boas. *Xingu: The Indians, Their Myths*. New York: Farrar, Straus & Giroux, 1973.

Viveiros de Castro, Eduardo Batalha. *From the Enemy's Point of View: Humanity and Divinity in an Amazonian Society*. Translated by Catherine V. Howard. Chicago: University of Chicago Press, 1992.

Waldman, Carl, and Alan Wexler. *Who Was Who in World Exploration*. New York: Facts on File, 1992.

Walker, Lynne. "The Royal Geographical Society's House: An Architectural History." *Geographical Journal* 146, no. 2 (1980).

Wallace, Alfred Russel. *A Narrative of Travels on the Amazon and Rio Negro, with an Account of the Native Tribes, and Observations on the Climate, Geology, and Natural History of the Amazon Valley*. New York: Greenwood Press, 1969.

Walters, Alan. *Palms and Pearls; or, Scenes in Ceylon*. London: Bentley, 1892.

Washington, Peter. *Madame Blavatsky's Baboon: A History of the Mystics, Mediums, and Misfits Who Brought Spiritualism to America.* New York: Schocken Books, 1995.

Weinstein, Barbara. *The Amazon Rubber Boom, 1850–1920.* Stanford, Calif.: Stanford University Press, 1983.

Whitmore, Timothy Charles. *An Introduction to Tropical Rain Forests.* Oxford, U.K.: Oxford University Press, 1998.

Wilford, John Noble. *The Mapmakers.* New York: Vintage Books, 2000.

Williams, Misha. *AmaZonia.* London: Misha Williams, 2004.

Willis, J. C. *Ceylon: A Handbook for the Resident and the Traveller.* Colombo: Colombo Apothecaries, 1907.

Wilson, A. N. *The Victorians.* New York: W. W. Norton, 2003.

Wilson, David J. *Indigenous South Americans of the Past and Present: An Ecological Perspective.* Boulder, Colo.: Westview Press, 1999.

Winter, Denis. *Death's Men: Soldiers of the Great War.* New York: Penguin, 1979.

Wolf, Howard, and Ralph Wolf. *Rubber: A Story of Glory and Greed.* New York: Covici, Friede, 1936.

Wood, Michael. *Conquistadors.* Berkeley: University of California Press, 2000.

Woods, William I., and Joseph M. McCann. "The Anthropogenic Origin and Persistence of Amazonian Dark Earths." *Yearbook Conference of Latin Americanist Geographers* 25 (1999).

Woolf, Charles M. "Albinism (OCA2) in Amerindians." *Yearbook of Physical Anthropology* 48 (2005).

Zweig, Paul. *The Adventurer.* Pleasantville, N.Y.: Akadine Press, 1999

Index

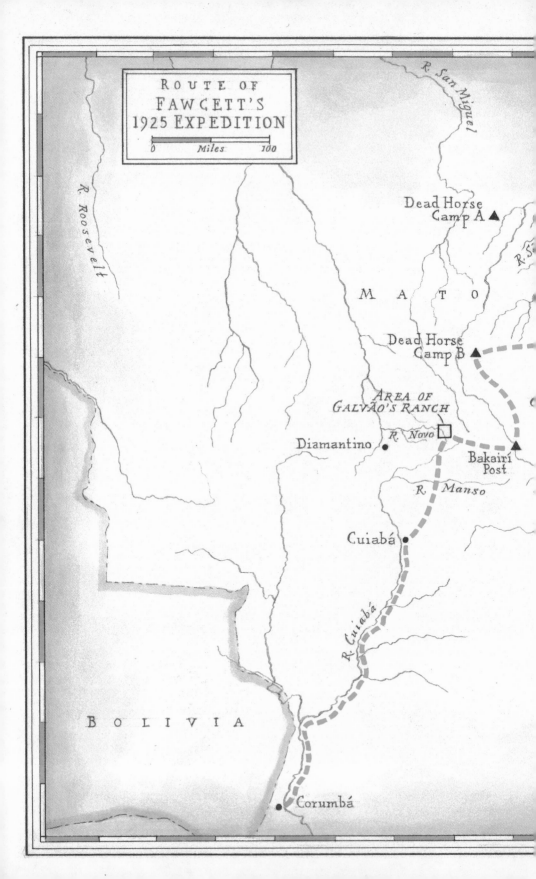